MALCOLM
BLIGHT

MALCOLM BLIGHT
PLAYER · COACH · LEGEND

Tim Watson & James Weston

Published in 2011 by Hardie Grant Books

Hardie Grant Books (Australia)
Ground Floor, Building 1
658 Church Street
Richmond, Victoria 3121
www.hardiegrant.com.au

Hardie Grant Books (UK)
Dudley House, North Suite
34–35 Southampton Street
London WC2E 7HF
www.hardiegrant.co.uk

All rights reserved. No part of this publication may be reproduced,
stored in a retrieval system or transmitted in any form by any means,
electronic, mechanical, photocopying, recording or otherwise, without
the prior written permission of the publishers and copyright holders.

The moral rights of the author have been asserted.

Copyright © Tim Watson 2011

National Library of Australia Cataloguing-in-Publication Data:
Watson, Tim.
    Malcolm Blight : a life in football / Tim Watson, James Weston.
    ISBN 9781742700243 (hbk.)
    Subjects: Blight, Malcolm. Australian football players—Biography.
    Other Authors: Weston, James.
796.336092

Cover design by Peter Daniel
Cover photography James Braund
Text design and typesetting by Cannon Typesetting
Typeset in Adobe Garamond 12/18.5pt
Colour reproduction by Splitting Image Colour Studio
Printed in Australia by Griffin Press

CONTENTS

Introduction		1
1	Two laps	5
2	The Peckers	8
3	Breakout	22
4	Rebuilding the Roos	30
5	Barassi	51
6	Love, hate	75
7	The coach, part I	88
8	Back to Oval Avenue	101
9	The coach, part II	119
10	One brutal afternoon	148
11	'Me, Big Chief Malcolm'	157
12	The Eagles	173
13	The Eagles, again	191
14	Catch-up	207
15	The big four	225
16	The Messiah strikes	242
17	September 1997	262
18	Back-to-back	281
19	Expiry date	305
20	Saints or sinners?	314
Epilogue		335
Acknowledgements		345

INTRODUCTION

THE FIRST BOOK I read about football was written by AFL legend Lou Richards, who wrote *Boots and All* way back in 1963. Fittingly, not long afterwards my next footy read emanated from Richards' sidekick, Richmond legend Jack Dyer, whose *Captain Blood* biography captured a fantastic time in the game.

For a kid growing up in country Victoria those books were a link to the real football world, a game that took place four hours away by car, which I saw two or three times a year if I was lucky.

I devoured both books. They sparked the passion I now have for reading sports books from all over the world.

When I retired from playing for Essendon I received offers to pen my own story; to be honest, I thought it was uninteresting, and declined. It took a conversation with my old coach Kevin Sheedy to spark an interest in writing. We were talking at his unofficial 'office', the bistro at the Hilton Hotel in Melbourne. Sheeds loves books and he felt strongly about how few books had been written about the AFL; we pored over books written about the NFL and NBA and golf and cricket, but so few good AFL books were available at the time.

Sheeds may have regretted that conversation, for the first book I wrote was about him: *The Jigsaw Man*.

Analysing my only senior coach's record taught me a lot more about the game than I could have imagined. Ultimately, it underlined the fact that football is a microcosm of life. If you go searching for perfection, you will probably more often than not be disappointed. This is best explained by a simple rule of thumb neatly borne out in the examination of the records of some of the greats.

A seriously great coaching record over a sustained period of time—say, a decade—will reap a win–loss record of 60 per cent. Which is to say, success *all the time* is impossible, but a two-out-of-three strike rate will ensure you'll not only keep your job, but be considered a winner.

The process taught me something else: there is no *one* way of coaching. Which leads me to Malcolm Blight.

My interest in Blighty grew from weekly conversations with former Geelong footballer Bill Brownless when I worked with him on SEN morning radio in Melbourne. It's not exaggerating to state that Billy loved Blighty, and many of the stories he shared during ad breaks are in this book. While Bill chose the more amusing anecdotes, and entertained me in his unique way, he also alerted me to what I believe is a fascinating story.

Malcolm Blight's story has the elements of a Hollywood script. Blighty is a legitimate legend of the game, an individual who is very much his own man—as you will read, out of the low point of his coaching career emerged a determination to do things his own way.

While Sheeds is a gut-feel instinctive operator, there is more of the sense of the academic about Blight and how he delivered

INTRODUCTION

success. Blight found it harder to get over defeat; Kevin moved on quickly. Yet what they have in common is a love of scoring and playing direct, exciting football.

Here's something else: they are both hard men. Of course, I knew that about Sheeds, but Blight's steel caught me by surprise. The external perception is that Malcolm was a laid-back bloke who did it easily and comfortably, occasionally drifting into the weird and sometimes unconventional. Kevin practised it openly, but Blighty did his best work behind closed doors.

The more of those doors I opened, the more intrigued I became. We were tackling a story on so many fronts: from a precocious Magarey Medallist for Woodville to the ground-breaking Ron Barassi years at North Melbourne, which yielded two premierships and a Brownlow Medal. A failed stint as the League's last playing coach led to a heroic return to the Woodville Warriors as a player (kicking 126 goals in his final senior season, no less) and then coaching them to their first ever finals win.

Yet in some ways, it is only then that Blight's real story begins.

What he achieved as an AFL coach is a textbook case in learning from your mistakes, and doing things your own way. At Geelong, Adelaide and St Kilda, he managed to take teams to grand finals five times in ten seasons, famously twice delivering the ultimate for the Crows. Throughout, he stayed true to himself, which worked with stunning success before failing with equally astonishing speed in 2001.

Each club's association with Blight is a book in itself—I've tried to cram them all into one, and hope I've done them justice.

This book couldn't have happened without Blighty's consent.

3

He refused at first, sending me in multiple directions before I eventually broke down his defences. It's a big decision to allow someone to write about you, and I'm sure he will not agree or even be pleased with every page, but I believe it's a balanced picture of a memorable, and remarkable, life in football.

As he said to me on more than one occasion, 'It's your book'. True, but it's his story, and it didn't have the typical happy Hollywood ending. Not all stories do—especially in football.

The St Kilda experience, for example, only adds weight to my belief that even the best only get it right two out of three times.

After his initial reluctance, Malcolm was generous with his time and his thoughts, and he only added to the mystique of one of the game's brilliant playing and coaching careers. The two words I most sought to avoid were 'mercurial' and 'enigmatic', simply because they are such clichéd tags in modern football. In Malcolm's case, it bordered on impossible for those descriptions not to surface time and again … it's been that sort of career. And he is that sort of man.

This is a completely different book than the ones I read as a kid in Dimboola. It has to be: football is a different game now; we view it, watch it and analyse it mercilessly, and, admittedly, I am part of that machine. I hope, though, that it not only explains a man who is far more complicated and driven than I suspected, but also—like Lou and Jack did for me—has the capacity to inspire others.

Tim Watson
Melbourne
April 2011

1

TWO LAPS

GIVE OR TAKE a dozen metres or so, the circumference of the Arden Street football ground is no different from the average suburban venue. White line, picket fence. Malcolm Blight knew it well, having completed hundreds of laps of the oval since first arriving at North Melbourne Football Club late in 1973.

But these two laps were different. Because 18 July 1981 would change Malcolm Blight forever.

Earlier that day, it was announced that Blight had stood down as playing coach of his Kangaroos, a position he had occupied only since the previous summer, when the great Ron Barassi had declared himself spent. For a man used to success, a player for a decade lauded among the very best in the country, whose confidence had elevated him to the status of a football god in two states, this was the ultimate, public humiliation.

Blight had hoped to find refuge first in the dressing rooms, then in his car and the slow trip home to his always-understanding Patsy. He had expected it. But his replacement as head coach, close friend Barry Cable, had other plans. He walked up to Blight in the dressing rooms.

'Malcolm,' Cable said, 'I want you out on the track. Get your gear on.'

Blight was incredulous. An hour earlier he had sat in a press conference and been exposed as a failure. The reasons were irrelevant. Six wins from sixteen games were not enough to save his skin, and the reign of the last ever playing coach in the Victorian Football League was over. It had been a difficult job; if overwhelming for a mere mortal, it was too much even for an icon like Blight. No matter that he had a list struggling with injuries. And no matter that he had planned his future with this job in mind, had walked away from a lucrative job in the transport industry to commit his heart and soul to a football club he had helped to engineer two premierships—its *first* two premierships—in his eight seasons.

Now he had to face the football world, which sat outside in judgement.

I have been there. I resigned from St Kilda after coaching the Saints for two years, but effectively walked before I was sacked. In your mind, there is no place to hide, and I didn't feel like talking to anyone, or even walking down the street, for months afterwards. Not many people get to fail as publicly as football coaches. When Malcolm told me the story my own anguish and disappointment, which is buried deep, was easy to recall.

'I couldn't believe it, but I got changed,' Blight recalled of that night. 'We used to do a two-lap warm-up at Arden Street, and those two laps felt like they took about 100 days. I've had a lot of TV cameras in my face, winning and losing grand finals, getting sacked, all of that. But for those two laps around Arden Street, every press, radio, television person was in my face. If I ever got close to jumping the fence and saying I've had enough, that time was it.

'I've been exposed before. Front page, back page, you name it. But this was a thirty-one year old with a family. I saw myself for maybe the next five or ten years coaching North Melbourne. For the first time in my life I really felt at home, this is where I wanted to be. And then, whack! Over. Then these two laps, the hardest thing I ever did in my life.

'During those laps, I decided that if I was involved in footy from that day onwards I would do it my way only, for ever and ever. During that period with North I had not been exactly myself all the time. There were other people feeding me things all the time, not all bad but not all me, either. So from the day of those two laps at North Melbourne, I changed as a person.'

2

THE PECKERS

DAVIS STREET, WOODVILLE lies three blocks to the south of Woodville Oval; Oval Avenue transects Davis Street, running north to border the ground. On the rare days that the Woodpeckers were hosting a match of importance in the 1960s, Malcolm Blight can recall the cars parked out the front of the modest family house in which he grew up. 'That meant there were about 4000 people at a game, when cars were parked all the way back to our house. But it didn't happen very often. We were terrible,' Blight explained.

Not that Malcolm or his brother, Barry, cared. Football was life. Life was football. They could not separate the two, spending hours booting rolled-up socks up and down their hallway for want of an actual football. A real leather one to kick in the street would have been a luxury in a suburb of war-commission houses. The boys had food on the table and clothes on their backs, but from an early age they understood you had to bide your time for those sorts of indulgences.

So Malcolm hatched a plan.

'I watched a lot of footy at Woodville and I'd always see these kids behind the goals in the street. At some point I figured out what they were there for,' he recalled. When the senior Woodville players kicked goals that carried the ball over the fence, the local kids would take off with the footy. It didn't happen in Dimboola, where I grew up—the club maybe had one or two decent footies, and everyone knew every kid. But this was the South Australian National Football League [SANFL]. In other words, serious football.

'After a couple of years I was big enough, maybe ten or eleven, and I had my strategy,' Blight said. 'I knew every house and back-yard heading away from the ground. Who had a dog, that sort of thing. So I'd planned the getaway, every inch of my escape route. I *dreamed* about it. Well, the second time I went behind the goals, standing in the street, I got the footy.'

Having secured his booty, Blight took off, jumping back fences and tearing through the streets to his house. He then confronted an even more relevant issue: what to do with his ill-gotten prize, knowing he'd 'get killed if anyone found out about it'.

The solution spoke of his paranoia. A wheat drum down the side of his house kept the family chooks well fed. He buried the football deep inside the drum, covered in wheat, and it stayed there for weeks as Malcolm 'waited for the cops to come'. Finally, he had the courage to retrieve it. It was as good as new, though the shiny leather would betray him, so he scuffed it up on the street before unveiling his find to his brother and telling his parents it belonged to another neighbourhood kid. He was simply borrowing it.

A trend was set that defined one of the game's all-time greats: whatever the challenge, and however cunning a strategy was demanded, Malcolm Blight would find the footy.

* * *

Like so many suburbs of Adelaide, Woodville is soaked in football history. A team carrying its name competed in the eight-team South Australian Football Association from as early as 1877, but the team we identify as having direct lineage to the Woodpeckers of the 1960s was formed in 1938. The team was part of an amateur league, the Port Adelaide District Football Association (PADFA), for three seasons before joining the second division of the South Australian Amateur Football League (SAAFL), and claiming the Section A2 premiership in 1941—the last year of competition before war halted it.

When the competition resumed in 1946, Woodville achieved the rare feat of securing the A1 flag in its first year after promotion, give or take a handful of 'suspended due to war' years. Captain-coach of that team was Horrie Blight, Malcolm's uncle. Jack Blight, Malcolm's father, played for West Torrens reserves in the pre-war years, while a cousin, George, played for Torrens in the early 1960s. It was a football-mad family, such that even in mid-summer the game was on everyone's minds. 'All the Blights would go to the Halfway Hotel on Port Road on Christmas morning,' said Malcolm, whose mother was one of fifteen children, his father one of eight. 'There were forty-six aunties and uncles and about three million cousins, and by about eleven o'clock they'd get to our place after a few beers at the Halfway. We talked footy the whole time.' The primary topic of conversation was the Woodpeckers.

The SANFL beckoned by the late 1950s, and Woodville joined the B Grade of the competition. Five seasons later, in 1964, they became a fully fledged SANFL club.

Looking on was a teenager who had grown up with split allegiances. While Woodville was his local love, its big brother Port Adelaide loomed to the immediate north and the Blight family had a connection: the parents of Rex Johns, a famous Port Adelaide premiership player of the late 1950s and early 60s, lived behind the Blights and occasionally babysat Barry and Malcolm. Malcolm was enraptured by the prodigious talent of Johns, who led the SANFL goalkicking four times and kicked 451 majors in just 134 games; the relationship, however tenuous, endeared the Magpies to him. But the contest for his heart was really no contest at all—he fell, heavily, for the unfashionable Peckers, for reasons both geographic and financial. 'They were four streets away and I knew how to get into the oval for nothing, so they were my team,' Blight said. 'I knew every player; they were my heroes. That's all I ever wanted to do, play League football with Woodville.'

With his 'borrowed' football, Blight and his friends spent every daylight hour on the weekends down at the Beverley Oval, home of his junior club, Kilkenny. Time would prove this to be a remarkably talented bunch of kids. Blight, of course, became a star. But the football CVs of a handful of those playmates also stand up to scrutiny: Ray Huppatz, John Cummins and Eddie Holland, for instance, all played SANFL and state football. 'We'd spend Sundays out there, maybe eight or nine of us playing on a full ground,' Blight recalled. 'That's when you learned to run. If you broke through you had twenty-three bounces and kicked a goal. Whenever I got the ball in any space, not many got it back off me.'

And he was getting it more and more often, be it on those long Sunday afternoons at Beverley or in local junior leagues. Twice he was runner-up in the competition's best and fairest in his early teenage years with Kilkenny, then he graduated to the captaincy at Woodville South's Under-15s. It partly fulfilled a dream, for that team trained on Woodville Oval. The first time you step onto a League ground the grass seems greener, the balls a deeper shade of red; the grandstands feed your dreams, and Blight thrived in it.

The following year, he eyed the chance to play Colts grade, a more prestigious Under-17s local competition. A growth spurt helped his chances, but local junior coach George 'Tuppence' Kersley suggested to the youngster that he would be a fringe player that season. Rather than train and only play infrequently, the sixteen year old decided to try out for Kilkenny's senior A and B teams. At the same time, Findon High School pressured its emerging junior to start lining up in their weekend team.

'It turned out I played for school Saturday morning, then played Colts when I could get a game and in the afternoon played for Kilkenny. So twelve out of twenty weeks that year I played three games of footy,' Blight said. 'It didn't bother me; I couldn't wait to play. I ended up playing in grand finals on three consecutive Saturdays. At Findon I kicked 5.5 from half-forward and we won [Woodville junior and future VFL player Craig McKellar was a teammate]. The Colts got beaten, but in A Grade for Kilkenny I came off the bench as a sixteen year old and we won a premiership.'

Kersley would be Blight's first genuine football influence. One drill in particular taught him the value of not only protecting himself, but also applying himself in training. 'Tup [Kersley] did an exercise where he'd throw the ball at you and you had to turn your body to protect yourself,' he said. 'His attitude was, "Why commit suicide?" I know some people say that's not very tough, but what's the point? It's always astounded me when kids just go for the ball and stick their heads out—that's not courageous, that's stupid. Anyway, this time I jumped in the air, mucking around, and Tup just tore strips off me.

'It was the first time anyone really got hold of me, got into me. He wasn't like that usually, either, so it was a good lesson in discipline, [in] how not to be a smart-arse.'

If Kersley was uncharacteristically harsh on Blight, it was perhaps because he recognised the precocious talent at his disposal. The local kid's height was outpacing his strength, but he lost none of his balance or mobility as he continued to grow into a willowy key position player. By 1968, he had left the Colts behind and was forging a reputation as a full-forward in the Woodville Under-19s. Looking on was a newcomer to the Woodpeckers who would play a pivotal role not only in the football maturity of Malcolm Blight, but also in the direction of the burgeoning star's senior aspirations.

*   *   *

For more than a decade from the mid-1950s, Noel Teasdale forged a distinguished career with North Melbourne in the Victorian

Football League (VFL). Having served the Kangaroos with distinction, including three years as captain and four consecutive best and fairest awards—plus the 1965 Brownlow Medal, awarded retrospectively in 1989 when the League recognised those who had lost on the 'countback' system—Teasdale decided to maximise his final few years in the game. 'After playing twelve years relatively injury free it was time to try and make an extra dollar by coaching,' Teasdale said. 'I got a very good offer for the time, from Woodville, a four-year contract, which I accepted.'

The bullocking ruckman was to earn $8000 and live rent-free in Woodville, a considerable step up from the seven pounds a game he recalled earning for much of his career at North Melbourne. When the news broke at Oval Avenue, players were intrigued about the cross-border replacement for departing captain-coach Peter Obst, who hailed from one of South Australia's revered football families. 'We were just starting to follow Melbourne footy on telly then,' Blight said. 'At the time it was a big thing, but I look back now and think it was Teaser's first coaching job, so I'm sure he would have been a better coach ten years later—that's not being disrespectful, that's just the truth. But, above all else, Teaser was disciplined and pretty tough on us.'

When the Kangaroos star arrived, he wondered if even $8000 was enough compensation for the heartache he suspected might unfold on the football field. 'They weren't that far removed from actually being amateurs, and in my opinion they were still sort of playing amateur football,' while he was a new coach. 'The year before they had won one game [and drew one, out of twenty matches], so I decided to develop the younger players and give them the opportunity to get into the footy team and develop them my way. From memory they had very good juniors so I was keen to promote all the young blokes.'

Those long Sundays of kicking the footy around Beverley Oval were by now well represented. Cummins had made his senior Woodpeckers debut in Round 1 the previous season, as had McKellar, and Huppatz played a single game late in the season. Under Teasdale in 1968, the trend continued: promising junior Colin MacVicar found his way into the seniors in Round 3, while Holland earned his promotion three weeks later. Yet, as was to become increasingly common throughout his playing and coaching career, Blight trod his own path to senior football.

'I went to Blighty, say, three different times and asked whether he'd like to play seniors,' Teasdale said. 'He wasn't ready for it; he used to say to me, "Well, I'm not really prepared to play seniors and your discipline thing is too hard for me. I like to have a gamble. I like to go out a bit and have some fun with my mates. So I wouldn't be able to discipline myself to do it".'

Most weeks Teasdale approached Blight and floated the idea of senior promotion. Each week he got the same response, although the coach could tell that his charge was becoming increasingly aware that his mates—those he wanted to play with—were featuring more and more in the seniors. Eventually, Blight relented, wandering up to his coach and declaring himself ready for the big step. 'I said, "Well okay, I will think about that for a few weeks, then we'll see where we go from there"', Teasdale laughed. 'That made him a little bit impatient.'

Blight was knocking down the door for selection. He had

played both Under-19s and reserves that year, winning the goal-kicking for the season in the latter despite playing only thirteen of the twenty games. By Round 12, Teasdale could deny him no longer. Pitted against powerhouse Glenelg, Malcolm Blight made his SANFL debut on 7 July 1968. The Glenelg Tigers were a fringe finals contender—they missed September action by a game that year—but their visit to Woodville Oval still presented the home side, which ended up winning four games that season, with a challenge. Blight handled the step up well, working out of the forward pocket and goal square to kick three of the team's 8 goals in an otherwise forgettable loss. 'There was a function that night but I was knackered, I ended up going home and going to bed,' Blight said. 'It was probably the only time in eighteen years of playing I didn't go out.' He played three more games in 1968, adding 2 more goals, before playing out the season in the reserves.

'Playing for Woodville was the dream,' Blight remembered. 'I could not believe it when I got a League game. That's all I'd been dreaming about for the past ten years. Nothing more. Didn't care if they were very good, I just wanted to play.'

That taste of senior football hardly ignited a career, though; rather, it introduced Blight to a new level of expectation from his teammates, his coach and himself. It's just that the latter was a little slower to pick up on it.

'Malcolm lived on his talent because he was just such a talented player,' Teasdale said. 'All the things that he could do … kick left or right foot, handball left or right hand. Take the specky mark. The abilities that you saw [Blighty had] throughout his career, his kicking and marking, were there from day one. His ability to read the play; all those things were quite evident. Only one thing I tried to break him out of—and obviously didn't—was that he would kick with his left foot all the time.'

Blight laughs when reminded of the apparent flaw in his game. Convention still dictated that kicking with the opposite foot was a carved-in-stone football sin. With Blight, they had not considered how refined that talent was, to the point where he considered himself a better kick on his left side than his right. Credit it to countless hours of practice, plus the influence of two childhood idols. One was childhood neighbour Rex Johns, who often favoured his left foot due to having had surgery on his right knee earlier in his career.

'Bob Simunsen was the other one' Blight said of Woodville's first League great, its captain and club champion in the Peckers' first SANFL season. 'He'd always go on his left and I'd go home and emulate him. Playing kick-to-kick as a little kid, we seemed miles away from the other end because I was nine and they were fourteen or fifteen, so I had to try to slam the ball onto my boot [when I was] kicking right-foot. But I didn't have to do that learning left-foot on my own in the street or backyard, so technically I was probably a better left-foot kick. And I practised it all the time; if I had 100 kicks, I'd kick ninety-five on the left.'

By 1969, the skinny kid had put on little weight but had added confidence. Teasdale knew he had a prodigious talent at his disposal—the question would be how to best utilise it. Another Blight trademark developed that year, one that remained throughout his career: few coaches knew exactly where to play him. Teasdale decided his gifted full-forward by now had the fitness to spend more time around the middle, while he also saw the benefit of instilling some defensive skills in the eighteen year old. In his first full season of senior football, Blight and his playing coach were primarily changing on the ball deep in defence, though Blight was also used to plug multiple holes as the Peckers' defences inevitably leaked.

'We used to interchange as run-on players in the back pocket,' Teasdale said. 'He also played for me at centre half-back. One day in his third or fourth season he played against Russell Ebert, who I think had won a Magarey Medal [the SANFL best and fairest] by then, and they were best and second best on ground. One played at centre half-forward and the other centre half-back. It was just a fantastic highlight, the way they played against each other. Blighty would run down the ground and do all sorts of things. So he played centre half-back, and I think he probably played in the centre. He played full-forward and probably centre half-forward, so he was a key player down the centre line and even a run-on ruckman.'

Blight played nineteen of twenty games in 1969, missing only Round 16 with injury. He kicked just 12 goals for the season, spending more time in defence waiting for Teasdale to finish his spell on the ball than in the forward role, which had been his meal ticket.

'We used to change in the back pocket, and if Teaser didn't have five kicks he wouldn't come off the ball. There were some days when I got pretty cold in the back pocket, resting on the talls,' said Blight, who found ways to keep himself occupied. 'I might have taken the highest marks of all time on six-foot-eight blokes, because you'd do anything to keep moving, keep warm. We weren't a very good team and the ball came down [to the back line] a lot, kicked up high. It was like Christmas some weeks.'

THE PECKERS

The Peckers won eight games in 1969, a new high-water mark. Huppatz was the team's standout player, winning the first of three consecutive best and fairest awards. And in Round 19, despite having no hope of playing finals football, Woodville produced the most telling result in the club's brief SANFL history—a defeat of reigning premier Sturt, which was en route to a fourth consecutive premiership. In some respects it was the high point of Blight's five-season stint with the Peckers, not for his personal achievements that day, but for the fact that Woodville had arrived as a threat.

With Huppatz, McKellar, Blight, Simunsen, Cummins and impressive first-year talent Ralph Sewer, who would go on to play almost 400 SANFL games, Teasdale's competitiveness came to life after half-time as Woodville chased down a 25-point half-time deficit to edge ahead in the final quarter. At the twenty-one-minute mark of the final term, Simunsen kicked a long drop kick into the forward line; according to commentator Ian Day, Blight soared over Sturt's Greg Wild 'like a 727' to claim a brilliant mark. He kicked truly, putting his team 26 points ahead. The game was essentially over. So too was the season, but the Peckers took bright hopes into 1970.

* * *

Woodville started the 1970 season well, winning three of its first six games, and was leading Norwood into the final term when Noel Teasdale's right knee first buckled, then gave way. Just as the ligaments tore in his joint, ending his playing career, the Woodpeckers' hopes essentially disintegrated. At thirty, Teasdale would not play again. He assumed non-playing coach duties,

19

struggling to make the transition but, now relieved of playing duties, more focused than ever on refining the talent at his disposal. Which was not necessarily a good thing for Malcolm Blight.

Teasdale's fire and brimstone playing-coach act evolved into a relentlessly driven performance as coach. And he soon had Blight in his crosshairs, unable to accept the now twenty year old's 'cruisy' attitude towards League football. By Round 14, he had seen enough. 'Malcolm used to like to have a punt and go to the trots and things like that', Teasdale said. 'This would have been something like being out late on a Friday night, which in those days wasn't allowed. It wouldn't have been a serious matter, but he was just going against the discipline routine and it had become a bit too common.'

So Teasdale dropped Blight. It was no small decision—the versatile utility had been named in the state squad and was destined for a top-three best and fairest finish, so Blight's form had been sound if not spectacular. 'I wasn't going great but wasn't that bad either,' Blight recalled. This was not a short-term issue, for Teasdale wanted Blight to elevate his commitment to the game, including giving away a passion for cricket. A natural sportsman, Blight had been promoted to A Grade for Woodville's cricket team and was toying with an early start to pre-season cricket training, but his football coach considered it unwise to split his energies. 'Teaser came up to me and said, "What do you want to do with your life? What do you want to do with your footy?"' Blight said. 'To be honest I hadn't thought of it that way, I just enjoyed playing with my mates and having a beer and a bet, and that's what I told him. So he dropped me.'

Club legend has Blight collecting north of 50 possessions in the reserves the following week. Little wonder he enjoyed himself, plus the $3 he pocketed for playing in a winning reserves side. He spent the money drinking, watching the seniors lose to Sturt, but Teasdale's lesson had not yet been absorbed. When asked the same question after Thursday training, Blight admitted he was quite happy to again just play footy with his mates. He stayed in the reserves, and the pattern continued that week: huge possessions, and a drinking session watching the seniors lose again, this time to North Adelaide.

'The next week the light went on,' Blight said. 'Playing with my mates was great but I hated losing, and I felt like playing seconds was losing. So cricket went. I used to pay a dollar for subscriptions to play district cricket, but I got $14 a game to play for Woodville. Well, I worked in the bank and I could count—that was twenty-eight beers' difference. So I stopped playing cricket.'

In the same fortnight that Blight spent time in the reserves, both Ray Huppatz and Craig McKellar suffered injuries that all but ended their seasons. With McKellar, Teasdale and Huppatz absent, the Peckers fell to ninth with just six wins, losing nine of their final twelve games. Hope was slipping away for a club that had appeared on the verge, but its brilliant young star was about to emerge.

3

BREAKOUT

During his eighteen years of senior football, Malcolm Blight was an All-Australian selection at both full-back and full-forward. He spent considerable time on a wing, at centre half-forward and at centre half-back, and recalls that in his playing-coach year at North Melbourne in 1981 he played as many as fourteen positions that season. 'One week for North Melbourne I went from full-back, rover, centre half-forward, to forward pocket to half-back flank.' The only position Blight never played at any length was ruck. At a tick under six feet 'in the old', or 182 centimetres, that's hardly surprising.

During his North Melbourne playing days, one day against Essendon at Windy Hill—with a gale bellowing to one end—I clearly remember him playing at that end of the ground all day. Full-back, full-forward. Full-back, full-forward. He was never out of the play, and he loved it.

Blight's awareness on the ground—his ability to read the play and contest so efficiently one-on-one—made him invaluable in practically every position on the ground. I'd argue, however, that he was never more damaging than when playing ruck-rover. Funnily enough, in the twenty-first century the term 'ruck-rover' is bordering on antiquated. Contemporary football demands a midfield rotation of as many as a dozen runners, supreme athletes with a 'clock on, clock off' mentality who produce high-intensity, almost manic bursts of speed through the middle.

The game's folklore credits Ron Barassi with popularising the role. Early in 1954, visionary Melbourne coach Norm Smith was searching for a role for Barassi, an athletic, bullocking style of player who was struggling to have an impact at half-forward. Struck by Barassi's combination of size, strength and mobility, Smith decided to try him in the ruck division as a combination of second ruckman and rover. Ruck-roving was born.

In 1971, Woodville coach Noel Teasdale had been using Blight to plug gaps. Having come through the ranks as a full-forward, Blight had spent time in every position up and down the Peckers' spine, but in Round 11 against North Adelaide he was assigned a ruck-roving role. Woodville entered the game at two wins and eight losses; powered by the mighty Barrie Robran, the reigning Magarey Medallist and arguably the premier player in the competition, North Adelaide sat on top of the table and was busy compiling the first of consecutive premiership seasons.

Woodville won by 24 points. Blight added 18 marks to his 32 kicks, but observers believe even those statistics do not give full measure to his performance that day. The *Adelaide Advertiser* noted that 'Blight stood out like a beacon in the face of an eight-goal onslaught' in the second quarter; Blight concedes he played 'a kick behind the game, I was sitting on the ball a bit' as the Roosters mounted their charge. Regardless of whether his numbers flattered him, that day was definitive proof that Woodville had produced one of the League's special talents.

A month later, that recognition was formalised when Blight made his state debut, lining up for South Australia against Western Australia at the Adelaide Oval. Pulling on your state jumper for the first time is an incredible buzz, and Blight knows he would have felt enormous pride that day ... he just can't remember anything about it. 'I got completely knocked out in that first state game,' he said. 'I reckon I had eleven or twelve touches to half-time and was going all right, but all I remember [is] waking up in hospital. I got kicked in the head, accidentally, but even so, just being there was building more momentum in my footy over those couple of years. Things were starting to happen for me.'

As the 1971 season drew to a close, Blight was playing his most consistent football. He now clearly figured among the Peckers' best handful of players, and was harbouring hopes of a strong 1972 showing. His coach would not be around to see it. His knee having betrayed his playing career, Teasdale had been unable to lift the Woodpeckers as he had hoped; they closed the 1971 season in last place, with six wins, after which his four-year contract expired. Rather than retain Teasdale, Woodville went to market, though it didn't look far: Barrie Barbary had been captain-coach of the reserves and was a logical replacement. The 1960 Magarey Medallist had left North Adelaide to try his hand in country football in the mid-1960s. He came to Woodville in 1967, playing serviceable football for the Peckers until assuming control of the reserves in 1971.

Teasdale left with regrets in his inability to both play past thirty and lift Woodville out of the cellar. Yet he got to watch firsthand the evolution of one of the game's rare talents. 'The very last game I coached was against Norwood at Norwood Oval, and they were always hard to beat there,' he said. 'Blighty was playing centre half-back and I spotted him running down the centre of the oval towards the end of the ground; he just took off. He got down to the goal square and took this magnificent mark and kicked a goal, which put us in front. We won the game. That was the sort of thing that he could do, just read the play, know when to run off [his man] of his own accord. Malcolm would do the spectacular thing and win games. You can't honestly say that about many players.'

Had Teasdale stayed, he would have witnessed one of the SANFL's watershed years as Blight the footballer came of age. Sadly, the Peckers were no better, winning seven games and finishing eighth. But Blight, recently turned twenty-two, was sublime. He kicked 44 goals from twenty games, winning the Woodville best and fairest award as he continued to fill multiple roles for Barbary. Blight represented South Australia at the 1972 national carnival and earned All-Australian honours.

Bill Sanders had been closely watching the maturing of the former Colts fringe player. Starting as assistant general manager of Woodville in 1968, and adding team manager duties the following year, Sanders also oversaw recruitment and sat on the committee. Even in a team featuring the star power of new captain Ray Huppatz, Blight had clearly elevated himself above the pack. 'He was breathtaking that season, just breathtaking,' Sanders said. 'Malcolm's game developed to the next level and it seemed to happen quite quickly. He'd be loping down the ground, bouncing a couple of times, most occasions kicking goals with his left foot but still cruising. Then he went up a notch. Whether as a ruck-rover or in the backline, he just dominated games.'

It was deep in defence that Blight made his most notable mark—more than one—that season. Bob Kingston was a former South Melbourne defender who had crossed first to Norwood, then, in 1971, to Port Adelaide, to prolong his career and make some money. An attacking full-back, Kingston was strong but injury-prone—so it proved in the interstate carnival game against Victoria, for he broke his arm in the first quarter. In search of a replacement, Croweaters coach Neil Kerley sent Blight to the goal square, on Peter McKenna.

McKenna was a handful. By 1972 (and given the severe knee injury Peter Hudson had suffered in Round 1 of the VFL season) he was the premier spearhead in the country. As revered as he was adored at Collingwood, McKenna had booted 143 and 134 goals in the previous two seasons, and was en route to adding another 130 this season. His record for Victoria was imposing; in seven games he booted 42 goals for the Big V.

'This bloke came down onto me, I took one look at him and thought, "He's not very tall, this will be easy",' McKenna said of Kingston's replacement. 'But I recall twice backing back to the ball and feeling these knees on my neck. He took two screamers.

Naturally I couldn't see it, but I could feel how high he must have been.'

If Blight was a stranger to McKenna, he was no stranger to the defensive goal square. 'In those early years at Woodville I'd invariably end up playing on a big bloke at full-back or in the back pocket,' he recalled. McKenna could not have been prepared for an aerial assault. Full-backs of the era rarely flew from behind and marked, preferring the convention of punching defensively at all costs. Not Blight, who stamped his presence on the carnival that Perth afternoon by taking 13 marks and reportedly gathering more than 20 kicks.

McKenna still enjoyed a successful day, the weight of possession from a dominant midfield making any full-back's job nearly impossible against a player of the Magpie great's ability. In fact, for all the Blight buzz that followed the game, McKenna kicked 8 goals on his way to leading the carnival goalkicking with 19 in three games. Because of Blight he changed his tactics, reverting to a fast-leading target instead of waiting in the goal square and challenging his man one-on-one. 'I didn't know he had that leap, but I found out the hard way, so I started leading up the ground. We had a very good side [Victoria accounted for ten All-Australians that season, while Blight was one of only two from South Australia] so I saw plenty of the ball. I remember thinking, "God, you're going to be a good player, probably just not at full-back",' McKenna said. 'And what a great player he was. He must have been a confident sort of guy even then, because I never got many blokes going for marks on me.'

Victoria won by 54 points. South Australia easily handled Tasmania but lost its other match against Western Australia, closing a largely unsuccessful carnival. Blight, however, secured a Seiko watch for his All-Australian selection. His stock was rising fast, and it was elevated to 'buy' status when the pundits sat to consider the Magarey Medal contenders late in the season. Blight was a runaway favourite, a near-unanimous prediction to become the Woodpeckers' first winner of the competition's best and fairest. Writing in the *Sunday Mail* in the lead-up to the Magarey Medal count, Bill Henderson said Blight 'has eye-catching style—spectacular marking and dashing speed. He has sustained his effort throughout the year'.

Blight had enjoyed a successful twelve months on and off the field. His football had caught the public eye, while his childhood sweetheart, Patsy, had caught *his*—they became engaged that year. With Woodville again not contending for the finals, his mind had switched off football by the time the count arrived, to the point where he chose not to attend. 'I didn't really want to go, to be honest, so we sat at home and watched it on TV. Mum and Dad were there, and I was engaged to Patsy at the time, so we sat on the couch.

'When it got close at the end, there was a bloke from the League sitting out the front in his car. They brought me in to the count.'

There was little tension in the closing stages on that Monday night: Blight polled twenty-one votes, five clear of the runner-up, Sonny Morey from Central Districts. The Magarey has a slight variation on the 'best and fairest' tradition of football leagues: it is voted upon the criteria of the player adjudged the 'fairest and most brilliant'. Blight, who wore the traditionally unlucky number 13, was exceptional on both counts, as was the party that night after local boy made good.

'We went back to Woodville Oval and gave the Magarey Medal the biggest send-off it had ever had,' he laughed. 'It was the night of nights. The local boy winning the big medal … anyone who lived at Woodville would have dropped in that night.'

As Tuesday dawned, so did the realisation that he had a game of football to play that day. There was a longstanding midweek competition in Adelaide called Bank Football, and, as an employee of the State Bank of South Australia, Blight was expected to be on duty against the Commonwealth Bank at Railways Oval. He had managed little if any sleep the previous night. It's fair to say the freshly minted Magarey Medallist was in no state to contribute at any level of competition. 'Normally I loved the bank competition because you got off work early and were excused from training that night,' Blight said. 'Not so much this day. The only way I was playing was full-forward with the wind, full-back against the wind. I didn't move. People just brought me drinks all day. Jeez, I was crook.'

Malcolm Blight was the toast of Adelaide town. In some people's eyes, it was time to conquer another city, just an hour's flight to the southeast.

4

REBUILDING THE ROOS

RON JOSEPH FIRST sought involvement in football when he was eighteen years old. It was 1964, the year after he'd left school, and Joseph applied—unsuccessfully—for the position of assistant secretary at Richmond. He persisted in his goal to find employment in the game, and within twelve months landed a junior role at North Melbourne. Internal bickering and politics over the development of a new social club had left the secretary's job open. Joseph knew an opportunity when he saw one, and despite his inexperience he secured the role.

The position of club secretary at the time was essentially the equivalent of today's general manager, plus any other duties that needed filling. It sure beat licking envelopes at Punt Road.

'But were we ordinary,' Joseph said. 'Something had to change.'

North Melbourne had joined the Victorian Football League in 1925, the same season as Hawthorn and Footscray. They became known as the Shinboners, harking back to an era when a number of players worked at the nearby abattoirs and when local butchers used to decorate their front windows with bones of that ilk. In the mid-1950s, the club assumed the Kangaroos moniker when the then club president Phonse Tobin wanted something 'characteristically Australian' for the club to identify with.

It took twenty seasons for them to play finals football, and another five to reach a grand final, losing the 1950 showdown to Essendon by 6 goals. That elusive premiership still awaited the club when Joseph walked through the front door of Arden Street, joining the club in an era showing few signs of competitiveness. North had finished no higher than seventh in the 1960s, and won three wooden spoons between Joseph's 1964 arrival and 1972. Meanwhile, across the city, the club at which he had first sought employment, Richmond, had lifted itself from perennial non-contention to the most ruthless team in the VFL. Under the guidance of administrators Graeme Richmond and Ian Wilson, the Tigers won flags in 1967 and 69, and would add two more in 1973 and 74.

Only twenty-two at the time, Joseph now admits to being 'petrified' of Graeme Richmond, who, by 1968, was running the Vaucluse Hotel while inspiring the Tigers' success. In desperation, Joseph that year placed a call to the popular Richmond pub. The man known universally as 'GR' answered the phone.

'Can I come and talk to you?' asked Joseph, who was prepared for rejection from one of the game's most secretive characters.

'Jesus, what would I want to talk to you for?' There was a pause, and a detectable sigh, before Richmond continued. 'All right, come and see me if you want to.'

When Joseph wandered into the hotel, he was granted just ten minutes with the Tigers powerbroker. But he gleaned a single piece of advice that became his mantra during the process of rebuilding a football club. 'I'll tell you one thing,' Richmond confided in his high-pitched shriek. 'You'll be known by the players you recruit. The money will look after itself if you've got good players.'

Joseph got to work. He had a substantial ally in Allen Aylett, who had joined the club board shortly after finishing a terrific 220-game career for the Kangaroos. A successful dentist, Aylett brought passion and effort to everything he tackled, and it was no surprise that by 1971 he was elected club president. With Joseph firmly in his camp, he set about changing the shape of modern football. Some have since accused the Kangaroos of seeking to 'buy a premiership'. It's not true—they were simply ahead of their time.

Aylett brought professionalism to the club. He introduced sponsorships and corporate entertainment, and promoted club coteries that raised significant revenue for the club. The club's much-feted grand final breakfast, born in 1967, fast developed traction in the corporate world and was televised by the mid-1970s. It would be 'poor old North' no longer, fuelled by a spirit of entrepreneurship and hard work that culminated in the construction of a new social club at Arden Street. 'It wasn't the Taj Mahal like Carlton or St Kilda's,' said Joseph, 'but it fit our culture and made a hell of a lot of money.'

Previously run on a bare-bones budget, the club was now a

REBUILDING THE ROOS

going concern … off the field. On the ground, the Kangaroos struggled under coach Brian Dixon in 1971–72, finishing ninth and last (with a 1–21 record in the latter season) and triggering the most significant recruiting coup of them all: the signing of Ron Barassi as coach. Just as he had been influential in developing the role of ruck-rover, Barassi had become an iconic figure in the game through his move from Melbourne to captain-coach Carlton in 1965. His defection was viewed in many circles as unconscionable—a Demons player since 1953, the captain and reigning best and fairest was tempted by a lucrative contract from the Blues to become captain-coach. For many, it represented the fatal blow for any vestige of loyalty in the game.

Barassi took the Blues to a premiership in 1968, and to another two seasons later in the game's most famous grand final. His 'handball, handball, handball' instruction at half-time in the 1970 play-off is firmly entrenched in football legend. Yet he was burnt out by 1971, and opted to pursue a career in business supplemented by media work. In his commentating role for Channel 7, he sat and watched his successor at Princes Park, captain-coach John Nicholls, take the Blues to the 1972 flag after they'd missed the finals in Barassi's last season. It was enough to fire his renowned competitive spirit, and North Melbourne knew it. 'That really dented his pride,' Joseph said.

On the pretence of buying a desk, Kangaroos board member Albert Mantello paid a visit to Barassi's furniture store. 'Albert came to my office at the showroom in Latrobe Street', Barassi recalled. 'We had a bit of a chat and I said, "Why are you here, Albert?"'

'Oh, I want a desk.' And a coach, he might have added.

As Mantello waded through the showroom full of office furniture, he steered the conversation to Barassi's passion for the game. 'Are you starting to miss football again?' he asked, before casually outlining the Kangaroos' plans. Barassi showed increasing interest as the conversation progressed, such that breakfast was organised shortly afterwards at the Old Melbourne Motor Inn. To both parties' surprise, an agreement was signed before the bill had arrived. 'Ron committed then and there,' Joseph said. 'He could see that we wanted to be successful.' (Many years later, as Mantello was inducted into the North Melbourne Hall of Fame, I interviewed him and discussed that breakfast. He laughed when asked if Barassi had wavered on the deal. 'Not with the $10,000 we offered him. [It took him] five minutes.')

Running in parallel to the Barassi negotiations was an intriguing VFL predicament. Mantello, who sat on the VFL board as North delegate, was reporting back to the Kangaroos that the League was spooked by a potential restraint of trade issue. A 'ten-year rule' proposal had been tabled in response to this concern—it meant that any player with ten years of continuous service to a club could effectively choose the club with which to play out his career. At every North committee meeting of 1972, Mantello declared the introduction of the rule was imminent. The Roos prepared to pounce.

Over the summer of 1972–73, with Barassi in their pocket, they used the rule and their inflated bank balance to secure Doug Wade, Barry Davis and John Rantall. Wade had been a star Geelong full-forward since 1961, kicking 849 goals in 208 games; Davis had been Essendon captain and was a three-time Bomber best and fairest (he later returned to Windy Hill and was my coach for three years); and 'Mopsy' Rantall was a brilliant defender who was later named in both North Melbourne's and South Melbourne's teams of the century. All are inductees in the AFL Hall of Fame. Joseph also came close to securing St Kilda's Carl Ditterich, who eventually used the ten-year rule to cross to Melbourne. Still, it was a stunning recruiting drive, made even more opportune by the fact that the ten-year rule was abolished inside of five months—clubs such as North Melbourne were seen to be pillaging the opposition.

It launched Barassi's maiden season in style. The Roos came within a half-game of the finals, winning eleven games and strengthening their football resources in the process, adding a pair of highly respected football minds to support the coach. Newspaper *Football Life* said of the club, 'Whatever the outcome of season 1973, nobody can say that North's bold, energetic executive hasn't pulled out all stops to arrest the club's down-the-ladder image. At the top are three imports, too—senior coach Ron Barassi and advisers Norm Smith and Bill Stephen'.

Ignited by Barassi's obsessive personality and a raft of new playing talent, the Kangaroos finally merited respect. They simply needed to keep securing talent, and a recommendation from former Kangaroos players and Woodville coach Noel Teasdale several years earlier was bouncing around in Ron Joseph's mind. 'Noel had rung me up, he said this fella Blight was casual but he could see his class and exceptional talent', Joseph said. 'He was worried about whether footy meant enough to him. So I went over and watched him … I just saw him do a couple of magic things. He might not have been best man on the ground but each time I saw him I thought, "Shit. We need him".

'We thought he could be a ruck-rover changing on a half-forward flank. He could play full-forward or centre, whatever you like. The secret is, don't go and look at a game and wait for a bloke to make a mistake. If he does one good thing, and our coaches are good enough, that one good thing can become ten good things. When I saw Blighty play twice, I knew he could play. He had something about him. And we had Barass.'

Teasdale's initial enthusiasm was tempered by his belief that Blight was not then mentally equipped for the VFL. 'Not for the things that were required. The disciplines and things like that, because he was very much a boy when he came up ... In many ways he was still a big kid.'

But by the end of 1972, Joseph pursued Blight and signed him to a Form Four, an agreement that tied the player to that club for two years should he choose to go to the VFL. Joseph did not hesitate, knowing that competition for signing interstate players was increasing and the Magarey Medallist's star was on the rise. 'If you waited, by the time you'd listened to your match committee and discussed it internally, someone like Graeme Richmond would have been over there and signed them,' he said. 'You really had to back yourself.'

Blight and Woodville teammate Ray Huppatz had both been approached by Footscray (Huppatz would eventually join the Bulldogs in 1974) but Joseph had learned his Graeme Richmond lesson well. 'Ronny sold me the dream,' Blight admitted. 'There were lots of things happening, Barassi was announced as coach, and not long after that the Wade–Davis–Rantall thing happened, so it was nice to sit back and watch that all happen while I was still

REBUILDING THE ROOS

in South Australia, then join it. Sometimes when you walk into a room you think, "That's for me". When Ron Joseph walked in, that was *that* feeling. Plus, North had only won one game [in 1972, after which Blight signed his Form Four], and I thought, "If I go there I might get a game".'

Given its history of being the have-nots, North was ironically becoming as hated as Richmond—both club and administrator—for its ruthless approach to signing talent. 'I flew to Perth to pinch John Burns, who was playing for East Perth,' Joseph said. 'Geelong thought they had Burns locked up but I flew over and signed him that night in the Parmelia Hotel. While I was there I heard about [Dick] Michalczyk, who had walked out on his WAFL [Western Australian Football League] club and gone to Adelaide, so I stopped off in Adelaide and signed him on the way home. Flying back I thought I'd probably spent five grand more than I should have, and was worrying about what I would say. But Aylett said, "Don't worry about it, mate, that's fantastic". That was the attitude.'

Next stop, Malcolm Blight.

Little did Joseph know that the man himself would soon be ready for a move. 'The weird thing was, I had this wanderlust, I even spoke with a couple of West Australian clubs around that time,' Blight said of life after the 1973 season. 'I just wanted to change my life, to this day I can't tell you why but I wanted to move and do something else. Patsy and I got married in early 73; she was keen to move, too.

'There was this feeling that I couldn't see myself spending the rest of my life working in a bank and playing for Woodville. I had always wanted to play 100 games for the club—that's probably why

37

I stayed in 1973. I figured 100 games put you in the top 15 per cent of players and it looked like you'd done something with your footy life. I enjoyed the bank but it felt like I couldn't go anywhere, because years of service was how you got your next job.'

Being a Magarey Medallist had a certain cachet in Adelaide. Blight's bank work by now consisted of visiting Rotary Clubs and schools, and activities such as teaching kids how to bank. With an open mind, he accepted a Joseph invitation to breakfast, and the Roos recall him being cagey about his decision to the point of being difficult. 'He was very much going to stay at Woodville,' Joseph said, 'and was just starting to settle with Patsy. I'm sure they both would have preferred another twelve months in Adelaide.'

Blight counters that he was simply waiting for the right moment. 'I didn't play hard to get. There was no plan. Something magic has to happen, words or money or whatever, something has to click. Anyway, I was pretty quiet, might have been hard to read.' The club brought Blight across to play tennis at Mantello's Toorak house and visit his Sorrento property, but the South Australian still wavered, returning home without a commitment. One final Ron Joseph plane trip to Adelaide was required, and he finally got his man in January of 1974.

Then it was a matter of securing a clearance. As the Roos were about to discover, getting Adelaide players to come to Victoria was no easy feat.

* * *

In the early 1970s, new trenches were being dug in the cross-border war between South Australian and Victorian football. The SANFL was a vibrant league, rightly proud of the talent pool it produced for a relatively small population base. When the Victorian clubs came knocking, it was a resented intrusion. The VFL was (and now, as the AFL, remains in some eyes) the arrogant big brother.

The poster boy for this crossover was John 'Diamond Jim' Tilbrook, the Sturt premiership star who was lured to Melbourne in 1971 for a king's ransom. Five years and fifty-three largely unremarkable games later, Tilbrook headed home, underscoring Victorians' belief that SANFL was a second-tier league and in the process deepening the South Australians' dislike for them. The Demons also attracted Tassie Medallist Graham Molloy from Norwood, but his 1970 move had equally underwhelming results: sixty-eight games in six seasons.

If those high-profile failures fuelled Victorians' anxiety about paying large transfer fees for SANFL talent, it did not stop them chasing.

Bill Sanders, a board member at Woodville at the time, understood the resentment from both parties, though he naturally sat on the South Australian side of the fence. Or, in this case, border. 'Well, South Australians were anti-Victorian. You know, "They're stealing our players to bolster their competition" sort of stuff,' Sanders said. 'But there was also the reality that it was the place to be if you wanted to play in the best competition. We were exposed to the [ABC highlights of the VFL] television show *The Winners*, and I can recall after our local SANFL games the telly in the corner of the rooms or the social club would be showing that, and there was always enormous interest.'

When he sat with North Melbourne president Aylett at a

Kangaroos game, Sanders could not be blamed for thinking it was a one-way street. He was seeking a trade for Blight as much as a transfer payment, keen to ensure the Woodpeckers' playing stocks remained relatively healthy. 'I remember a possible trade of players with North Melbourne, meeting with Aylett and sitting in the stands. Every time a name was raised, Aylett was, "He's untouchable, he's untouchable". Not one player were they prepared to let go.'

Annoyed, the Woodpeckers requested a sizeable transfer fee to release their best player. They had already seen Craig McKellar depart for Richmond in 1971, weathering a lengthy transfer battle and holding their ground for a $20,000 fee, which the Tigers finally paid. The excellent history of the Woodville–West Torrens Football Club, *Best of Both Worlds*, details that McKellar had been paid $216 for his 1970 season in the SANFL ... minus $5 for the team photo. His first season at Richmond yielded $2000, plus the revelation that 'I wanted to see how far I could go'. The understandable temptation was growing for a number of SANFL players.

Huppatz, too, was keenly sought after, with Carlton and Essendon treading a path to his door. He eventually signed his Form Four with Footscray, which constructed a shed in his backyard in a bizarre form of compensation. After winning his fourth Woodville best and fairest in five years, he decided to take the VFL plunge for the 1974 season. The decision meant Huppatz was denied a place on the Woodpeckers' footy trip at the end of the 1973 season. Obviously, taking VFL money still counted as a black mark against your name for the locals.

Blight did not care. In 1972, when he won the Magarey Medal, he had earned $500 for a season's work. North Melbourne offered up to $10,000 for him to change the colour of his stripes. As Blight had noted earlier when assessing the financial merits of playing cricket versus football, he could count, but there was more to it than a financial argument or the sense of wanderlust he was experiencing. There was the challenge to affirm to himself that his football had merit. 'This is the honest truth: I've never thought I was god's gift to footy,' Blight said, conceding a fear of failure often gripped him and eroded his confidence. 'I loved it, but in every game I'd go to the toilet three times before we ran out. I never, ever thought I had the game beaten. Footy is just mentally and physically tough, so I never took it for granted.

'Also, I didn't play in premierships in those early days, I didn't know what September was, but all these other players around me were playing finals footy.'

Blight wanted to be a part of it. Woodville, however, wanted its pound of flesh. 'McKellar, Blight, Huppatz. It was almost like we were victims of producing this talent that departed all at one time. Suddenly a swathe of players were heading to Victoria,' Sanders said. 'We were realistic. As much as [SANFL] club officials beat their chests about it, ultimately there was not much we could do about it until the evolution of the national competition and the arrival of the Crows [Adelaide, in 1991].'

The Peckers demanded $30,000 for Blight's services, the highest requested transfer fee to that point. They refused to budge on the terms, but when North Melbourne officials finally agreed they found their Woodville counterparts had developed cold feet. It led to an almost comical exchange of phone calls and letters, until Joseph finally decided to settle the matter. Or so he thought.

'Woodville played hardball,' Joseph said. 'When they changed their mind, we went over with thirty thousand in cash and left it there. It wasn't like they couldn't cash the cheque or anything, it was cash.'

Woodville secretary Brian Watson was instructed not to accept it. 'They were pushing the briefcase across the table and we were pushing it back,' Sanders laughed. 'Then they went out and got a bank cheque drafted to the Woodville Football Club, thinking we'd have no choice [but] to accept it. Ultimately, we accepted on the basis that Malcolm might have been able to go for nothing anyway,' he added, referring to possible intervention from the National Football League.

Had Blight been aware of the charade surrounding his departure, it might have given him a better sense of what to expect when he walked into Arden Street. Under Aylett, the Kangaroos had transformed themselves into a marketing machine, stealing a march on opposition clubs by being wise to the media and its influence. 'North was headlines,' Blight said of the strongest impressions of his arrival. 'Names on dressing gowns. Big sponsorship. There were businesspeople at training, watching on, they really embraced the whole club. I was like, "*What?*" And I think a lot of other clubs in the VFL would have been "*What?*" Barassi was a walking headline, Allen Aylett was a super name. [Marketing manager] Barry Cheatley was bringing out all these auctioning items and marketing ideas. Medallists were coming from everywhere. It was an incredible place to be.'

Blight was aware of the reputation that preceded his new coach. He expected Barassi to be difficult, but felt that, having turned twenty-four a month before the first game, and with a

Magarey Medal to his name, he was hardly an unknown rookie who would be pushed around. But the new signing had two things going against him: one, Barassi paid no heed to reputation, and two, the coach hated South Australian football. 'Barass had a thing about South Australia,' Joseph admitted. 'He thought they were taught the wrong way. He had it in for them, and he certainly had it in for Blighty. But he wanted him anyway; he was going to cut the Magarey Medallist champion down to size. I'd have to say Blighty wasn't confident in his first three years, basically because Barass knocked the guts out of him.'

It did not help that Barassi's primary assistant, Ray 'Slug' Jordon, had an equally passionate dislike of all things South Australian. And Blight also had to adjust to a training program that was light years ahead of the regime at Woodville. In his first week, for instance, he was confronted with a 20-kilometre run. 'To that point I'd never even run three Ks at once,' he said. 'I chafed and I hurt my groin, and for the next six weeks I struggled.' Barassi noticed his man was battling, but he continued to push and prod the newcomer with the big reputation through a pre-season Blight has never forgotten. Though the South Australian could not have known it, it was flattering treatment from his coach, who had quickly become aware of the Woodville recruit's potential. Barassi was always toughest on the talented.

'I was wary of them falling into that trap that "I don't need to train like the others",' he explained.

Wayne Schimmelbusch was a long-time teammate of Blight, and captained the Kangaroos when the latter became captain-coach in 1981. He was aware his coach could be fierce on the talented

MALCOLM BLIGHT

members of the group, in particular Blight and gifted wingman Keith Greig. 'Barass had a theory that they had more ability in their little finger than the rest of the team had combined,' he said. 'And he always thought that he could get more out of them. Both of them. Blighty copped it on the chin and went on with his game.'

Blight continued to hear the negativity heading his way: 'Barassi and Slug were the same,' he said. 'You heard second hand, "Another fucking interstater," while Slug was pushing up his younger blokes.' But this was, in truth, parochial grandstanding. The Kangaroos lured Blight and Western Australian star midfielder Barry Cable to the club in 1974 for the simple reason that they were among the country's best players.

Blight was quick to prove his value. He made his VFL debut in Round 2, 1974, performing well enough to earn media votes. 'Thank goodness for that; the papers basically said, "At least he can play a bit," so that took a lot of pressure off,' he said.

Schimmelbusch had played his first game the year before Blight arrived, and liked what he saw of the newcomer. Well, most of it. 'My first impressions were fantastic kick, fantastic mark,' he said. 'But it became fairly obvious that while he had all this ability he also had a lot of bad habits, which Barassi was always on his back about. I mean, he would fly from fourteen-deep and try and take these speckies all the time and Barassi was always on his back about that. I reckon it took him two or three years to get himself out of that.'

Blight kicked 10 goals in the three weeks from Rounds 11 to 13, and was being used as a spare-parts man, just as he had been at Woodville. But the workload took its toll, as did the stress of

44

REBUILDING THE ROOS

the move east and perhaps even the news that Patsy was expecting their first child. 'I felt like I was getting into it but I got glandular fever. It meant I missed the last six or eight weeks and I felt like I'd fallen off the perch. Patsy was pregnant and she was sick, so it wasn't a great time.'

For a debutant, it was a promising season in a team that responded brilliantly to Barassi's drive. Blight's season finished after Round 20—in all likelihood he had been unwell for a period of time before being diagnosed, so his fifteen-game, 17-goal return for his first VFL season was respectable. There was a positive: the coach's tirades softened when Blight fell ill. But when the Kangaroos marched on to the grand final, only to lose to Richmond, it did not make Blight—who pined to play finals football—feel any better.

*   *   *

Though they had reached a grand final for the first time since 1950, the Kangaroos knew they were well short of the competition benchmark. Richmond had just secured back-to-back premierships and had a core of talent that suggested its run had not ended. But North Melbourne, having won sixteen home and away games, was clearly on the next tier, which made its start to season 1975 all the more incongruous.

The Roos lost to Hawthorn, Melbourne, Carlton and Fitzroy—an embarrassing 30-point loss at Arden Street—to open the campaign. Of those teams, only the Hawks had made the finals the previous year, and Fitzroy and Melbourne had filled the bottom two places on the ladder. What happened next has stuck in Blight's mind ever since, helping craft his ideal of football club management. It's also a good example of how, when you look back, you don't remember many of the games of football you played over the years, but you always remember the valuable lessons learnt along the way.

During the week that followed that loss to the Lions, the playing group was gathered in the rooms when the president walked in. 'Allen Aylett stood up at a meeting. There are strong football clubs and there are those who think they're strong—now, this was a strong football club,' Blight said. 'Allan got up and said, "See this bloke here, his name's Ron Barassi. You are the playing group. While I am president of this football club, this bloke is coach. Whatever he says goes. Any more whingeing about this bloke, and you can go. Come and tell me you have a problem, and I'll personally pay you out and you can go. Has everyone got this message?"

'"If you think you can find an ear to whinge to because your coach says something's not good enough, then leave right now." Things clicked from there. When you look back on what some football clubs have done in certain circumstances, if only they had the balls ...'

Joseph and Aylett had engineered the meeting, having sensed discontent in the camp. The playing list was relatively experienced and 'full of characters and fiery types', Blight recalled, which made for an interesting dressing room. Especially when you were losing, and Ron Barassi was on your tail.

'Barassi was pretty upset that we lost the grand final to Richmond in 74 even though Richmond was a far better side than we were,' Wayne Schimmelbusch said. 'At the back of his mind he would have had blokes that he thought could play in premiership sides and blokes that couldn't. And he wasn't prepared to go on with blokes that, even though we didn't have anyone better, he knew wouldn't play in a premiership.'

It meant for potent dressing-room chemistry. An experienced, unhappy playing list meets a determined, single-minded coach. Blight used to wonder at how sparks did not fly more often. 'We had really strong personalities, a lot of thirty year olds. That intrigued me. Look at the guys who played then: Arnold Briedis, fiery. Burnsy, fiery. Gary Cowton, fiery. Phil Baker, fiery. Denchy, Kekovich and Chisnell, fiery. There were seven or eight who were really good players but they had a lot of fire in them—fancy trying to handle *them*? You knew there was a lot of aggression in the team. And Barassi was the same. Some of the team meetings were outstanding. I don't think I ever said a word, and if I did he would have bitten my head off. For me it would have been throwing petrol on a fire.

'But if anyone thought they were a star in that group, they were pulled back. Others might have perceived we were full of egos, but internally that wasn't the case.'

The Aylett speech put an end to the grumbling. The president had made clear the expectations for the group's behaviour, while underscoring management support for the coach. In five minutes, he re-established the rhythm of a football club.

'Barass had a clever way of sensing when blokes were getting ahead of themselves, or whether they needed a pat on the back,' Joseph said. 'He was a good people manager, even though he could be destructive as well. You put up with that. In 1975, we thought Davis and Wade were not going to play again [after that year], and we'd probably seen the best of Rantall ... here are these three ten-year players and we've finished sixth in 73, and been thrashed by Richmond in the grand final in 1974, so this was it. I said [to Aylett], "Will you come and have a talk to Barass. I'm hearing there's trouble in the camp".

'That changed the mood of the place. Come July, Barassi is still roaring his head off and blasting blokes, but by then they didn't care. We were winning.'

Which is another lesson in football: winning beats losing.

Blight had settled well in his second year, being used primarily at centre half-back with an occasional pinch-hitting role at centre half-forward. By now, his leap and timing were on show—notwithstanding teammate Schimmelbusch's reservations—and it was no surprise when he was selected to play for Victoria in an unusual interstate knockout carnival. Playing alongside him in the Big V would be Findon High School teammate Craig McKellar. These were the days prior to the state-of-origin concept, and with so much interstate talent playing in Victoria it was hardly surprising that the Vics rolled through the carnival undefeated. The official carnival program assessed Blight's performance in that season to date:

Was probably unlucky not to have been chosen in the state team earlier this year but will no doubt give a good account of himself in such select company. Has been doing well in club games. High flying type who kicks the ball well and is a clever player on the ground.

48

North continued to grind away, working towards a .500 winning percentage; when they squeezed past Fitzroy in Round 14, the Roos had managed to climb into the top five with a 7–7 record. They were not considered contenders, but they had regained some respectability. In Round 15, on 12 July, they defeated Carlton in the rain at Waverley Park. At that point, the Blues and Hawthorn were considered the two dominant teams of the competition, both sitting five wins and an enormous percentage clear of third-placed Richmond.

It was North's first statement of sorts, but Malcolm Blight was nowhere to be seen. 'After playing in the state team I got glandular fever again,' he explained. 'I was really crook, not physically well at all.'

He was absent for Rounds 14 through to 17. When he returned, he found himself being used more as a forward as Barassi sought to refine his team before what was looming as a return to the finals. Blight kicked 7 goals in the next four games, getting a taste of what his coach had in store for him. A 5-point win in Round 19 over Richmond at the MCG all but secured a berth in September—it put North two wins and percentage clear of sixth-placed Collingwood, which it had thrashed the previous week. Barassi's men entered September having won seven of their last eight matches.

North accounted for Carlton in the first final. After starting the season 13–1, the Blues had the staggers—a run of outs sparked by that Round 15 loss to North. In his first final since junior football, Blight kicked 3 goals that Saturday afternoon, a major fillip for a confidence level still lagging due to the lingering effects of his ill health.

That win earned for North a second semi-final engagement with Hawthorn, the only club it had not beaten that season. The Hawks were laden with talent, but it was not one of the big names who had the better of North that day; incredibly, first-gamer Michael Cooke, who had been recruited from amateur club Old Carey, played at full-forward and kicked 4 goals in a low-scoring game. It was enough to lift Hawthorn into the grand final, and relegate the Kangaroos to a preliminary final meeting with Richmond at Waverley, the first time the penultimate game had been moved away from the MCG.

This time the weight of North talent simply overwhelmed the reigning premiers. Barassi and his team had come a long way from that Round 4 meeting. A rematch with Hawthorn now stood between the Roos and that elusive premiership.

5

BARASSI

THERE IS A snapshot of the 1975 grand final that Malcolm Blight remembers with clarity. It is not when teammate and captain Barry Davis received the premiership cup, holding it aloft to soothe a club's half-century of heartache. Nor is it the lap of honour he had been waiting his entire football life to join. Rather, it's a passage of play during the last quarter, when Blight was flattened by Hawthorn opponent Leigh Matthews.

Collecting the ball at half-back, Blight played on and dodged around Matthews. Or, at least, he tried to. The Hawk rover left his arm hanging out and it collected Blight across the face. Dropping to his knees, Blight recovered to take his free kick, and the Roos remained in control. It was a day memorable for so much Kangaroo joy, a post-match celebration that Blight remembers as a blur of joy and emotion. Yet he can specifically recall the sting of Matthews' forearm and what followed.

'Matthews coathangered me. Next thing I know Barassi was screaming, "Go tell Blight, *you can't play on in a grand final!*" What's all that about; here's the Super Coach, *handball, handball, handball* a few years earlier … and now I can't play on?' Blight laughed when he told the story, but was shaking his head at the same time. He could not ignore the irony of Barassi's instructions, given that in the 1970 grand final Barassi had instructed his players to play on at all costs. I suspect he was conveniently ignoring the basic difference in the scenarios—his Carlton team was 44 points behind, and simply had to try *something*, whereas North was protecting a lead in the last quarter—but it's an interesting insight into the relationship between the two men. There is an unquestionable father–son sensibility at play; Blight was clearly eager to please the senior figure, but equally frustrated, even now, twenty-five years later, by being forced to operate as what he perceived to be a marked man.

'Sometimes I wondered …' he said, trailing off. 'Sometimes I played in spite of him, you know, "Will you just get off my back today?" I know I've done it to players as a coach; sometimes you go too far with someone. But Barass would get you down and you'd stay down.'

It was not just Blight, of course. Dual Brownlow Medallist Keith Greig was perhaps the most elegant and gifted player of that Kangaroos era; beautifully balanced, fast and spring-heeled, Greig was awarded the captaincy in 1976 after Davis retired, which made his relationship with Barassi all the more unusual.

And it was not just Barassi. Kevin Sheedy could be really tough on players during my time at Essendon, none more than ruckman Simon Madden. At one stage, Simon was not only dropped to the

52

reserves, but found himself on the bench in the twos after turning up late. The year after he arrived, Sheeds took the captaincy off Simon, who never got it back. Kevin was not as confrontational as Barassi. He would hope the penny would drop via the message. Put it this way: Simon became one of the greatest ruckmen in the history of the game.

But Kevin also had people looking out for signs in those players as he sought to figure out which ones he could push, and how far. At North, Ron Joseph played that role for Barassi, and he could see the impact that Blight's relationship with his coach was having. 'Barassi was the bloke who needed someone behind him,' he said. 'He needed somebody to stand in the coach's room against the wall and watch the eyes of the players when he was getting stuck into them. Then quietly move in and take the player out to dinner or have a chat.'

The venue of choice for the Blight–Joseph counselling sessions was The Steakhouse in Doncaster, in Melbourne's outer eastern suburbs. 'Patsy would ring me up and tell me how low Malcolm was … I'd go out and we'd talk until one o'clock in the morning,' Joseph said. 'Barassi was pretty torrid with him, and Blighty basically used to say he was going to go back to Adelaide after three years when his contract was up.

'I used to calm him down. "Look, Barassi is the coach. If you're going to be a champion, you've got to adjust to him. He's the boss. Get down there tomorrow night and cop the next tirade."'

Which Malcolm Blight dutifully did.

Remember, Ron Barassi was far and away the biggest name in football at the time. Ted Whitten had this definitive larger than life status, but Barassi was the Super Coach. No one questioned him. In my first playing year at Essendon, 1977, I was asked to come in to *World of Sport* at the Channel 7 studios. Bobby Davis greeted me and showed me around—it was like a smoke night, a big crowded bar, only it was Sunday morning. And it was chaotic. It felt like there were 100 people in there, but no one held the room like Barassi.

Davis introduced me. 'Ron, this is Tim Watson.' Barassi shook my hand, then turned to whoever was standing next to him. 'This is ridiculous,' he said, referring to me, 'playing a kid at fifteen years of age.' It was like I didn't exist, but he was talking about me. When you were as big as Barass, you could get away with anything.

The *Sun News Pictorial* on the Monday morning after the grand final added weight to the Super Coach legend. On the front page, the headline referred not to the Kangaroos' drought, nor to their best players that day. Instead, it screamed, *Barassi, you beaut!*

And why not? The coach had primed his men for the contest, and they jumped out to an early lead they never relinquished. By half-time it was 20 points, and would have been more if not for the efforts of key Hawk defender Peter Knights, in many eyes the game's best player. But 10 goals to four in the second half blew the final margin out to 55 points, a decisive result that, according to the *Sun*, more than justified the $1 million the Kangaroos has spent on players in the previous three seasons.

The theme song was being sung by the North fans well in advance of the final siren. More than 110,000 packed the MCG, and impartial fans—as there always are on grand final day—would surely have enjoyed the sight of a club's premiership drought coming to an end. It was not the biggest story of the week that followed—that belonged to the third meeting of Muhammad Ali and Joe Frazier, the 'Thriller in Manila'—but it forever changed the perception and sense of self-worth of a football club.

When the siren blew to end the grand final, Barassi soared off the bench like a rocket. Blue jacket, collar and tie, killer moustache. Buttoning his jacket, he ran to the middle of the ground, joining his jubilant players as the realisation set in: the Kangaroos had finally won a premiership. Blight can vividly recall the overwhelming sense of elation he felt, having achieved his goal of not only playing finals football but winning a premiership. 'Let's just say when the siren went I knew what to do, I'd watched enough of those [post-match celebrations].'

Blight was not the Kangaroos' best that day, but he was far from their worst. Having played much of his football at centre half-back or centre half-forward that season, he was assigned an unusual role in the grand final. Teammate Doug Wade was in the last of his fifteen seasons of League football; he was hampered by injury and had missed large chunks of the season. Wade kicked 47 goals in fifteen games that season, a useful contribution but less than his remarkable career average of 3.95 goals per game across 267 matches. Barassi recalls contemplating dropping Wade for the grand final, but Wade, who sensed it might be his last game of football, pleaded his case to the match committee—an argument perhaps based as much on sentiment as value—and survived. Provision for Wade's lack of mobility was therefore required when the Roos designed their game plan, and Blight became the fall guy.

'Doug was on his last legs, so they came up with this plan that I play in the forward pocket and contest every single ball in the air,' Blight said. 'Doug would do the pushing and shoving. I was just standing there waiting for the big bombs to come down. I jumped at everything in the first half but couldn't catch a cold. Doug kicked two or three and it was "Barass, you're a genius". We were 20 points up at half-time.'

When you watch the game footage, it looks like the plan worked. Blight was present, but not a presence—he rarely looked in position to actually mark and the forward line looked too restricted for both Wade and Blight to be effective. This was an era when a long kick to position was standard; when it happened, Wade claimed the ball off the back of the pack time and again. Like his earlier contemporary, Hawk star Peter Hudson, he had that rare gift for reading the play a half-second before his opponent, making many of his goals look simple.

Just after half-time, a long Sam Kekovich kick hit a pack about 20 metres out from goal. This time, Blight chose to shark the pack rather than climb on it. He gathered at top pace as the Hawthorn defenders stood flat-footed, and snapped from the pocket with, yes, his left foot. It was his last taste of life deep in the forward line that day. 'Peter Knights was killing us, he was on fire,' Blight said. 'I went to centre half-forward [to Knights] and got a few touches. I didn't blitz Knightsy by any means. And I couldn't mark anything; I was just off. Then at three quarter-time, Garry Farrant went off so I went to centre half-back.'

Then, the blessed relief of the siren, with North 55 points to the good, and the blur that followed.

'Others were swapping jumpers, but there was no way known anyone was going to get mine,' Blight said. (It is one of four jumpers he keeps to this day, having given away much of his memorabilia to Variety Club auctions—he kept the 1975 and 1977 premiership jumpers, the lace-up Woodville jumper in which he received his Magarey Medal on SANFL grand final day in 1972, and the Victorian number 1 jumper he wore when he captained the state in 1979. 'Even when I did swap I always tried to get the same number. I wore 13 for South Australia and swapped 13s with Peter Bedford in a state game.')

Blight does not recall his coach's post-match address. Nor does Barassi remember saying anything of note. Joseph actually better recalls a moment from six years earlier, when then-Carlton coach Barassi was writing a column in the Melbourne *Sun News Pictorial* called 'Column 31'. 'He'd written this article in collaboration with [journalist] Greg Hobbs, saying North Melbourne should be in the VFA,' Joseph said. '"They've never won a premiership, never had a Brownlow Medallist, never had a leading goalkicker." I was really angry, because I knew how hard we were working. We didn't have Aylett's direction or Barassi's know-how then, but there was still a genuine commitment to the place.'

And now there, in the corner, was a premiership cup.

*   *   *

When Malcolm Blight arrived at North Melbourne, he signed a three-year contract. He and the club could not have dreamed that their premiership hopes would be fulfilled so quickly, although Blight these days smiles when he looks at the playing list of the time. 'That's why we played in six grand finals,' he said of the strength of the team, reading off the names, 'when you see a list like that.'

There was no logical reason why the Kangaroos would not again be competitive in 1976. Though Doug Wade and Barry Davis bowed out on a premiership high, having vindicated the club's use of the ten-year rule, and John Rantall returned to his original love—South Melbourne—Arden Street was still dense with talent.

The perception was (and is) that North had bought a premiership, specifically through the use of the ten-year rule, and it's a storyline supported by these facts: Davis won best and fairests in 1973 and 1975, bookending Rantall's win in 1974. Wade led the goalkicking in his three years at the club. They certainly got value from that five-month window in early 1973, but Joseph contends that that was only part of it. 'There are a lot of myths, but in the 75 premiership side Frank Gumbleton, Peter Chisnall, Barry Goodingham and Gary Farrant all came to North Melbourne in the days of Form Fours. Any of the clubs could have signed them, and we beat all the big clubs for their signatures. There was just as much work going on [in] the Ovens and Murray and [other] country leagues, getting Sam Kekovich and Gary Cowton.

'In 1969, David Dench arrives and plays 275 games. In 1970, Keith Greig arrives and plays 294. In 1973, Schimmelbusch comes along and plays 306. That's getting up to 1000 matches that came out of Pascoe Vale and Brunswick.'

Besides, argued Kangaroos assistant coach John Dugdale, it was simply the wheel of football life turning for a club that had long been taken advantage of. 'Many times over the years we had players signed and other clubs came and offered them more money, and off they went,' Dugdale said. 'Alex Jesaulenko was signed on a Form Four by North, so was Dick Clay, then the richer clubs came in and took them. We even went up and played a practice match in Kyabram to give Dick's local club some revenue. Six weeks later Dick was at Richmond because they paid him.

'We used the [ten-year] law well, and we might have thrown some money around but a lot of that is exaggerated. Don't tell me other sides wouldn't have done it if they'd had the money or the opportunity or the initiative.'

Of the team that lined up for Round 1, 1976, only Blight (Woodville), Barry Cable (Western Australia), John Burns (a Tasmanian playing at East Perth) and Graham Melrose (a Sandover Medallist from East Fremantle who crossed in 1975) had been significant interstate signings. Burns had been a star in the grand final, kicking 4 goals and figuring in the best. Cable was contracted and would play through to the end of 1977. Melrose was cursed, missing both North premierships with injury. But Blight was the signature the club now craved, as he was coming out of contract after season 1976.

'I knew he was a brilliant player,' Barassi said. 'In fact, in our box at North there would have been, perhaps including coaching and playing, a thousand games of experience. And we reckon on an average, once every two or three weeks, one of us would say about something that he did: "How did Blighty do that?" I mean, he was miraculous.'

Miracles did not take place on the field in 1976, however, a season Blight refers to as 'the Crimmins year'. Hawthorn captain

Peter Crimmins had been diagnosed with testicular cancer after the 1974 season. He played the first seven games of 1975 but extensive treatment and chemotherapy reduced football to the least of his priorities; Crimmins sought to come back for the finals but coach John Kennedy could not find a place for him, putting team over sentiment. Tragically, Crimmins did not play again—by the following year, the cancer had clearly won its war, and he died three days after his team's 1976 grand final triumph.

The Hawks played inspired football that year, closing the home and away season in second place and defeating minor premier Carlton in the second semi-final. Meanwhile, North had presented coach Barassi with another horror start—three straight losses to open the year and a 1–4 opening. However, just as they had recovered twelve months earlier, the Roos got back on track. And in the game in which they got back to a .500 win–loss record, a Round 10 game against Carlton, Blight produced a post-siren moment that has been immortalised.

Just over 25,000 people attended that game at Princes Park. As Blight says, if you believed everyone who said they were there for 'that kick', the official attendance 'was 233,000 … and I can't believe the seven and eight year olds who were there!'

Visiting the Blues at Princes Park had long been a brutal task, but it was seldom a more difficult challenge than during that era. Between 1975 and 1982, Carlton had a 72–14 record at home, plus two draws. Of those fourteen losses, four came against its co-tenant at the ground, Hawthorn, so with genuine visitors it was 72–10—and one of those ten came courtesy of Malcolm Blight's right foot.

The scene is worth setting. Blight had moved to a more permanent centre half-forward role that season. Carlton entered the game at 7–2, North Melbourne 4–5. In Round 6, the Blues had dusted off Hawthorn by 40 points—the Hawks' only loss of the season to date—and they were warm favourites this week. It seemed a safe bet, even more so when the home side led by 13 points entering time-on of the last quarter. The Blues had led all day, including a 27-point edge at the long break, and their near invincibility at home seemed set to continue.

Then Blight out-marked his direct opponent, Mark Maclure, from a Xavier Tanner kick. Commentator Lou Richards declared him to be '70 metres out', but in truth it was closer to 50. A solid drop punt split the middle for Blight's second goal of the term, and the margin was 7 points. Then Peter Chisnall streamed through the middle of the ground and found Blight leading wide to the forward pocket in front of the Carlton Social Club stand. Five metres in from the boundary, he attempted an audacious 'checkside' kick— or 'banana' as Victorians would better recognise it—from about 35 metres out, and it arced through for his fourth goal of the day. The Kangaroos were back to within a point, but the clock seemed likely to beat them.

Carlton surged forward, but Blight's teammate Mark Dawson claimed possession and roosted it forward to a one-on-one … Blight versus Maclure. Side by side, Blight simply out-positioned his man and claimed a one-grab mark. Sensing the urgency, he trotted quickly backwards to prepare to take his kick, and was assessing his options when the siren went. North trailed by 1 point.

Immediately, he raised his arms and put the ball behind his head. His body language read 'anguish' as teammate Keith Greig wandered across. 'What am I going to do here?' Blight asked him.

'Why don't you just try kicking it?' was Greig's amused response, although Blight's question referred to the style of kick. 'I thought I might have got there with a drop punt.' But he rightly fancied his form with a torpedo, and knew the extra distance might be required.

Commentator Mike Williamson described what happened next: *'Now, Blight would have to kick this, oh, he'd have to kick it 85, 90 metres. It's not over yet, what drama here at Princes Park ... Malcolm Blight, it's a big kick, it's a mammoth kick ...'*

The commentary was drowned out by the crowd's reaction. How anyone spoke is difficult to fathom, as the kick took the breath away. It went through post-high, landing about ten rows back on the terrace. And it was straight. The Kangaroos won by 5 points in arguably the most famous, and certainly the most talked about, moment of Blight's playing career. He was chaired off the ground amid a sea of North supporters. Williamson, a showman who added colour and a sense of fun to the coverage of the game, capped the moment perfectly. *'Oh, I've seen it all now,'* he said. *'I. Have. Seen. It. All.'*

The result is without question, but the query remains: how far did Blight kick the ball? There were no 50-metre arcs to give us perspective on distance in the 1970s, and Princes Park was notoriously short, so kicking from two steps past the corner of the centre square, as Blight did, could be slightly misleading. The ground was listed as 165 metres long. Only Collingwood's

62

Victoria Park and Essendon's Windy Hill were officially shorter—each by about 1 metre—while grounds like Geelong and Footscray were both 18 metres longer.

Playing my home games at Windy Hill, I liked Princes Park because it was a similar size. It felt wider, but the length meant our game plan—kick it long and direct to the forward line—worked just about as well. When we went to Footscray or Geelong, we felt lost. But even on that relatively small ground at Princes Park, Blighty's kick was a monster. Melbourne University students that week went to Princes Park and measured the kick, reckoning the kick to be 83 yards, or 75.8 metres. It's as safe an estimate as history provides.

Blight believes he has three kicks on videotape that were longer. Anyone who watched him kick torpedo punts—both left and right foot—would have no trouble believing that claim. Indeed, during his coaching days at Geelong, fifteen years after that Princes Park marvel, Blight would be kicking torpedoes back and forth with his assistant coaches in the middle of Kardinia Park while his team completed its warm-up laps. 'The boys would be jogging along, watching Blighty roost these torps, thinking, "Jesus, he's still a better kick than any of us",' Billy Brownless said. A decade later, as Adelaide coach, Blight could still land them from 65 metres out; he was forty-nine at the time.

'I'd do them forever, it was good fun, just kicking the footy,' he enthused. 'There's a certain skill to the torpedo. Doug Wade could do them, too. You almost had to aim for the left-hand goalpost, because if you hit it right they actually cut back with drift to the right.'

Lost in the drama of that goal was a more salient point. Not only had the Kangaroos climbed into the top five for the first time that season, but the result confirmed Blight's potential as a permanent forward target. He had started playing centre half-forward more often that season, and it would become an increasing trend as his VFL career evolved.

The club needed Blight in attack. Wingman Wayne Schimmelbusch led the club goalkicking that year as five players kicked 30 or more goals in the vacuum of Doug Wade's retirement. Sam Kekovich managed just eight games in 1976 before crossing to Collingwood for one final, largely unsuccessful season. Brent Crosswell could be highly dangerous but was not always played around goal. And injury would erode the consistency of Arnold Briedis as his career marched on.

Blight's 5 goals that day took his tally to 47 goals in forty-three games. Notably, he kicked 90 in his first four years, but averaged 70 *per year* from 1978 to 1982.

Just as the Roos had used a win over Carlton to gather momentum in 1975, their Princes Park escape in 1976 triggered a phenomenal run. They won nine out of the next ten to cement a club record third consecutive finals appearance. But, guess what? The sole loss in that mix was to Hawthorn by 8 points in Round 13, a classic showdown at Arden Street. It was as close to the Hawks as North got that season.

'Hawthorn beat us five times that year,' Blight recalled of the 'Crimmins year'. 'Two in the day, one in the night [series] and two in the finals. There's a message there: they were too good.' (The night game was actually the final of the national club championship, played in Adelaide. Hawthorn defeated North by 8 goals in the last edition of that series.)

Memorably, the Roos squeezed past Carlton in a 1-point preliminary final, Blight having 22 kicks, 12 marks and 6 handballs to figure among the best. But nothing could stop the Hawthorn momentum that year, and only the Hawks' inaccuracy (they kicked 13.22 to 10.10) kept the grand final remotely competitive.

It is hard to overestimate just how physical those Hawthorn sides were. In my first pre-season, Essendon played a practice match against them at Glenferrie Oval, where they had not played home and away footy for years but still used as their training base. It was terrifying, especially for a teenage kid. They were so much bigger and stronger than we were, and on that tiny ground it felt like there was no room to move. Don Scott, Leigh Matthews, they were everywhere. Little wonder, then, that Blight was tired— playing (and losing to) Hawthorn five times in a year would do that. Though he had missed three games through niggling injury in 1976, it had clearly been his most consistent and successful season.

Yet the call of Adelaide was running through his veins. A trip home seemed to convince him that a return to the Woodpeckers was his likely choice, having proven to himself he could measure up in the VFL. His three-year contract had expired, so the option was his. 'I went back to Woodville and thought, "That's it". But I also took some time to think about things. Things unfold for certain reasons, and after a while I thought, "No, that was all right [at North]". And Ronny [Joseph] came up with a very good offer at the time.'

Blight managed his own affairs. He never found it uncomfortable, believing that 'if you're talking, you'll get there. It was just me and Ron around the table'.

It's an understated description of a process that Joseph found draining. 'Malcolm and Patsy had flown to Noosa, on Queensland's Sunshine Coast, for a break,' he said. 'After seven or eight days I followed them up and talked about him playing on. I'd just re-signed Greig, Dench, Schimma, [Ross] Henshaw, Briedis, eight others on contracts. We signed Blighty on a five-year contract, but it was a totally new dimension of payments compared to the others. I didn't feel like coming back from Queensland because I couldn't look Grieg and Dench and those blokes in the eye.'

In Joseph's eyes, however, it was the most significant football decision of Malcolm Blight's playing career. 'His leadership came out after he'd made his decision to commit to a five-year contract,' he said. 'The relationship between him and Barassi became much stronger, there was a bond that developed that hadn't existed in the first three years.'

* * *

Arnold Briedis spent the morning of the 1977 grand final watching a replay of the last quarter of the 1975 edition of football's biggest day. Briedis hoped his performance this afternoon would be equally as positive as that day of two years earlier, when he had kicked 4 goals in the final term as the Roos clinched the premiership.

Twelve hours later, as he sat at a sombre grand final night dinner, Briedis pondered the bizarre events of the afternoon. 'Looking at that last quarter of the North Melbourne–Hawthorn grand final in 1975 … made me feel so confident,' Briedis told *The Age*. 'I never dreamt anything could be so bad. Fortunately, there is always next week.'

His statement raises two questions: what happened to Briedis that September Saturday of 1977, and how could there be a next week? This, after all, was a grand final.

A relatively accurate kick for goal, having compiled a 65 per cent conversion rate over his 161-game career, Briedis kicked 0.7 in the 1977 grand final. His team kicked 9.22, and it took a strong finish against Collingwood, which it trailed by 27 points at three-quarter time, to secure a memorable draw—only the second in grand final history. In one fifteen-minute spell in the second term, Briedis kicked 4 behinds as North simply could not put away the opposition. It looked to have been not just wasteful, but decisively so.

Under the inspiration of new coach Tommy Hafey, the Pies were within a decent thirty minutes of achieving the unthinkable. After all, they had come from last in 1976, having won just six games, and improved to a League-best eighteen wins in 1977. But just as history sat within their grasp, a withering Kangaroos final quarter actually edged North a goal in front in time-on. Magpies forward Ross 'Twiggy' Dunne then famously marked and goaled for Collingwood to draw the game.

On the siren, and the realisation that another seven days and two more gruelling hours lay ahead, most players from both teams slumped to the ground, exhausted. In frustration, North ruckman Peter Keenan lived up to his nickname—'Crackers'—and began a wrestle with opponent Rene Kink. 'It is just a terribly empty feeling,' Keenan has since recalled of the minutes that followed the siren. 'I remember Gary Cowton pulled me off Rene and said, "Come on, we have to come back next week, come back to this bastard of a place."

'We all just went and collapsed around Barass, went to our tribal leader.'

If Briedis was tormented by his performance, Malcolm Blight was shattered. An early mistake was to haunt him all day; Blight centred the ball but missed his target, and the turnover directly resulted in a Collingwood goal at the other end. 'At quarter-time I couldn't get out of [Barassi's] way. He just gave it to me,' Blight said. 'Normally I got there late and he got someone else first. But he absolutely barrelled me, and this was after I got a few touches early. He screamed, "You don't even think that's a mistake, do you?" Well, I reckon I know I stuffed up. Then he said, "Go to the forward pocket, you lair".'

For the next two quarters, North Melbourne failed to kick a goal, and Blight barely touched the football as Collingwood broke away to what appeared to be a decisive lead. As he headed to the huddle at the last change, he saw a fuming Barassi from a long way off. 'At three-quarter time, Ron yelled, "Johnny Byrne, you've done nothing, get off!" I thought, "Beauty, I can go back on the ball". But as he walked away, and the huddle was breaking up, he called, "Blight, come back here. You're off. Byrne, get back on". I sat on the bench in the last quarter.

'I was pretty peeved, but what do you do given we came back from 27 points down? Some things you bring on yourself, crap happens and you cop your lot in life. A bad kick is a bad kick, but if we all got demonised for one bad kick the game would be poorer for the exercise. I thought it was pretty harsh. I sat there and watched the last quarter with strange emotions like everybody else.'

North kicked 5.7 to 1.4 in the final term to salvage the draw, actually forging ahead before Dunne's late heroics for the Magpies. That evening, Barassi gathered the North players and their families. His speech holds a special place in club folklore, for it touched on the relationship between players, their families and the town they live in. 'Barassi got every player in the room, with their partners,' Blight recalled. 'He said, "I want you to leave the players with me for another big week. I'm sorry, but this premiership will be a famous premiership, which we'll win. We need you to support your partners for another week".'

The coach outlined how the team would cope with the largely uncharted waters of a draw. The only previous grand final draw had occurred in 1948, when Essendon kicked 7.27 to draw with Melbourne (the Demons won the replay). Even before the final siren that day, Barassi had sensed the nature of the week ahead would strain the players mentally, so he decided to strike that night.

'Straight after a game is usually a time when you've got their concentration,' he said. 'You know, their real, real concentration. I remember, before the bell went, looking across the ground and totalling up in my mind what points I had to make. And one of the things that struck me was that this was a very unusual situation and all these people in Melbourne would be giving you advice. You know, bloody uncles and aunties and dads and kids and mates … well, that's not a good thing. It's a nice thought, but advice? No. And that was one point that I made, that it's best if you only have one voice; it makes sense for you to listen to me. Not just because I am your coach but I have had experience in grand finals. Don't take any notice of anything else. I said the same thing to the girls, because the girls are part of the picture.'

It is a frequently referred-to speech. Many rate it among his finest moments, another foundation stone in his monument. Barassi was at this stage the very epitome of the Super Coach, an uncompromising man on a personal mission. Wayne and Daryl Schimmelbusch recall the extent to which that drive had portrayed itself earlier in that finals series. 'Barassi gave us a lot of one-on-one training stuff in the finals that year,' Wayne said. 'He put me on my brother because he knew that, as far as competing against each other, we'd be at each other's throats. Ron had told me he was thinking about putting Daryl in the side. We were throwing ourselves into it, but I ended up breaking Daryl's leg at training. Oh shit, we both heard the crack. All Barassi said was, "Well, that's how I want you to compete this week".'

If Barassi's calm, measured speech made sense of the non-sensical, eerie mood of the dressing rooms, and the week that lay ahead, by early the next morning Barassi was back on form. According to Ron Joseph, 'Barass came into my office. He was in his gear, his jumper and socks. He opened the door and said, "I'm going to drop Blight, and don't you fucking tell any of your mates—it's between you and me. Okay?" I thought, "We've got some dramas here".'

By referring to Joseph's 'mates', Barassi meant chairman of selectors Max Ritchie and selectors John Dugdale and John Wymer. But Barassi had already told them. That Sunday morning the players had undergone rehabilitation at the St Kilda Baths. 'Ron came to us and said, "I'm going to drop Malcolm Blight". He was adamant,' recalled Dugdale. 'There was no way known we were dropping Malcolm, because you knew he could be best on the ground the next week. Barassi was getting carried away. But at the Tuesday training night, I said to Blighty, "Make sure you train well this week because he's thinking about dropping you. You've got the support of the other three of us".'

All these years later, I still find this story unbelievable. Blight was not the most consistent player in the team, but he was nowhere near the worst. More to the point, he was a potential matchwinner, and had proven as much more than once. I still can't decide if the coach was serious, although it seems he was: all parties (except Ron, who unfortunately can't remember) recall that Barassi still wanted to drop Blight on the Thursday night. First, however, Blight was called in to plead his case. His contribution the previous week had been 10 kicks, 2 marks, 4 handballs and 2 behinds. It was his lowest statistical production for the season, but Blight had starred against Richmond in the semi-final a fortnight earlier, kicking 2 goals and gathering 30 touches. This was hardly a form slump.

'In a formal sense it was the first time I was called in to the selectors,' Blight said. 'They asked whether I thought I should play. Of course you'd say yes. Then they asked what I thought my form was like last week. I said something like, "Well, it was pretty hard in a forward pocket. I'd obviously made a kicking error and the coach thought strongly enough to get me out of the action. Given all that, it's not my decision. I think we'll win, we're good enough, and they [Collingwood] missed the opportunity, not us.

You'll win it with or without me. I've got nothing else to say. Let's go to training".'

When the match committee met later that evening, Barassi was outvoted by the other three selectors. Blight survived. 'It was the only time in my life I outvoted the coach,' Dugdale said. 'But what's the point of being on the match committee if you're not prepared to put your opinion on the line?'

As was customary, the selectors then went to the President's Room for a drink. Barassi stormed in. 'I want to see you, you and you,' he said, pointing fiercely at Ritchie, Dugdale and Wymer and leading them back to the club offices. 'We'll still win the premiership,' the coach said once he'd closed the door, 'but what you fellas did to me was totally wrong. It's my fucking head on the chopping block, not yours.'

The vote was never mentioned again.

Two days later, as the players ran onto the MCG for the grand final replay, Blight was his usual last out of the race—which was his habit, dictated by superstition. His coach was waiting for him, and Blight found himself fixed by that famous stare. 'Barass grabbed me by the arm and said, "If I was a praying man, I'd pray for you today".' The coach walked off. The player's blood ran cold.

The Kangaroos might have blown their chance seven days earlier, but they were not to be denied in the replay. Barassi that week spoke about his team remaining 'loose and lucid' during their preparation for the replay, and his men clearly enjoyed the Barassi edict to 'sharpen up, but not much more training'. By game day, with another crowd verging on 100,000 returning to 'that bastard of a place', North was favoured in a game played in bright sunshine

BARASSI

and perfect conditions. Indeed, it was ideal weather for a shootout, and that's what eventuated: while the Roos were again inaccurate, kicking 21.25, it didn't matter. Five goals up at three-quarter time, they won by 27 points. Briedis kicked 5.3, redemption for sins of the previous week, while Blight, with 27 possessions, 2 goals and 6 hit-outs, was widely considered in his team's best three players. 'I was fresh as a daisy,' he said. 'It was like I just joined the Melbourne Cup at the 600-metre mark because I hadn't spent a penny the week before.'

* * *

Blight averaged 22 possessions and a goal per week in 1977, his most consistent production to date. He was splitting his time between ruck-roving and half-forward, but his most notable contribution—aside from playing in a premiership—came in Round 12 at Arden Street. The ground was so wet that day that the reserves game was abandoned. Late in the final term, with North trailing Hawthorn by a point, Blight ran into goal and, from 20 metres out, his scrubby kick tied the game with a point. As he kicked, he was pushed in the back, so he was offered the kick again. Naturally, with a chance to win a low-scoring game, he took it.

'Schimma missed one from the goal square that day, that's how bad the mud was,' he said. 'As I got there to kick, I ran out wide because there was a huge mud patch there. That was my mistake.' The kick slewed off the side of his boot and finished out of bounds on the full. Hawthorn hung on to win by a point, and many years later Blight, as a coach, would describe the moment as 'the low point of my career'. The Roos had their revenge in the preliminary final, crushing the Hawks by 11 goals. '[Hawthorn coach] David Parkin mentioned it after the [Round 12] game,' Blight said. '"We beat them in the dry, we beat them at night, now we beat them in the wet",' he said. 'That got a fair mention in the finals series when Hawthorn was eliminated.'

The incident highlighted a fundamental part of life at Arden Street in that era: life was seldom boring with number 15 in the game.

6

LOVE, HATE

AFTER THE 1977 grand final triumph, after the torn-up telephone books had been swept out of the MCG gutters and the hangovers had settled, Malcolm Blight was getting on with his summer when the telephone rang. It was his coach, Ron Barassi. 'I made a terrible mistake,' Barassi said, casting back to the grand final rematch. 'I didn't give you a vote in the best and fairest [for the grand final].'

Before Blight had a chance to reply, Barassi continued. 'What are you doing now?'

Barassi invited Blight to the Australian Open tennis, held at Kooyong in December 1977. 'We had a huge day,' said Blight. 'A lot of good drinks and laughs, a lot of good times. Honestly, the world had lifted off my shoulders. In 78 he hardly said a word to me, and I played so much more consistently.'

If anything had been missing from the Blight arsenal, it was that word: consistency. Teammate Wayne Schimmelbusch has put forward that Blight's maturity as a player was only becoming evident in this period. 'I thought he obviously had a lot of ability but I don't think he got the best out of himself in his first few years,' Schimmelbusch said. 'But by 1978 he was a genuine superstar. He really blossomed into someone who was actually using his talent. You should be playing your best football when you're twenty-seven, twenty-eight, around that age, because you've learnt all you can; you should be putting it all together. And Blighty certainly did.'

Schimmelbusch said Blight's biggest flaw was his ability to 'go missing for a week, or two' earlier in his career. Which is what makes his 1978 output jump off the page: Blight started the season brilliantly, averaging 25 touches and 3.5 goals across his first month. He was playing ruck-rover, and changing forward with John Byrne, who spent perhaps 60 per cent of his time on the ball. It meant Blight could spend effective time in attack while being used through the midfield, a configuration in which he was never more dangerous.

He kicked 7 goals against Fitzroy in Round 7, and 8 against both Richmond and Melbourne as the year unfolded. All the while the Kangaroos were winning, getting to the halfway mark of the season with a 10–1 record and top place on the table. The defending premiers were showing no sign of slipping, and neither was Blight.

He was also enjoying the presence of former Woodville teammate Ray Huppatz, who had crossed that year from Footscray. Two long injury absences took the edge off Huppatz's season, but he was a quality contributor in the finals.

LOVE, HATE

By the end of the home and away season, Blight had clearly compiled the best of his five seasons in Melbourne: just short of 18 touches a game, plus 77 goals, across twenty-two weeks as North claimed the minor premiership. In Round 21, he had clocked up his one hundredth game for the Kangaroos, his benchmark for having made something of his football career. A month later, another achievement. Approaching Brownlow Medal night, a strong Blight showing seemed a formality—his subsequent win was widely regarded as the worst-kept secret in Melbourne.

Blight polled in nine games, including five best afield performances, and his twenty-two votes left him one clear of an opponent he knew well: Hawthorn's Peter Knights. Blight became the first player to collect both the Magarey and the Brownlow medals. 'Feeling healthy was a big part of it, but really it was about Barassi leaving me alone,' Blight said of his season. 'He obviously coached me, just like anyone else, but I didn't feel like he was into me all the time. I don't remember much of the night itself. It was grand final week, obviously, which makes the night and even the medal a secondary sort of thing.'

But Blight knew he had been in rare form that season. There were afternoons when he knew he was destined for a strong showing, and it would come easily to him. 'Some football days it just happened,' he said. 'You're in the zone. You could read the bounce of the ball, just before it bounced you could see the word Sherrin and how it was going to bounce, almost in slow motion. Sometimes you could see the same when the ball was in flight; you knew exactly where it was going to go. Why it doesn't happen all the time, every game, who knows?'

The Kangaroos had booked yet another berth in the last Saturday in September. As seemed almost inevitable for the time, so had Hawthorn. The pair had met in the semi-final a fortnight earlier, when the Hawks had led all day; Blight went goalless for the first time all season, despite gathering 16 touches and kicking 2 behinds. It forced North into a preliminary final against Collingwood, who pushed them all day without success. A 12-point Kangaroos victory confirmed the grand final rematch.

What followed was one of Malcolm Blight's most disappointing days in the game.

'I ran into [Hawthorn player] Richard Walter in the first five minutes and ripped my groin to bits,' he recalled. 'I went off the ground. John Tickell was the doctor; I used to get a lot of injections but on this day he went for his big one and managed to paralyse my whole right side. Back on the ground, I went to run into Kelvin Moore and realised I couldn't jump. I was thinking, "Tick, what have you done?"'

By half-time, with the Kangaroos 4 points ahead, Blight was no better. He was lying on a treatment table when Barassi barged in. 'What's going on here?' he demanded, and after a brief examination it became apparent that there was no answer to offer except the obvious: Blight's day was all but finished. He finished the afternoon with 4 kicks and a handball. 'Someone wrote after the game that winning the Brownlow Medal obviously affected me,' Blight said. 'But I couldn't run.'

The Hawks ground out a 3-goal win, claiming their second flag in three seasons, both against North Melbourne. This grand final aside—he was clearly hampered—Hawthorn was the one team that Blight could honestly say gave him constant trouble. In his 178 games for the Kangaroos, Blight had a losing record against just two clubs: Carlton, narrowly (8–9), and the Hawks, glaringly (7–17). On a personal level, he averaged one more possession per game against Hawthorn than against other opposition teams, but his goalkicking productivity fell away.

The wide range of his opponents in both height and strength highlights the breadth of roles he played across those twenty-four games against the Hawks. 'David O'Halloran got me a few times, but then Alan Martello got me four or five times, too,' he said. 'Peter Knights, Michael Tuck, lots of different blokes.'

On paper, the Hawks came to control North Melbourne fortunes, yet Blight believes the rivalry is the natural course of football. 'In every era, playing or coaching, there's always a rival team,' he said. 'In the 1976 grand final we had six blokes tagging, including [Keith] Greig on [Leigh] Matthews. They'd beaten us so many times; we had to try something. Other times, we got them.'

* * *

The concept of state-of-origin football was introduced in 1977. It meant that if you were a South Australian, you played for South Australia. Simple. But not every interstate game adhered to that rule, even in the years that followed its introduction. Hence, in 1979, Malcolm Blight captained Victoria in a non-carnival game against South Australia at the Adelaide Oval.

The game was to throw up two moments that to this day Blight still finds astonishing. The first took place before the bounce: as he addressed his players in a team meeting, Victorian coach David

Parkin was adamant that his team should kick against the wind if Blight won the toss. His captain argued vociferously against the idea. 'We went away from the team meeting and discussed it further,' Blight said. 'Eventually I told him I wouldn't do it, and I wouldn't lie to him either. I was the one who made the call, and I was a big boy.

'The debate was pretty strong. He thought that we'd be fitter and stronger and we'd overrun them in the end. I told him that I grew up there and the expectation was that Victoria would hit hard early, be really aggressive. Plus, I had two golden rules in footy: first, don't badmouth opponents—that's one of Barassi's and I totally believe in it. Second, don't give a mug an even break. That's what I thought we'd be doing by kicking into the wind.'

Victoria won the toss, and Blight kicked with the wind. At quarter-time, they led by close to 7 goals. The crowd had been taken out of the game, and the visitors cruised home.

When he returned to North Melbourne training later that week, the first person he saw was Barassi. And, for the second time in a week, Blight experienced a tirade from his coach. In front of the team, Barassi gave Blight a dressing down about his right to captain Victoria. 'I thought I was in a really nice place, had played in another premiership, won a best and fairest and Brownlow, then I got this barrage', Blight said. 'He just couldn't see the sense of a South Australian captaining Victoria. I seriously didn't even think about it; by that time I'd been in Melbourne for half a dozen years and it was the done thing.'

The moment passed, but Blight knew the goodwill he had built with his coach at Arden Street was as fragile as ever.

LOVE, HATE

Perhaps Barassi was more on edge about South Australians than usual because of the influence of two more prominent Croweaters in that 1979 North Melbourne squad. In the off-season, Joseph had lured two enormous SANFL names to Arden Street: Graham Cornes and Russell Ebert (Huppatz remained on the list, though he would miss the entire season with a knee injury).

Cornes turned thirty-one a week before the first round; Ebert was eighteen months younger. Throughout their twenties both men had dominated the SANFL competition. Cornes had been a star for Glenelg, an athletic, spring-heeled player who had won three best and fairests for this club. Ebert had won three Magarey Medals by the time he came east (he would add another in the following year, making him the only four-time winner of the SANFL best and fairest honour). In total, Ebert represented South Australia twenty-nine times throughout his career, Cornes on twenty-one occasions.

'Both were unbelievable, absolute quality players,' Blight said. 'Russell flew back and forwards, which made it very difficult for him. Played a number of games, many off the bench, and had a lot of possessions. Was he at his peak? Probably not. He was a fit thirty, but he was thirty. Russell did a remarkable job to even get close to playing at his best.

'Graham was an out and out ruck-rover, but he was slight. One of the things I noticed when he first came here was that, while he was a great high mark in South Australia, where he could move packs in Adelaide, here he couldn't do that. [Opponents] were just a touch bigger.'

Ebert and Cornes made their debuts in Round 1. Cornes kicked 2 goals and had 15 possessions; Ebert had 17 and 1. It was a bright start, but it was not long before their fortunes began to tread different paths. Ebert locked down a midfield role, and did not miss a game that season despite the difficulty of commuting each week from Adelaide. 'He was a professional player,' Schimmelbusch said. In Round 2, Ebert had 20 kicks, 10 marks and 12 handballs. 'He looked after his body and was a very, very good player ... one of the better players that I had seen, and I saw him towards the end of his career,' Schimmelbusch added.

Cornes, meanwhile, reminded Schimmelbusch of a young Malcolm Blight—clearly talented, but hampered by the habit of dominating the SANFL without needing to impose himself physically. 'You were never going to change what he was at that age,' he said. 'If he had come over earlier I'm pretty sure he would have been a good player.'

It seemed the coach felt the same way. Although Cornes had kicked 10 goals in the five games he played up to Round 10, Barassi had seen enough. 'We played Hawthorn in Sydney in 79 [Round 10], the first game back when the League started playing games in Sydney again,' Blight explained. 'We got away to a flyer, I think my first two kicks went down Graham's throat—he was playing full-forward. He kicked one and missed one. I reckon that was it for the day; we led by 5 and got beaten by 51 points.'

Cornes had 5 touches and kicked 1.2. Barassi approached Blight after the game and said quietly, 'I'm sending your mate home, he's not going to cut the mustard'.

Cornes headed home that week. The irony of the decision? Due to a standout interstate carnival, including winning the Simpson Medal for best afield against Western Australia in the 1979 Perth Carnival, Cornes secured an All-Australian jumper that season.

Meanwhile, Ebert arguably improved as he adjusted to the pace of the game and the lifestyle he was demanding of himself. He averaged 29 touches a week for the six games leading into the finals as North finished the home and away season in second place. Their seventeen wins was the highest total of Blight's VFL career, but they were two astray of a Carlton team that had controlled all comers in 1979. In the second semi-final, the Blues had twice as many scoring shots to sink North by 38 points. And in the preliminary final, Collingwood led all day to end the Kangaroos' season ... and Ebert's career at Arden Street.

Ron Joseph believes that list was good enough to win a premiership; the Kangaroos had split their home and away results with Carlton that year. He even goes so far as to blame the coach for driving Cornes out. 'Barass was unfair in his analysis of Blighty and in fact all South Australian footballers; in my mind it cost us a premiership with Ebert and Cornes,' he said. 'Even though I think I probably recruited them too late, to have not made the grand final with that list was a loss. Cornes had gone after a few months; Barass gave him no encouragement at all. Ebert was more the Schimmelbusch type, do his job, pack his bag and go home each night.'

Perhaps the coach's interest was waning. Late that season, after a Round 20 demolition of Melbourne, Malcolm and Patsy invited the coach over for dinner. Over a late-night glass of port, Barassi let slip that he thought his time at Arden Street was coming to an end. It was the first time Blight considered that he might not play his career out under the Super Coach.

*   *   *

Season 1980 presented VFL fans with a mix of potent teams at the top of the table. North Melbourne seemed the equal of them all, defeating reigning premier Carlton, Hawthorn and South Melbourne in the opening nine weeks. That meant there was only one other side in the top five they had not met, and Richmond sat in the diary for a top of the table showdown in Round 10. Though the Tigers led all day, North fell by just 7 points. It was enough to confirm their confidence that they would be there in September.

But it was their last high point for the season. Ageing ruckman Mick Nolan managed just three games in his final season, although the 1979 arrival of Brownlow Medallist ruckman Gary Dempsey had relegated Nolan to secondary duties anyway; Huppatz, too, was playing his final VFL season, having not fully recovered from his knee injury. Heavy losses to Collingwood and Geelong threw Barassi's men back into the pack.

In Round 18, lowly Melbourne visited Arden Street, setting the scene for perhaps the most infamous clash between Barassi and Blight. Tight on the boundary in the forward pocket in front of the social club, Blight was trapped on his left side and tried an audacious left-foot checkside kick. It sailed through for a goal, giving the Kangaroos some breathing space in a closely contested game.

The runner came out immediately and dragged him to the bench.

'Left foot?' roared Barassi down the telephone line. 'Centre the ball!'

'I joined Ross Glendinning on the bench', Blight said. 'I didn't even bother telling Ron there was no one there [in the centre] because I did look. Anyway, Ross goes on and Schimma comes off.

Then Schimma goes on and Greigy comes off. He was shelling peas for my benefit, and I didn't come back on until three-quarter time.'

In the Monday *Truth* newspaper, Barassi castigated Blight for what he perceived to be an undisciplined act that broke a golden team rule. '*We have a rule,*' he wrote, '*centre the ball.*'

Blight confronted his coach at training. 'Ron, there was no one there', he said. 'There was a bloke three or four metres away so I had time before I kicked, and I had a look. No one.'

Barassi turned on his man. 'You wouldn't kick one out of twenty from there!'

To prove his point, that Thursday night at training he organised for Blight to take twenty shots from the same spot, only this time Barassi was the man putting pressure on him … and he had the entire team line up to watch. After ten attempts, Blight had kicked 4 goals, hit the post twice and kicked 4 behinds.

As the fourth sailed through, Barassi wheeled on his heels. 'That's bullshit,' he said, and walked off the ground.

The general manager of that year, John Dugdale, laughed about the snapshot of his former coach and his '*Centre the ball!*' edict. 'Blighty could do the phenomenal things that a lot of people couldn't do. That was Malcolm Blight; he did a lot of those things naturally. He wouldn't go out to think, "I'll kick a left-foot goal from the boundary"; it was instinctive.'

It was a light moment in the year that never quite clicked for the Kangaroos.

In their return match with the Tigers, in Round 21, they fell by 11 points at home. They had fallen to fourth place and were summarily dismissed by Collingwood in the elimination final.

It reversed the result of the other final those two teams had played that season, a memorable play-off for the Escort Championship night series crown. In time-on that night at VFL Park, Blight had picked up a loose ball and snapped from directly in front, bringing North to within a point. From the centre bounce, Collingwood managed to score a point, leaving the Roos 2 points adrift with the clock ticking. As rain began to pour down, Ray Shaw added another point. From the kick-in, Xavier Tanner received a free kick and played on, booting long to Blight and direct opponent Billy Picken, who was worked under the ball to concede the mark.

At some point in the seconds that followed, the siren went. You cannot hear it on the replay. Blight did not hear it on the ground. Most importantly, nor did the umpires. Blight played on—which technically would have ended the game—and passed to teammate Kerry Good. By now, it was apparent the siren had gone but had perhaps malfunctioned, for it was muted compared with its usual blast when it sounded again.

As Collingwood supporters poured onto the ground, closing to within 20 or 30 metres of Good, he kicked truly. The goal stood—a correct if controversial decision, as the umpires have to hear the siren and signal the end of the game for it to be officially over—and the Kangaroos won by 3 points. Blight laughs about the night, having been asked the question 'Did you hear the siren?' hundreds of times in the years since. No, he said, he did not.

Arguably, then, North Melbourne took something from the season: a night premiership. But they lost something, too: the passion of their coach. Barassi could not maintain the rage with which he had driven his players.

LOVE, HATE

To this day, Schimmelbusch feels deflated when thinking about that summer. 'Barass drove us pretty hard but the results were there; we played in five grand finals in a row,' he said. 'You play football to play in finals. If he doesn't drive us hard and we don't make grand finals, then you would be just as upset with him. It just didn't make sense to me that he took that attitude [losing his passion]. Okay, he said that he was tired and he wasn't as motivated as he was, perhaps. He said the players weren't responding to him so he left. I was disappointed about that.'

Perhaps he's missed the point. Coaching is like a marriage—if both parties are not fully invested, it is inevitably doomed.

'Barassi was a very strong character, a tremendously honest bloke and a man of integrity,' John Dugdale said. 'He had a fear about him. His coaching was all about basics, about avoiding the basic mistakes. You often think back, you would have liked to have played under him yourself; he had that sort of aura about him. Look, he got the best out of players because he made them concentrate. That was the way he ran the place. But when your time is up, your time is up. No one knew that more than Ron.'

7

THE COACH, PART I

JOHN DUGDALE AND Malcolm Blight were enjoying a beer one night late in 1979. As the topics chopped and changed, Dugdale threw in a question from left field.

'Are you interested in coaching?'

Blight already knew his answer. Only months from turning thirty, he was interested in both the patterns of the game and what made those who play it tick. Not only did he respond in the affirmative, he also added that 'funnily enough, I've been taking notes'. If it was the first wheel turned in a succession plan, it was a subtle one.

The Kangaroos still had Ron Barassi at the helm, but the magic, if not the message, seemed to be wearing off. North performed well during the 1980 season, winning 14 games, but their upset at the hands of Collingwood in the elimination final was their earliest September exit since Barassi had taken them to the grand final in 1974. In isolation it was hardly a disaster, but the coach was proving to be high maintenance for the football club. Barassi, whose contract was to expire after 1980, had financial troubles.

'The club helped him out as much as it could,' explained Ron Joseph, detailing a plan hatched several years earlier. 'We got on well with Dick Seddon at Melbourne, who had taken over as chief executive. Seddon agreed that if North didn't renew [Barassi's contract] Melbourne would take an option on his services. I was in a moral dilemma as the chief exec of North to do that, but at least there was a sum of money there to get Barass going again. Then, after 1980, Barassi said to me he was finished.'

Dugdale had seen it coming. Though he was unaware of Joseph's dealings with Melbourne, he recognised a coach whose expiry date was approaching, and fast. 'Ron was going through the motions in 1980, he was as flat as a tack,' he said. 'And I suspect he knew he was going to Melbourne. He wasn't the same Ron Barassi; I thought he'd run his race at North Melbourne.'

The Demons were true to their word, appointing Barassi soon after the season to bring home a favourite son following a fifteen-year absence. After a period of extended success, North Melbourne needed a coach. They flirted with Tom Hafey, who was entrenched at Collingwood and had taken the Magpies to the 1980 grand final. After a series of conversations, Hafey turned the Kangaroos down; he felt morally bound to Collingwood.

'We felt there was another premiership in Malcolm Blight and Gary Dempsey, David Dench, Keith Greig, Schimma, all of those blokes who were senior footballers and would respond to someone like Hafey,' Joseph said. 'When he said no, we didn't have another string to our bow. Ray Jordon and Barassi thought Blighty could do it as a playing coach, although I thought it was unfair. But we didn't have anywhere to turn. This was certainly late September, into October. So Blighty became playing coach.'

'We thought Malcolm had the brains and ability to be a coach,' added Dugdale. 'And we wanted a North Melbourne person. We hadn't had one for ten years, and we thought Malcolm was the man for the job.'

The most recent playing coach in the VFL had been Alex Jesaulenko, who had taken Carlton to the memorable 1979 premiership. Memorable because Jesaulenko had been such a brilliant presence in the game, but also for the fallout during the summer that followed. When Blues president George Harris was ousted at a fiery annual general meeting, Jesaulenko's allegiance to Harris saw him depart too; 'Jezza' was snapped up by St Kilda in 1980. Yet his success in 1979 meant the concept of a playing coach in 1981 was not far-fetched in some people's minds ... certainly not in Malcolm Blight's. 'I had probably started to coach a bit on the ground,' Blight said. 'I didn't want Barassi to go, to be honest, but there were games when I started to wander a bit in my head, thinking more about *the* game than *my* game. People at the club were really positive about the idea of it. I had some ideas to freshen the club up. I changed training a fair bit and tried a few things.

'I mean, I was brought up with the words "Super Coach". Barassi taught me stuff. We used to go to the Channel 7 studios and see either the game we had just played or the team we were

THE COACH, PART I

playing the next week. I hadn't been exposed to a lot of this, and Barassi just talked as the game was played. I listened to everything, even the bad stuff, and there was plenty of that. I started picturing a game of football much more than I had before. Up to that point it was all about playing—chase it, get it, kick it.

'No one would have known, because I was quiet in that group, but those sessions and just being around Barassi titillated me for coaching.'

The Kangaroos opened the 1981 season well under their new leader, hosting South Melbourne and handing the Swans an 8-goal loss. But Round 2 exposed the playing coach plan for what it was, especially in light of the man in the opposition coach's box. North Melbourne headed to Windy Hill to tackle Essendon; our new coach, Kevin Sheedy, had taken his coaching role on the proviso that it was full-time, the first coach to carry that status into the season. 'I was going to be up against some of the best ... I couldn't match them doing the job on a part-time basis,' Sheedy reflected in his book *The 500 Club*. 'It was like playing catch-up football, I had to play catch-up coaching and the only way I could do that properly was full-time.'

History—and two premierships within five years—suggests Sheedy was right in his assessment. Coaching *was* a full-time job, so adding the responsibilities of playing—and playing well—was to be Blight's biggest challenge. He started that Windy Hill afternoon brightly, kicking 4 goals to half-time, by which time his men led by a goal. As the game progressed, however, he became ineffective as he juggled the demands of both player and coach. 'I ran around in the last quarter, playing on the ball, and didn't get a kick', he said.

'I spent the whole quarter telling other blokes what to do and did not touch the footy once. I was worrying about seventeen other blokes.' Essendon won by 12 points.

At the time, journalist Michael Sheahan was senior football writer for the now-defunct *Herald* newspaper in Melbourne. A veteran of forty years of covering League football, he had sensed a shift in the wind during the early 1980s, although he also understood North's decision. 'There was a growing view that you couldn't do both jobs,' Sheahan said of being playing coach. 'The only thing is that, with Blighty, you thought, "Well, you can't actually do this but maybe Blighty could because of who he was".'

Despite his growing concern about the viability of the role, Blight's men had climbed to 6–4 and fourth place when they thrashed Melbourne by 129 points at Waverley. It was to be the best moment of the season, though, as injuries began to erode the depth of an ageing list. Keith Greig had torn up his knee in Round 7, his season finished with just three games to his credit. Blight himself missed three early games and Arnold Briedis managed just six for the year, while premiership wingman John Cassin was traded to Fitzroy. Only two players, Ross Glendinning and Gary Dempsey, managed to play all twenty-two home and away games.

After that high against Melbourne, the Roos lost to Carlton and Essendon in successive weeks, and were then humiliated at Geelong by 114 points as an injured Blight looked on from the coach's box. Three Roos had played less than five games that day but the malaise went deeper than youth or injuries. The famously competitive North spirit was missing, and losses followed to Richmond by 43 points and Hawthorn by 60. A trip to Waverley and a 34-point loss

THE COACH, PART I

to Fitzroy turned the season into a 6–10 disappointment, and made up the coach's mind.

'No one ever said, "You're not doing it." It was more a "Look in the mirror, something has to change" thing,' Blight said. 'The match day stuff was hard. Occasionally the runner [former team-mate John Rantall] couldn't get to me, or the communication thing was really difficult. At half-time of one game, I said to a player, "I want you to play a bit higher, get some space behind you." He told me he'd just received a message to do the opposite, to get back. Someone on the bench was giving a different message to what I was thinking.

'[It was] no one's fault: I didn't do it my way; it was circumstances, not individuals. In the end it clearly wasn't working, which gave me three options: give the coaching away, stop playing—which I didn't want to do—or keep going. The scoreboard gets you. You have to be honest, that's where it counts. I felt the team would get better quickly, and it was a reasonable list, but it wouldn't be me in charge.'

Blight had thrown in a promising job with a transport company to commit himself to playing and coaching, picturing a graceful, timely playing twilight followed by years of coaching at Arden Street. He had just bought a house, too, confident that he could comfortably surf Barassi's substantial wake in the short term before placing his own stamp on the club. 'But no one got me [fired] at North Melbourne. *I* got me [fired].'

'Giving him the job was the mistake,' conceded Dugdale, who was the assistant coach in the box that season, alongside reserves coach Colin Kinnear. 'It was too bloody hard. In the box we tried not to interfere but we could obviously see things better than Malcolm could. And if Blighty wasn't playing well himself, it was too hard to then be managing other fellas on the ground. The days you're struggling, and you can't play well every week, it became hard to give a bloke a blast.'

In Round 14, the Kangaroos had headed to the MCG at 6–7 to take on the defending premiers, Richmond. It was the scene for a mistake both comical and revealing, depending on your perspective. Steve McCann lured an opponent to him and wafted the ball to an unattended Blight in the goal square. Blight turned around, took several steps and booted the ball through … for a point. What he thought were the goals were the behinds. While he has an explanation, he also concedes 'that moment probably sealed it for me mentally'.

'I half went to sleep because I thought [McCann] was going to have a shot. I'd gone across on the angle a bit like a goal umpire to get behind his kick, then he handballed to me,' he said. 'The goal umpire started to move to the other side of the goalpost. So I just ran in and kicked what I thought was a goal, straight past the goal umpire.'

The mistake was so bizarre that when the ball returned to the centre square, Richmond's Geoff Raines turned to Wayne Schimmelbusch and said, 'Has Blighty got the shits with you blokes? What did he do that for?'

Dugdale believed that error, while innocent, 'told you where Malcolm's mind was at'. And the aftermath highlighted Dugdale's belief that leading by example when you are playing poorly had become too difficult for a playing coach. 'We kicked poorly,' Blight recalled, 'and I kicked 4.8 that day. I said after the game, "We need to spend more time with our kicking". And I'd kicked four out of my twelve chances. I'm not sure the message got through'.

Blight had played a handful of first-gamers that year, and five players that day had less than ten games to their credit. But, seeking to lead by example, he had played himself in fifteen different positions in sixteen weeks, always looking to plug a hole in the forward or back line, or on the ball. And it was simply wearing him out. Wayne Schimmelbusch believes the task was beyond most people, but especially one most commonly playing from the goal square. 'Playing from full-forward, it's pretty hard to get a picture of what's happening up the ground,' he said. 'You'd have to be pretty confident of who was calling the shots in the box. And even then it probably wouldn't matter.'

Throughout, Joseph had been watching his close friend slide into a funk. By the nature of his deeds—the Brownlow Medal, a best and fairest, two premierships, the 1976 goal at Carlton—Blight had become a larger than life figure at Arden Street. Combined with his natural confidence and forthrightness, and what psychologists would call an 'alpha dog' presence, the Blight charisma had played a significant role in his assuming the coaching role in the post-Barassi era. Now, Joseph simply saw a man under pressure to hold down two jobs. 'You could see the stress and tension he was going through,' Joseph said.

On the night of the Fitzroy loss, Blight had organised a player function at his house. Joseph attended, noting a sombre mood of surrender in the group and its coach. He arranged for a Monday-morning breakfast with Blight in the familiar confines of the Old

Melbourne Motor Inn, a regular Kangaroos haunt. It was apparent to Joseph that Blight was not mentally capable of continuing both roles, so he kicked off the conversation with a blunt directive: 'There are three things you can do,' he said to Blight. 'You can leave things exactly as they are; there's six weeks to go and we'll ride it out. You can quit as a player for the rest of the year and just coach, and see how you go. Or you can quit as coach and just play.'

Blight responded: 'What do you think I should do?'

'I'd play,' Joseph said. 'Why put yourself through this heartache and stress, when you've still got two or three great football years? You can coach forever when you finish.'

Joseph believed that former Kangaroos star Barry Cable 'would run across the Nullarbor Plain to coach. So we went to my office, rang Cable and asked him if he'd coach. He said yes, so that was that'.

Cable had retired after playing an instrumental role in the club's 1977 premiership, accepting an offer to captain-coach East Perth. He led the Royals to a flag that year, and played on until 1979. If any player had the reputation and stature to take over it was Cable, who like Blight was revered in two states for his football talent. A board meeting during the week confirmed Cable's appointment. 'Word got out,' Joseph said. 'Mike Sheahan rang me and asked me if it was true, and I said no. But I was about to go into a meeting and that was exactly what was going to happen. Sheahan was furious. It was all pretty emotional. Then Blighty goes out forty-eight hours later and kicks 11 goals at Footscray.'

This might be the most astonishing aspect of a remarkable week in football. Seven days after coaching his final game at North

Melbourne, Blight drove out to the Western Oval, contemplating his playing future. He was thirty-one years, 159 days old when he entered Bulldog territory that day, having two nights earlier endured the intense humiliation of those endless, embarrassing '100-day laps' on Cable's insistence. The last thing he felt like doing was playing football, but he also knew the game offered an escape of sorts. 'I wasn't dirty on anyone except myself,' he said. 'I didn't play in spite of anyone that day, didn't worry about anything else, I just played.'

Blight had 23 possessions, took 12 marks and kicked 11.7 as the Kangaroos broke their losing streak with a 9-point win. Of all of his achievements, this is still the one that caught me most off guard. That famous kick after the siren at Princes Park had been a single moment; his performance at Footscray took an exceptional combination of courage and talent to front up in the first place, and then to produce a show like that. After the game, he didn't even change or shower—he simply got in his car and headed home, still a whirl of emotions. It tells you he might have sleepwalked through the game on talent alone.

Blight kicked 8.6 a week later against St Kilda, another win, before his body and perhaps spirit gave in against Collingwood in Round 19. His season was finished, as was his coaching dream.

* * *

If there had been any doubts about Blight's capacity to continue to perform at VFL level, they were laid to rest when he divested himself of coaching duties. Cable anchored him deeper in the forward line and the results were stunning: 22 goals in the three weeks he played before the end of his 1981 season. If it highlighted his talent, it also underscored his value to the Kangaroos. But as he entered the summer of 1981–82, he was torn about his playing future.

Shortly after the season finished, Joseph found himself in his close friend's backyard in the Melbourne suburb of Highett. It was a recruiting visit of sorts, focused on re-affirming a club's interest in bringing its star player back. Blight had invested everything he had in filling the Barassi void. A man not accustomed to failure, he was putting into place the philosophy that had evolved during those two slow laps of Arden Street: do things his way. Step one was an ultimatum of sorts; he would return to play, but only if certain players were traded or released. Blight then rattled off his list. Joseph couldn't believe his ears but he knew Blight was serious. After a lengthy discussion about the former coach swallowing his pride, Blight settled on three non-negotiables—Gary Dempsey, Stephen Icke and Brian Wilson—who he felt had let him down during his tenure as playing coach. If they went, he stayed.

'There were more than that. Blighty was really disappointed with a lot of the senior players,' Schimmelbusch recalled. 'But that's the nature of coaching. When he went to Geelong and Adelaide, and even St Kilda, I bet he felt the same way about a few senior players.'

'He got stuck on Icke, Dempsey and Wilson,' Joseph explained. 'So I rang Cable the next day and told him. Cable, to his eternal credit, said we'll get rid of Wilson and Icke but not Dempsey. So Icke and Wilson went to Melbourne.' In 1982, nineteen-year-old Brian Wilson—by then at his third club, having started with Footscray before crossing to North—won the Brownlow Medal.

THE COACH, PART I

In the same season, Steven Icke won the Demons' best and fairest. All these years later, Joseph still muses about those trades. 'I think we overreacted.'

Joseph played his final card in convincing Blight to return, appealing to his legacy in the game. 'Who is going to be the Ron Barassi or Ted Whitten in twenty-five years' time? It could be you,' he said that night in the backyard. 'There is so much you can achieve as a person by swallowing your pride.'

Blight stayed. He retained lingering issues about playing on at Arden Street in 1982: 'Did they need the old coach sitting in the background? I'm not sure if I want to be here, not sure what I want to do'. His new coach, though, had plans. Cable saw in Blight the perfect roaming target to utilise in his first year as a senior VFL coach. Spending more time up forward from his Brownlow Medal season of 1978, Blight had led the Kangaroos' goalkicking for three of the previous four seasons; 1982 was to be the ultimate extension of that opportunity, as he played only at centre half-forward or full-forward, settling into the permanent spearhead role.

Despite missing four games, Blight kicked 103 goals for the season. The effort equalled former teammate Doug Wade's club record, and made Blight only the second Kangaroo to break the season century mark. His consistency across the season was remarkable. 'He showed a lot of character, I thought, sticking around and playing on, and playing that well,' Schimmelbusch said. 'And that was one way to stick it up everybody, I suppose.'

Blight's hundredth goal for the season is a revealing glimpse into both his mentality and that of the Kangaroos. Receiving a free kick against Hawk full-back Kelvin Moore right on the

99

MALCOLM BLIGHT

quarter-time siren of the semi-final, Blight kicked truly from about 40 metres. He punched the air with both arms and received some handshakes from opponents, then trotted to the huddle, having put his team 10 points ahead. There was no fanfare, no crowd invasion, and the moment passed with little more than commentator Doug Bigelow's 'There's Magical Malcolm' reference as the camera zoomed in.

The overriding emotion was … well, a lack of emotion.

It hardly seems surprising that, after the game, when the Kangaroos had been overrun by 52 points, Blight turned to Dugdale in the rooms and declared, 'I'm out. I'm finished'.

'It was the end of the year and I was itchy [to move],' he conceded. 'So I did.'

8

BACK TO OVAL AVENUE

THE SEEDS FOR the late 1990s success of the Adelaide Football Club were sown fifteen years earlier in the front bar of the Saracen's Head Hotel in Carrington Street, Adelaide, where Malcolm Blight met John Reid for a chat about footy. It was a discussion enjoyed over several beers, then several more. Blight's credentials by this point opened any door in Adelaide, not least those of the Saracen's Head, which was owned by his former Woodville coach, Noel Teasdale. From his precocious early days at Woodville, through his storied VFL career with North Melbourne, Blight's place in the game was secure despite his brief, unsuccessful fling as Kangaroos senior playing coach. Yet those sixteen weeks in charge at Arden Street proved more than a random flirtation, for they left in Blight a residual sense of feeling unfulfilled.

The Peckers offered to scratch that itch. After the 1982 season, in which the club had won a single game and finished last, Woodville's administration decided change was in order. A new jumper was commissioned; out went the vertical stripes, replaced with a more contemporary panel-and-logo style. They also revealed a much-needed new sponsor and, in some ways a sign of the ultimate rebranding, changed their name from the quirky Woodpeckers to the more imposing moniker of the Warriors.

Then, on 8 October, they announced they had secured a new coach: Malcolm Blight.

It's hard to imagine a deeper line being drawn in the sand. For so long the poor cousin of nearby Port Adelaide, the Warriors had called upon one of their favourite sons to resurrect the football club. This was not a reach back to a better time, because even during Blight's playing days prior to his departure for North Melbourne, they had finished no higher than seventh. But there was a feeling it was the club's last chance to reinvent itself; in fact, there was an undercurrent of sentiment that the club was living on borrowed time and always had been.

Woodville, the critics argued, had such a small local zone to choose from in such a parochial competition that it had long been impossible to build a culture of sustained success. '*What can you say about the Woodpeckers, jammed into territory too small to rake up a good Mini League side?*' journalist Doug Thomas had penned in the *Sunday Mail* back in 1971. 'The club was squeezed into the western side of the city between Port Adelaide, West Adelaide, West Torrens and North Adelaide,' added Bill Sanders. 'It had never enjoyed a large [recruiting] zone to provide us with the depth of players we needed. Every now and then someone like Malcolm came along but we struggled an awful lot.'

If Blight was seeking a challenge, he found one. The same could be said for Reid, who that night entered the Saracen's Head with a history in the game that lacked the national profile of his drinking partner's but was in its own way impressive. A former South Adelaide senior player and coach, he had enjoyed a successful coaching stint at Port Augusta before returning to the city to fill the role at Woodville as Blight's assistant. The men shared a belief in hard work and having the appropriate support structures in place. They were keenly aware of the task that lay ahead: Woodville had won eight games in the last three seasons, and in each of those years had finished last of the ten SANFL clubs. In many ways a new mascot, jumper and coach was a last shot at survival after two decades of borderline non-competitiveness, for the club had played finals football just once, in 1979, suffering an 11-goal loss to Norwood in that solitary appearance.

Blight's signing lit a flame of interest in the club. Membership increased by 120 per cent, an important boost for a club teetering on the edge of a financial cliff. Sanders was not an official of the club that year, having only recently completed a regional posting for the Bank of South Australia. Yet his relationship with Blight from the latter's playing days gave him a connection. 'When I came back from the country I was content to just watch Woodville as a spectator,' he recalled. '[Club chairman] Kevin Angel told me he wanted to change the name and jumper, but also to recruit Phil Maylin, John Roberts and Malcolm Blight. Given I had history with Blighty they asked me to approach him about coming back as a player. I went to visit him several times in Melbourne, him and Patsy. Sitting there, talking about footy and coming back, we weren't really making much progress, it was all pretty general. Out of the blue, I said, "How about coming back and coaching?"'

Blight sat for a moment before responding. 'Now, that's got appeal,' he said.

'It was his first strong, positive response to returning to Woodville, and probably sent the message that coaching had his interest,' Sanders reflected. 'So I asked him the direct question, "If you were appointed coach, would you come back to Adelaide?" He didn't really pause this time, he just said, "Yep".'

Blight's thinking was typically forthright. He had failed in coaching once, but it helped him identify the coaching opportunity that suited his goals. 'There were still some scars there from 81,' Blight recalled. 'I thought, if I'm ever going to coach again, and I want to do it entirely my way, where's the worst football club in Australia? It just happened to be my home club, which had won one game [that season].'

When Sanders returned to Adelaide, he delivered the news with the understanding that the Warriors had an incumbent coach, Rod Olsson, who had a year remaining on his contract. Angel and general manager Jim Hewitson barely hesitated. Get Blight. Sanders summed up the opportunity: 'The club needed an injection of enthusiasm and, well, *Blightism*'.

If the idea was sound, the Warriors had not counted on the climate surrounding Blight's departure from North Melbourne. More than a couple of hurdles stood in the way of a transfer: there were 50,000 of them. The Kangaroos believed Blight had been paid in advance (as part of his coaching termination lump-sum payout) to finish playing until the end of 1983, which would honour his original playing-coach contract. The confusion surrounded what portion of that payment related to playing, and what percentage to coaching. To this day, both parties stand firm by their position.

'North had paid him money and I had to get fifty thousand back,' Ron Joseph argued. 'By this stage Bob Ansett was the club chairman, so I explained to him what I'd done, and calculated that on the fair side for Blighty he owed us fifty grand, so we wouldn't clear him.' Blight puts the figure at closer to 'ten or eleven, maybe twelve thousand'.

'But that wasn't the point', said Blight, who at the time was becoming increasingly frustrated with the Kangaroos' administration. 'They wouldn't listen.'

And the Warriors simply could not afford the transfer fee. 'So the National Football League [the game's governing body] revoked Malcolm's permit to play,' Sanders explained. 'North wanted fifty thousand for his clearance and we had nothing like it. We launched a media push from this end and used a couple of connections in the Melbourne media, appealing to the supporters and followers of football: how can you deny this guy, who had been such a champion for your club, the opportunity to play and coach back with the club he started? That gathered some momentum for our side.'

A white knight then emerged in the form of a local Woodville businessman, not a football follower but a man who smelled the injustice of the situation. He offered to foot the transfer fee out of his own pocket. 'He was actually American,' Sanders continued. '[He] didn't follow Aussie Rules but saw that Malcolm was being denied the right to play. So the money was there, but we decided to sit tight rather than offer the money to North, because it felt like public opinion was running our way.'

The deadline for clearances was 12 noon on a Friday. Sanders was tipped off that the North Melbourne board had called an extraordinary meeting that morning to discuss the matter.

'All of Adelaide was into us,' Joseph recounted. 'We held our ground for a while but we were getting letters from supporters: *"Why are you doing this to such a champion, hasn't he given us enough?"* That sort of thing. So I went to Bob Ansett and said we just had to clear him, we were on a hiding to nothing. We couldn't win this one.'

Fifteen minutes before the clearance deadline, Sanders received a phone call. Blight's clearance was approved without a transfer fee. 'And we ended up being fifty thousand better off,' he said, 'because the benefactor decided the money could stay with the club.'

If Joseph was disappointed by the nature of the transfer, it was not helped when Blight later admitted the club would have paid. Both men were in a hotel overlooking the Albert Park golf course one night. If push came to shove, Blight then admitted, he would have played on at North Melbourne. 'I just said, "You fucking idiot",' Joseph said. 'After all that had happened, our friendship was never the same.'

* * *

Overcoming a transfer drama to satisfy a coaching urge seemed likely to be the least of Malcolm Blight's problems. 'My first cheque bounced,' Blight said. ' *"Refer to drawer."* I rang up Bill Sanders and said, "Bill, you know how I used to work in a bank with you? When you got *Present Again* it meant exactly that: *Present Again*. But *Refer to Drawer* means you have to go back to the bastard who wrote the thing out. What happened?" He said, "We've got no money".

'What could I say except "Shit",' Blight said. 'I suspected it was tight but didn't think there'd be a *"Refer to Drawer"* with the first cheque. I wasn't sure what to do, so I started marketing the club. We created a "Gold Key Fundraising Club", knocking on doors trying to raise money.'

If the money side of it was disastrous, the football side of it might have been even worse. There could be no magic fix. Blight used forty-five players in his first season at Oval Avenue as the Warriors managed just four wins, albeit including a memorable triumph over perennial powerhouse Port Adelaide (their third win over the Magpies in twenty seasons). The honour board on the clubroom wall paints a telling picture about the weight of responsibility that the club's prized new signing carried in that 1983 season.

> Coach: M Blight
> Captain: M Blight
> Best and Fairest: M Blight
> Leading goalkicker: M Blight (54)

Far from being discouraged, Blight and Reid, joined by chairman of selectors (and best man at the Blight wedding) Colin MacVicar, adjourned in the week after the season to reassess yet another wooden spoon performance. The outcome largely centred on professionalism and fitness, with individual programs developed for every player who survived a brutal cull. Incredibly, twenty-six of the fifty-odd players on the list moved on that summer, either via retirement or because Blight's standards were simply too high for a large slice of the existing talent.

The turnover triggered an intensive recruiting campaign. On weekends, Reid would head to the north of the state and Blight would head south, or across the border into Victoria. 'I was marketing, fundraising, coaching this horrible team then driving around Port Augusta, the Wimmera, Mount Gambier, anywhere they played footy looking for talent,' Blight said. 'Our criteria was to recruit good people. No more dickheads. Once we got half an inkling that a bloke could kick, we did the networking—"What's he like? What's his family life like?" We got into their backgrounds.'

There were other benchmarks. If you had won a competition best and fairest or been leading goalkicker, it was naturally a solid endorsement ... but only if you passed the personality test.

While 1984 delivered another four-win, wooden spoon season, this Warriors team was now younger, more disciplined and more competitive. There were highlights—8 goals in the final twelve minutes to upset reigning premier West Adelaide, for instance, and the end of a twenty-six-game home losing streak. At thirty-four, Blight remained among the team's standout talents; on the day Woodville ended that turgid run of outs at Oval Avenue, he gathered 30 possessions and 16 marks against Sturt. It was a rare high point in his playing season, but Blight could see signs of progress. Winning his first of successive club best and fairest awards was an East Gambier recruit, Kevin Harris, who fitted the Blight mould: he had won a competition best and fairest, but, more to the point, he was a popular, hard-working and respected rover who went on to play six seasons with the club. Over Blight's first two years, he signed eight players from the Mount Gambier area as he rebuilt a club's self-respect.

'In twenty out of twenty-two games in 1984 we kicked 100 points, so the system was working,' he said. 'Four wins, four wins, six wins in my first three years, but we were getting closer. Even when we got successful though, it was hard work. I honestly believe those five years took ten out of me.'

In 1984, Blight kicked 44 goals from eighteen games, a decent return in a lowly team, but he was becoming increasingly aware of his hourglass sands running dry. His Achilles tendon hurt. His back ached. He even resorted to abandoning football boots for running shoes during a handful of games, having broken a toe and been unable to get his boot on—which made 1985 all the more remarkable, and unexpected.

Malcolm Blight had kicked 13 goals after a fortnight of football in his final playing season. The Warriors then played West Adelaide in front of 2975 people at Richmond Oval. He kicked 14 straight. Blight was not always the most reliable converter around goal, often taking snaps from difficult angles that had an impact on that efficiency—the previous week, for instance, he'd kicked 7.10 against Central Districts. But even by his career standards (his goals to behinds VFL record was 444.280, or a 61.3 per cent efficiency rate) this was an astonishing day out.

By the mid-year state-of-origin fixture against Western Australia, he had kicked 59 goals in nine games, having missed Round 4 with injury. His form was so impressive—and sentiment so strongly in his corner—that he was selected for a sixth and final appearance for his home state, and he would captain South Australia for the first time. Blight travelled to Perth and kicked 6 goals as the Croweaters annihilated WA by 87 points.

Just as he had finished his playing days in the VFL with a century of goals, Blight closed out his SANFL playing career with a century ... and it was a big one. He passed three figures in Round 18, booting 8 in a thumping win over Norwood, and iced his year with 12 straight in his final appearance at Woodville Oval in Round 21. For good measure, he added 6 more to his tally in his final game, a 38-point loss to eventual SANFL runner-up North Adelaide at Prospect Oval on 7 September 1985. Though the Warriors finished last for a record sixth successive season, they managed to win six games. And their playing coach booted 126 goals. That, said Blight, was enough.

'When I told Bill I was going to finish they were a bit disturbed but I felt the system was there by now,' he explained. 'Andrew Taylor and Stephen Nichols, Kevin Harris from Mount Gambier, Ralph Sewer, there was some good talent there.'

Sewer was one player for whom Blight held a special fondness. It is generally considered that North Adelaide's Barrie Robran was the pick of the SANFL talent to turn their back on testing themselves in the VFL environment. In the national club championships of 1972, Robran was the standout player in the final against Carlton; his coach that year, former Richmond premiership player Mike Patterson, noted that 'Barrie can match [any Victorian] in any phase. I've seen him do things that the best players over there have been unable to accomplish'. Blight held Sewer in similar reverance.

Sewer's nickname—'Zip Zap'—perfectly captured his frenetic, high-energy and powerful style. 'He was a smaller Gary Ablett senior,' Blight said. 'The most destructive little player I've ever seen. Tough, left foot, quick, I played with him and coached him too. It's a tragedy that he never came across [to Victoria]. He was a star, a sensational player, he could hurt you with this big goosestep and he just ran past blokes.'

Blight's goalkicking exploits in 1985 earned for him a third All-Australian jumper, thirteen seasons after his first. Only a fellow South Australian, the remarkably durable and consistent Craig Bradley, spaced his first and last All-Australian honours across a longer time frame (1983–97). Blight did not win the club championship—hardened rover Harris claimed the honour. And Grantley Fielke took the Magarey Medal with fifty-four votes, streets ahead of Blight's twenty-nine. But when you consider his ailing body and commitments as captain, coach and primary spear-head, those twenty-one games of football in 1985 sit in rare air, and were fitting closure to one of the game's better playing careers.

Bill Sanders, his lifelong friend and club chairman during that Warriors era, put it most succinctly: 'Malcolm squeezed the very last drop out of himself—he gave everything he could as a player'.

* * *

I can't help feeling that the mystique of Malcolm Blight in the Adelaide football scene earned him a period of grace others might not have received. The competition ladder doesn't lie, and after three seasons under Blight the team had extended the club's wooden spoon streak to six. But you couldn't fault his player turnover and commitment to change, and this pre-season quote told me plenty about why his approach would ultimately work. 'Off the ground things have certainly sharpened up,' Blight told the *Football Times Yearbook* during that pre-season. 'I've always believed and hammered home at Woodville that you have got to get your act in order off the ground first—that means from administration down to players ... There's been a lot more planning and preparation this year.'

If the absence of Blight the player left a hole, it was ably filled by Stephen Nichols, who from that season would top a goal-kicking century in three consecutive seasons. Blight's former North Melbourne teammate, Darryl Sutton, had tipped Blight off. Sutton was coaching North Hobart and liked what he saw in the Sandy Bay spearhead, who had played seven games for Geelong in the early eighties. Blight had expanded his recruiting zone well past Mount Gambier and even south to Tasmania; the deadly efficient Nichols was one catch, and his Tasmanian state-of-origin teammate Michael Templeton another. There were a half-dozen new names to add to his list. By Round 5, 1986, the team had claimed back-to-back wins and climbed to fifth.

The end of his playing days allowed the coach's imagination free rein. Early that season he watched the game at Richmond Oval from the crowd seated opposite the grandstand wing, seeking a different perspective. He was training his young team on Monday, Wednesday and Friday nights; that final session was because he liked getting to his players after they had finished work for the week, so they would switch onto footy.

One pre-match address featured an opposition jumper stretched out across a coathanger and hung in the middle of the room as Blight spoke. He had cut a heart-shaped hole in the jumper and held the cut-out heart there with double-sided tape. Theatrically, the coach tore the heart off the jumper to leave a symbolic gaping hole where the opposition's hearts lay. Yes, that reads as ridiculous, just as it did when Blight explained it. 'We lost, but hopefully not by as much as if I hadn't done it,' Blight laughed.

Central Districts that season had a new coach, Kevin 'Cowboy' Neale, hero of St Kilda's 1966 premiership win. 'Cowboy wanted to bring weights into their system so he took over half the visitors' rooms to build up his gym. The visitors' was like a dogbox,' Blight said. 'So while the seconds were on, we did a warm-up on the ground, behind the goals. I'm not sure anyone had done that before. Another time I had noticed that we were running onto the ground like scraggy dogs and I thought, "Why not run out as a tight bunch?" So I said, "I want you to be so close you'll smell the bloke next to you." I guess our philosophy became "Go home and cry, or try something." By the time we got to 86, I'd made more mistakes than any other coach in the League, but because we were on the bottom no one cared. I was having fun trying things.'

The coach's actions against Port Adelaide in Round 9 caught the most attention. After a bright season start, the Warriors had lost three on end when they travelled to Football Park to meet Port. Trailing badly at three-quarter time, Blight split his men into groups and had them conduct end-to-end training drills during the changeover, to the amazement of both the modest crowd and the opposition. He later claimed it was in response to his team constantly missing targets by foot, adding that the drills did cause some improvement in the final thirty minutes. 'We kept coughing up the ball; I was pretty angry,' Blight said. 'Can I yell at them again? No, I'm doing my own head in. So I said, "Listen, we've given away the footy too much, for Christ's sake we're going to do some lanework. Just a little training drill." From memory we won the last quarter by a few goals.'

Now someone cared. The *Sunday Mail* observed the bizarre instructions as the last straw for a frustrated coach: *Blight Boils over in Day of Drama*. The Warriors were trounced by 11 goals, and a week later sat midway through the season on the foot of the ladder. Again. As of that moment, it was fair to assess the Blight experiment as a failure if you read the local press, as the knives remained out for Woodville. More to the point, the balance sheet told a dire tale, prompting the administration to gather the players for a chat that week.

'After the Port thing, the following Monday night we addressed the players,' Sanders said. 'Chairman, general manager and the president … on what we saw as a real problem within the club. We stressed to the players that unless there was a turnabout in our performances, we were in real danger of amalgamating, or merging, or folding. It was a crisis, the situation was pretty desperate.'

Then something clicked. Blight might take credit for the lanework. The administration might claim to have flicked the switch. But a players' meeting seemed the most likely cause. Captain Max Parker simply said the players had 'had enough of losing'. Training started an hour earlier that week—when Blight arrived at five o'clock, to his delight his men were already mid-session.

In Round 11, Woodville flogged Central Districts by 101 points. In the fortnight that followed they downed flag favourite North Adelaide and South Adelaide, before stumbling to Glenelg. By now, Parker was gathering his men on the ground before games in possibly football's first version of 'the prematch huddle'. Woodville, which had played finals football once since entering the SANFL in 1964 and had never won more than four on end, triumphed on seven straight weekends. Though they fell to lowly South Adelaide in the final week of the home and away season, wasting the opportunity to secure a double chance, the Warriors had earned a place in September action.

Their first opponent? Norwood in the elimination final. South Australia's weekly football newspaper *Football Times* previewed the game: '… one thing hasn't changed—Woodville still lack finals experience,' wrote Michelangelo Rucci. 'And there lies the tragedy of the form side of the competition missing the double chance. Had the young Woodville players been given the chance to play in a final—just to get the feel of playing in the big time—they would be a better proposition for the grand final. That is Woodville's penalty for starting the season so poorly. Woodville—and the tactics of Blight and assistant coach John Reid—can beat Norwood. Whether it does win is in the hands of the 20 men Blight chooses to determine his destiny.'

The Redlegs were (and remain) a perennial SANFL strength; since Blight's debut in 1968, they had won no less than seven premierships prior to this meeting. The Warriors had not won a single final. Ever. So the first thirty minutes came as a surprise. Against the wind, Blight's men led by 23 points at the first change. If Norwood had the names, Woodville countered with commitment—their tackling and pressure had established a lead that flew in the face of their finals inexperience.

Norwood, however, was certain to make their charge, and with the wind in the third quarter they closed to within 9 points late in the term. If ever Blight's men would be tested, it was now. When Templeton kicked their first goal of the final term, the Warriors were on their way.

With a 'Woodville ... Woodville' chant reverberating around Football Park, a final-quarter onslaught broke the club's finals drought with a 43-point triumph. 'It's equal to the biggest buzz I've had in footy,' Blight recalled. 'For Woodville to finally be recognised as a team, given my history with the club and the area, was an enormous thing for me. Obviously winning a premiership would have been better but for the club to finally be taken seriously was really satisfying.'

The Warriors then confronted Port Adelaide at Football Park, in front of the largest crowd the club had ever attracted: 39,086. Given that, as a kid, he had supported the nearby Magpies yet coveted a Peckers senior jersey, there was a synchronicity in the largest game in the club's existence. Maybe the occasion got to them in the opening term. Six goals behind at quarter-time, the Warriors were back within a kick by the half. Every time Port threatened to break away, telling goals kept Blight's men in touch, and it was a Nichols snap from 40 metres that eventually sealed a 1986 preliminary final berth.

The fairytale ran a chapter short. Against Glenelg in the penultimate step, the Warriors were wasteful in the final term, kicking 2.10 in the final thirty minutes to fall a kick shy of the eventual premiers. The defeat still haunts men who played in that game, but Blight's post-season column in the annual report would prove to be an insightful assessment of where he found himself. *'Any inflated ideas about the coming season will soon be brought back to earth if all of our energy is not directed to the one aim.'*

How those words must have rung true as Blight sat in a Hobart airport on the eve of the finals the following year, 1987. His flight had been delayed for several hours. When he'd retired from playing, he had secured a role with SPD Transport in the Adelaide suburb of Wingfield. Within twelve months, Brambles had taken over SPD, and Blight quickly climbed the ranks to national manager of the transport side of the group. It said much for his organisational and people-management skills, but it had a heavy impact on his capacity to coach a football team.

On this Friday night, as the Warriors poured onto Oval Avenue for their final training session before the finals, Blight sat in Hobart and pondered his future. 'When I couldn't get back for that final training session, I couldn't believe it. The back half of the year became a real struggle timewise and emotionally. Actually, I could feel myself not entirely committed.'

What followed the next day was hardly a surprise. The Warriors had had the staggers through the latter half of the season, slipping from 11–5 to finish the home and away season at 12–10, still good enough for fifth and a return to September. It's too simplistic to tie Blight's increasing work commitments to the team's form malaise; injuries had eroded the depth, and too many players found them-selves out of form as the home and away season drew to a close.

What followed next *was* a surprise. At three-quarter time of the elimination final, with his team trailing by more than 10 goals, Blight stunned the playing group by announcing that he was retiring as coach. 'I went up to him and said, "That wasn't a very good call, Malcolm",' 200-game veteran Ian Dettman recalled in *The Best of Both Worlds*. '"What do you expect us to do now for the last quarter? Go out and bust our guts while you're giving it away?"'

Blight later admitted his timing could have been better, but an overwhelming sense of fatigue drove his decision. Little wonder the 63-point deficit blew out to 102 by the final siren—the man who had restored hope and respect in a football club was leaving.

Work duties would see him relocate to Melbourne. Blight believed he had done all he could in reshaping the football club of his youth. It had increased talent, a stronger financial base—having recorded a profit in three consecutive years—and, most importantly, it had shed its reputation as the competition's whipping boy. 'Blightism', which in other arenas might simply be called tough love, had worked its magic. 'He was brutally honest, particularly with players' performance,' Sanders summarised. 'You could be forgiven for thinking he was too harsh in what he said or what he did, but his record speaks for itself.'

9

THE COACH, PART II

THERE IS SOMETHING inherently country about Kardinia Park. Geelong is hardly a small town, but it has managed to retain some of the niceties of rural Victoria, many of which are evident at its football ground. The rickety timber Past Players Stand, built in 1945, might be the best example. Until 2009, it sat in the forward pocket like the anachronism it was, much like the general vibe at the entire ground.

For a country boy, it felt like playing country football, only without cars encircling the ground. And back then it was a big trip down the highway. This sounds laughable now, given interstate trips and constant travel, but we used to fret a bit about how to prepare for it. I spent one trip to Geelong in the back of Simon Madden's kombi van. On another occasion, short-lived teammate

Barry Day, an aircraft fanatic, stopped en route at Avalon to watch the jets take off. I was late for the team meeting.

By 1988, the ground—it was not yet a stadium—was flying the flag for suburban football in the Victorian Football League. A lot of local grounds were on the threshold of extinction as match day venues. In fact, North Melbourne had last played for premiership points at Arden Street three years earlier. Essendon had only three more seasons at Windy Hill; St Kilda vacated Moorabbin twelve months later. The Western Bulldogs sought a new playing home in 1998, while Collingwood—effectively the last, proud bastion of inner-city football identity—deemed that Victoria Park was no longer suitable for matches after season 1999.

I was lucky enough to play at all of them. Some, like Moorabbin, were primitive beyond belief. But they all had character and represented a unique challenge in a time when black or white shorts—and even Essendon's horrible red ones—meant something.

Football was changing, and so was its coverage. As Channel 7 had been the main broadcaster of the game, a handful of names provided the soundtrack of the game: Mike ('*I have seen it all*') Williamson and Lou Richards had a commentary style that was unmistakable in the 1970s. Either that, or it was Doug Bigelow and Drew Morphett bringing country people *The Winners* on the ABC. But more names were being added to the commentary box. When Malcolm Blight's phone rang early in 1988, Channel 7 sports executive Gary Fenton was on the other end of the line, sounding him out about joining the commentary team.

'It was around that time that North Melbourne also rang,' Blight said. 'John Kennedy was coach and they asked me whether

I wanted to come down and effectively be an assistant. But I said I was committed to work, and I needed to do a fair bit of flying around, so I said no. But commentary? Why not? It might be interesting. There were games in all states so it suited me, it dovetailed nicely with work.'

Blight took straight to the role, bringing a combination of acute observation and left-field thinking, plus a sense of perspective. He was proving the model of an analyst as Fenton sought to create a more traditional, US-based style of commentary team: a game-caller coupled with one or two analysts. Bruce McAvaney later shared a commentary box with him and noted how Blight the coach and teacher was never far removed from Blight the analyst. 'Malcolm's ability to break down the game off a camera was brilliant,' McAvaney said. 'I liked talking to Blighty because not only could he give you big-picture things about footy but he can actually show blokes how to play. A lot of coaches can't. They have great big-picture stuff and are organisation wizards, but Malcolm can show a bloke how to hold a football, or point to a spot that you have to get to. And that comes through in his television work.

'His tactical sense was fascinating, and he was instructional. I got so much practical sense out of a bloke that could be a bit airy fairy, like Sheedy at times, but even the zany stuff made sense with Blighty.'

Blight adeptly juggled football commentary with his work for Brambles Transport. It gave him balance, and he enjoyed the opportunity to watch the game without living and breathing it. You can sense that what made him successful in football gave him an edge in business: terrific people-management skills, competitiveness and, above all, a clear sense of process equals result. 'I loved it, loved the industry and the working with people side of it,' he said. In fact, every time Blight drifted back to the transport industry he experienced a rapid rise.

His year at Woodville had taken its toll but almost against his will his orbit again transected football's gravitational pull, as a cry for help from Kardinia Park piqued his ego and his interest.

The 1988 home and away season closed with Geelong languishing in ninth place, extending a finals drought to seven consecutive years under three coaches. Just as they felt it was time for another change, Blight was opening eyes and ears with his work on Channel 7. Then–Geelong president Ron Hovey remembers watching the telecast of a Cats game that year and being drawn to the simple philosophies spun by the South Australian analyst. His general manager of the time, Ken Gannon, was also aware of Blight the media performer. 'What [his time in] the media was able to provide, and what everyone could see, was Malcolm's thoughts on football,' Gannon reflected. 'During that twelve months in that Channel 7 time he was there for everyone to see what he thought of players, game plans, the direction of the whole game. The media provided that opportunity to evaluate Malcolm. Likewise, him being in the media meant he would know how to handle the media … He didn't see it as the enemy.

'The growing reality of football at the time … was that the League was putting increased pressure on the clubs to make sure they were open with the media, rather than hide things away or be a closed shop. It was all about building fans, bringing people into the circle.'

THE COACH, PART II

The contract of incumbent coach John Devine had expired. The day after it was announced that Devine was not returning, Gannon placed a call to Blight. They agreed to meet in the latter's Maribyrnong office, and it quickly became apparent that both parties were interested in extending the conversation on a more formal basis. Shortly afterwards, Blight found himself in front of the Geelong Football Club board, which had convened at club director Colin Carter's house in Melbourne's inner east. The interview, for want of a better word, did not start well. 'Someone said I had to write a board paper each week,' said Blight, who responded to the request with typical candour: 'You've got the wrong bloke'.

'I understand if you require that, but I'm not the right bloke,' he explained. 'Wasting time on reports is not me—I'd rather go out and have a kick with a kid. Talk to me at the start of the year and the end of the year; if it's not good enough give me the flick. They could come into any team meeting, into the rooms, it wasn't like I wanted nothing to do with them, but my energy had to go into the players.'

If the board was taken aback, it also sensed the club had struck on the innovative mind required to drag Geelong back to competitiveness. Since the departure of Billy Goggin after season 1982, the Cats had tried a big-name coach in Tommy Hafey, then Devine's laid-back style. In Blight, however, the entire room identified a spark that had the room full of club directors buzzing long after he had departed. 'We approached Malcolm, so he wasn't selling himself, we just wanted to hear what he had to say. He was very honest and open, he promoted a free spirit we were looking

123

for,' Gannon said. 'The board knew they'd get information either informally or reporting back through the football director. But to come to a meeting every week? No. Malcolm knew he would be evaluated by his results.

'Really, he was the realisation within the board that we had to step forward and do things better, he brought the innovation to the club that we needed.'

That meeting in Colin Carter's lounge room created precisely the environment in which Blight could control an audience. 'People were mesmerised by him,' said *Herald Sun* chief football writer Mike Sheahan, a one-time colleague on football talk show *On the Couch*. 'After doing shows with him, we'd all go to the Botanical [Hotel] and he would hold sway in the room, almost like a pied piper. It didn't matter if you were John Worsfold or John Elliott, he was such a great storyteller and so magnetic that he was the centre of attention.'

McAvaney added his own perspective. 'Malcolm has a healthy ego. He commands attention,' McAvaney said. 'He needs to be treated socially and thought [of] as something out of the ordinary. The minute you do that you're on a similar wavelength. That sounds like I'm being critical, but that's Malcolm. He walks into a room, opens his mouth, and you listen.'

I'd spent a little time with Malcolm and seen signs of that. Talking to him about this book, it struck me how right Sheahan and McAvaney are. The guy is, well, intriguing. The Cats board never had a chance. Blight blended charisma with a classroom approach, outlining to them the way he thought the game needed to be played. Keep it uncomplicated, stick to a plan, allow for the occasional tweaking to sharpen things up. On the strength of that sales pitch, Malcolm Blight was the new coach of the Geelong Football Club.

*   *   *

Andrew Bews knew exactly who his new coach was, and had done for more than a decade. Just as I used to go out of my way to watch Blight play when I first came down to Melbourne, Bews and his mates made a point of catching the Blight show whenever the opportunity arose. 'Two or three years before I started senior footy [in 1982], Blighty was still playing,' said Bews, Geelong's first rover at the close of 1988. 'A car load of us used to jump in, we were all sixteen, seventeen, eighteen, plodding around the Geelong Under-19s or seconds, and we'd watch him playing at the Western Oval against the Bulldogs. We didn't go to watch the Kangas or the Bulldogs, we went to watch *him* play. We were probably a little bit in awe of him.'

Blight had not starred at Kardinia Park during his playing days, kicking just 8 goals in five trips down the highway, but his arrival as coach had the playing group buzzing. Gifted midfielder Mark Bairstow recalled the 'breath of fresh air' that energised the dressing rooms that summer. 'John [Devine] was a great player and a great Geelong man but there seemed to be different people going in different directions', Bairstow said. 'Even when I arrived in 87 there seemed to be a few factions within the team. It wasn't actually a team, more like all these bits and pieces. A country bloke like me coming to a League club probably would have thought they would all be bound together and pushing in the right direction.

But it seemed like there were different people doing different things within the club.

'From the start Malcolm was trying to be different. Even at training, if you arrived early, you knew straightaway there was something going on. That's how he liked to be, to keep you guessing.'

A similar mix of excitement and uncertainty hung over a conversation between Ken Hinkley, who had graduated from the Cats' Under-19s, and new arrival Andrew Rogers, who had played for Blight at Woodville before spending season 1988 with Essendon. 'What's going to happen here?' Hinkley recalls asking Rogers as pre-season training commenced.

Rogers laughed. 'I've known Blighty for a lot of years; I've given up trying to figure him out. You have an idea of what will happen and it will almost be the opposite.'

Rogers should have known what was coming, though. Blight's pre-seasons at Woodville were torturous. Now at VFL level, what followed was confronting to all. 'Every club I went to had been in a position of not winning,' Blight reflected. 'The first thing I learned was to eliminate a negative factor you've got complete control over. Is the bloke a really good kick or a great reader of the game? You haven't got control over that but you can work on it. Are they great decision-makers? You can teach them, but there's still not that immediate control. But get miles in their legs and discipline in their running? I could do that.

'Get fit, and you get less breakdowns when you get to the ball skills and the games themselves. We were part-time, after hours, not the full-time nature of today when you basically train twelve

THE COACH, PART II

months of the year. So these guys would go away for six to eight weeks and not look after themselves and drink too much … What I wanted was control of their heart and their lungs and their mental toughness. Find out who could stand the pressure.'

The playing group embraced the new regime. Bews believes a handful of players would have sought a clearance had no coaching change been made—like Bairstow, he had enjoyed Devine's company but felt the club had not progressed. Under Blight, the players at last seemed prepared to commit to the common cause.

'Malcolm had a belief that the fitter you could be the better you would be,' Bews explained. 'Everybody understood that and was trying to achieve that. It was probably the first really solid pre-season, blokes were nearly sick doing it. And not for the reasons of having a night out before, like in the old days. This was a whole new level of commitment, getting people prepared to play his brand of footy.'

The coach understood the potential sting of a savage pre-season; Blight's cross to Arden Street had been a similar slap in the face. 'Going from Adelaide to Melbourne was a rude awakening. I might have cruised around in Adelaide a bit, but it was hard to cruise when you're spewing every three steps under Barassi.'

The shadow of his former North Melbourne coach seemed to accompany Blight to Kardinia Park. Centreman Paul Couch recalled Blight would frequently mention Barassi during conversation, a point of reference from which his entire football experience was understandably drawn. 'One time I said, "How come you are so hard on us?"' said Couch. 'And Blighty said, "I'm not too bad compared to Barassi." Barassi must have been awful in what he

127

used to say to some of the players to get a spark out of them, to see if he could get a lift out of them.'

Just as Barassi had sought results through discipline, Blight channelled similar virtues, but an under-rated aspect of the Barassi—and therefore Blight—philosophy was an eye for detail. Such as ensuring the players knew how to tie their boots properly. 'He actually said one day, "Righto, guys, how do you tie up your boots?"' recalled Billy Brownless, a Blight favourite throughout his stint at Kardinia Park. 'Someone said, "Just normal, you tie the knot on top." And Blighty said, "No, wrong. What happens if we are a point down in a grand final and the siren has gone and you're having a shot at goal? You drop the ball on your boot and it hits that knot. It just skews a little bit and goes through for a point and you lose the game. That can happen." So from then on I reckon we all tied our boots up on the side instead of on top.'

The coach also insisted his players trained in correct attire: footy socks and shorts, and no running tops: 'Train in what you play in'. And he introduced rubber garters to keep players' socks up. 'Initially I think they just chopped up some rubber gloves to use', Brownless said. 'We wore garters a lot if it was pre-season training, especially if it was wet because he believed you looked tired and slow with your socks down. From then on we would always have our socks up.'

The coach began to introduce his rules, packaged in a handbook that each player received in the pre-season. The book featured 'negotiables' and 'non-negotiables', and a series of instructions detailing Blight's philosophy on the game. These rules would come to control their football lives. 'A big one in the handbook was *The*

Aim of the Game', Paul Couch recalled. 'And the aim of the game was to kick goals quickly. It wasn't about defending, it was about kicking goals.'

Of all the aspects of the Blight file, I found this among the most interesting. My football experience and learning rotated largely around Kevin Sheedy, who spent as much time stopping other teams as getting us to score ourselves. Most coaches' balance would be similar, and that mix has skewed largely to the defensive end of the spectrum in recent years.

But attack would be the defining approach of the Blight years at Geelong. Bairstow believes the coach gave his men 'free rein'. 'He wanted them to execute their skills and have a go. If it didn't come off, well it wasn't the end of the world. A lot of coaches, when you made a mistake it was as if the heavens bloody fell in. But Malcolm was a bit more free-willed and let you go a bit.'

It's a common attitude among his players, though it doesn't sit entirely comfortably with the handbook. For all of that freedom, transgressing the rules of the handbook was forbidden.

No u-turns.

When in doubt, kick long, hard and high.

If you can kick a torpedo you are allowed to keep doing it until it fails. Then not again.

'He was a bit crazy with his rules, but from our point of view they were creating a bit of discipline,' Bews said. 'Having them in written form meant we could go over and over them. We knew a lot by heart by the end of that first pre-season, to the point where he would call us in and say, "Right. Rule 1?" And we would go through every rule that he had.'

Your good luck is my bad luck, then man up.

Couch laughed at that one. 'You only got three goes at it. If you were playing off an opponent and he got a lucky break, and got the footy, that was his good luck. If you weren't in place for the second contest and he got it, that was your bad luck. And if you got beaten the third time, you just man up.'

The number 'three' related to another similar rule. 'Make a mistake once, you're being silly,' Blight recounted. 'Make it twice, you're a fool. But if you ever do it again, look out. One, two, three, that's enough.'

The new coach was keen to understand the culture of the club, and quickly became aware of a misconception about the way the Geelong players related to their city. It was assumed that the Cats were seen as giants in a tiny country fishbowl, turning heads in the city wherever they went. Blight discovered the opposite was closer to the truth. 'When you got to know the boys, you realised the perception of them constantly getting a pat on the back when they were walking down the street was wrong,' he said. 'When they were losing they were getting slagged more than pats. The losses hurt more than the pats on the back felt good. So they actually hid a bit—it wasn't quite what I expected it to be.'

As Blight soon learned, the same applied to Gary Ablett.

If ever a coach was equipped to understand or manage Gary Ablett, it was Malcolm Blight. Blight had been one of the most enigmatic yet talented VFL players of the 1970s; Ablett took those characteristics in the 1980s and amplified them, maybe ten-fold. It did not help that he played in a small-market town. In Geelong, famously, Ablett was referred to as 'God'. The record Ablett had compiled since his 1984 signing with the Cats fairly sparkled, though it only told one side of the tale. He averaged more than 60 goals per season in those five years; even more impressive was the nature of his football. 'He was the most explosive player I've seen,' Blight recalled. 'A lot of times it was goals but a lot of times it was splitting the game open with sheer power, splitting a pack.'

I agree with Malcolm: Ablett's football was a force of nature. By definition, this made him unpredictable, such that he was an ongoing source of maintenance for club and coach. 'He took a lot more looking after than the normal player,' Ken Gannon conceded.

In 1988, for instance, Ablett pulled out of a Saturday game on the Friday afternoon, citing injury. The following day, he turned up at the ground and began to get changed, preparing to play as if nothing had happened twenty-four hours earlier. Rather than at least being challenged, he ran out that day with the Cats and played four quarters. 'Me no like,' Blight concluded sharply when recalling the story.

Like Blight, Ablett looked at training as a chore. Unlike Blight, he sometimes chose to simply not turn up. There was no clause relating to this in the new coach's handbook, but Blight instinctively knew what to do about it. A January 1989 conversation between match committee member Greg Wells and Ablett triggered a memorable meeting between coach and player. 'Gary pulled out of training one Sunday, he said he was not going to be there,' Wells said. '"Going to church, is that all right, Wellsy?" So he's not there, and Malcolm decided it was time for a talk.'

Blight asked Wells and a handful of others if there was somewhere quiet he could take Ablett. They recommended the Balyang

Sanctuary, about 2 kilometres to the west of Kardinia Park. 'Gary wasn't doing his fair share of training, and that was not on,' Blight said. 'The star system didn't work, he just missed too many so I figured I had to tell him he had to be more serious than this.'

They met in the car park and went for a walk along the edge of the duck pond. Blight kicked off the conversation; Ablett listened. 'I reckon you can play, and I can help you have a great career,' the coach said. 'But if you don't train, you don't play. In fact, you can finish up right now. That's how serious I am. Either go home and get your gear, and come to training, or I'll get Ken Gannon to come and see you and pay you out. You can go and do whatever you want to do. Pretty clear, isn't it?'

Blight continued to outline his expectations. As he spoke, the pair came to a modest bridge that spanned the pond. Blight strolled to the middle of it and turned around, facing Ablett. 'I'm going this way; you can come across the bridge with me. Otherwise ...'

There was a pause.

'Gary, take your time, but I'm serious. Very serious. We're going to be a good footy club whether you're here or not.'

Ablett pondered his options before responding. 'Okay Malcolm, I'll go get my gear.'

As training finished that night, Ablett was walking up the race with his teammates. Blight stopped him. 'Gaz, the 200s and 400s, you missed out on them last week,' he said. 'Off you go, do them now.'

Cats runner Dean Schulz took Gary back onto the ground to complete the catch-up work. 'That changed the whole psyche of the group inside [the rooms],' Blight said. 'I was doing it for him, but it became obvious for the discipline of the group that it was useful. Blokes with talent that waste it—and we've all seen them—I felt it was a criminal football injustice. With Gary I even said, "Do you want to go to another club? Aren't you happy here? Don't waste what you've bloody got".'

Ken Hinkley has followed Blight into coaching. He has tried to take that message with him, figuring it as liberating to not tie your hopes to certain players. 'Footballers acknowledge the "supers" a bit,' Hinkley said. 'He was a little bit different, that was fine. Gaz was one of them, he's a different sort of a person, but on game day he performed better and harder than anyone else. But Malcolm wasn't frightened to lose a great player, because in his mind it gave him another thing he could do with someone else. That's a great belief to have.'

Blight tried to be even-handed, drawing together a group of senior Cats and discussing the Ablett issue. Sunday was the primary concern, as Ablett's increasing involvement with religion saw him more interested in church than training. The players agreed that Ablett would receive an occasional 'leave pass' in return for extra work during the week. By Round 1, most club parties seemed comfortable with Blight's treatment of the superstar. Even the player himself.

'If you ask around, a lot of them don't like Gazza because of how he got away with a lot of things,' Couch said. 'But, shit, I was happy that he was in my side. You know, a player like that, they only come along once every hundred years.'

* * *

In 1989 Geelong embarked on one of the more celebrated home and away seasons in the modern game. They had hardly been terrible under previous coach John Devine, although ten wins in 1988 was three shy of a finals berth. From the outset of 1989, however, it was clear that they would now be playing attractive football under their new mentor.

In Round 1, they kicked 17.21 to lose to North Melbourne by 2 points. The following week, at Kardinia Park, they broke their coach's duck by dismantling the visiting West Coast Eagles: the 95-point home win seemed to follow the Blight formula—the Cats had conceded 11 goals, but kicked 26 of their own. 'Malcolm liked to let people's natural flair come out,' Bairstow said. 'He was always about taking the opposition on, which is a great way to play from a player's perspective.'

The Cats won three of their first five games, in Round 4 dropping a disappointing game to Fitzroy by a point at Princes Park. They returned to the same venue to meet the defending premiers, Hawthorn, in Round 6. Allan Jeans' men had figured in every grand final since 1983, and they had formed one of history's most transcendent teams. Which is why the first sixty minutes of the game shook the footy world. At half-time, Geelong led 17.6 to 9.5, having led by as much as 56 points in time-on of the second term.

I had to read that score twice to make sure it was right.

Blight had not tricked anything up, preferring instead to back his men against the talented Hawks. 'We'd been up–down, up–down, so I thought we'd try something different', Blight said. 'Now we're going to play man-on-man. If your man comes off, you come off. It was the first time I'd done it. Let's have a look and

THE COACH, PART II

see what happens against the premiers. We decided that Ablett didn't have the motor but he was quick, so we played him wing–forward pocket. He basically kicked five or six from the wing in the first half.'

Hawthorn defender Gary Ayres recalled the disbelief in the dressing rooms at the long break. 'It had been a Blitzkrieg, all-out attack,' he said. 'When you are in a side like Hawthorn it was a strange feeling because it very rarely happened that a side could dominate us. But it certainly showed that Geelong was going to be a much, much improved side … and that game ended up being a complete shootout.'

The Hawks, of course, figured out what Blight was doing. Just before half-time, Ablett's direct opponent, Robert DiPierdomenico, was sent to a forward pocket. Blight sent Ablett with him, effectively taking his man out of the game. Hawthorn then mounted a counter-assault after the break, but Blight stood firm, resolutely refusing to change tactics. 'That was one Blighty lost, I reckon,' Wells said. 'The strategy was, "You are playing on a bloke, you beat that bloke. Where he goes, you go." They woke up to that. But the amount of ball that was getting down there was incredible. That convinced me. I thought, "Shit. We've got something going here. If we can be that far ahead of that lot at some stage, we've got something".'

The Cats made unwanted history that day—Hawthorn produced the second-greatest comeback from a half-time deficit, winning by 8 points despite 9 goals from Cats forward Gavin Exell. 'Being eight goals up at half-time,' Blight reasoned, 'my thinking was that we only need to kick four more and we'll win it. I just

135

didn't know they were going to kick fourteen. But it was pretty scary how good we could be, actually.'

If the result depressed anyone in Geelong, the events of the following Saturday washed it away. Led by 8 more majors from Exell, the Cats kicked 35 goals to hand St Kilda a 20-goal thrashing. In Round 8, they kicked 26 more, then added 32 against Richmond and 23 against Collingwood to complete a stunning stretch of football. Geelong averaged 28.18 across those five games, going 4–1 to rise to fourth on the ladder. Throughout this period, Blight was as predictable as anyone with his mannerisms could be. He still liked to catch people off guard, but when his teams were winning—at any stage of his career—he liked to say, 'The players never heard from me'.

Greg Wells agreed. When interviewed for this book, he suggested it should be called *Don't Go down the Same Path Twice*. 'Malcolm's undying belief was that if you had lost, you would never follow that same pattern again', he said. 'You have to change something or otherwise you'd get what you're given. If you were winning, though, sit tight—he'd be quiet and content.'

That was true, but only to a point. For even in good times Blight harboured a capacity to verbally confront his team to such degree that, two decades later, players recall those moments more strongly than most others. 'He would berate players, which they tell me is what Barassi did to him,' Brownless said. 'He would personally berate players in front of the whole group, in front of your teammates. Oh, it was unbelievable.'

If there is a single aspect of his time in football that Malcolm Blight regrets, it is this character trait. Yes, he at times used his temper as a premeditated weapon. But there were occasions when he admits to having lost control, usually immediately after two hours of battle. 'After games I found it difficult because of what I might say,' he said. 'I had to hold back. If I was honest with myself I never knew if I was doing the right thing or the wrong thing, and I'm not sure I always got that right. Sometimes you should shut up. It's why we always had a chat in the box before we headed for the rooms. If I just rushed out, I could be uncontrollable.'

Every player interviewed has his own experience of a famous 'Blighty spray'. They typically related to the breaking of a team rule or discipline, inducing frustration in the coach that required an immediate response. If Blight was predisposed to having a short fuse—and I think he was—it was certainly not bred out of him during his seasons under Ron Barassi.

From the comfort and distance of time most speak of those verbal assaults with affection, though Bews believes 'he really did some damage to individuals and he probably cut a few of their careers short'.

'God, he could get livid sometimes,' he said. 'You were always wondering if he was going to go and physically attack somebody. The vein would pop out the side of his head and … he would really get very wound up and people would get very concerned.'

'It would not wash with players today,' said Mark Neeld, an assistant coach at Collingwood who played three seasons under Blight at Geelong. 'Blighty's sprays were sometimes very personal and critical. It doesn't happen like that today but society has changed, too. Footy's a part of life and it often reflects current community standards.'

For his part, Couch does not hesitate when recalling his 'favourite' Blight barrage: half-time of the 1991 elimination final, with Geelong trailing St Kilda by 19 points. 'We were getting beaten so it looked like we were going to get knocked out straight-away,' he said. 'All the on-ballers were shithouse. Toby [Bairstow], Bewsy, Garry Hocking, all of us. The concrete was pretty thick at VFL Park but we could hear him coming down the stairs, roaring and yelling and going off his nut, screaming, "Those fucking on-ballers, I'm fucking sick of them".

'He slammed the door. "Right, Couch, Bairstow, Buddha [Hocking], Bewsy"—I think Gazza got hauled in too—"you're fucking rank. I'm sick of you bastards not getting a kick." He was off his head, red in the face. "Right you bastards, if you don't all get a kick in this second half I'm taking you off. You've got five minutes. I don't care if I take the fucking whole lot of you off, we're playing with fifteen at the moment anyway. Remember, we have to win the ball because our back line is fucking useless!'

Blight's defenders sat nearby, and suddenly, indirectly, found themselves included in Blight's spray courtesy of his unflattering description of their ability. 'He couldn't care less if they could hear him. I mean, you could hear him from outside VFL Park, he went berserk,' Couch laughed. '"Anyway, who's that fat bastard, the full-forward for St Kilda? What's his name?" Blighty was so mad he had forgotten Tony Lockett's name.'

The tirade continued. For the record, Lockett kicked nine—hence Blight's dismay—but the Cats won by 7 points.

'There's no doubt that when you're screaming you can lose control,' Blight said. 'Some things you shouldn't say. But in the

A star is born—Malcolm Blight shows off his 1972 Magarey Medal, awarded for being the standout player in that SANFL season. (Newspix.)

Finally ... in their 50th year of League football, the Kangaroos savour success. From left, Arnold Briedis, Peter Chisnall, Sam Kekovich, David Dench, Frank Gumbleton, Doug Wade, Malcolm Blight, Mick Nolan, John Rantall, Wayne Schimmelbusch and Garry Farrant run a lap with the 1975 premiership cup. (Newspix.)

Malcolm Blight takes in the final quarter of the drawn 1977 grand final from the sidelines, having been exiled to the bench by coach Ron Barassi. (Rennie Ellis.)

In his last game as North Melbourne coach, Barassi addresses his men during their 1980 elimination final loss to Collingwood. (Rennie Ellis.)

Above: Having been floored by Geelong's Mark Yeates, ailing Hawthorn star Dermott Brereton heads to the forward line to recover in the opening—and defining—minutes of the 1989 grand final. (Getty Images.)

Right: Gary Ablett Snr and Malcolm Blight during a break in a 1990 contest. Blight was often accused of providing special treatment for his star, but Ablett rewarded his coach's approach by being the dominant player of his generation. (Newspix/Brett Faulkner.)

Trailed by assistant coach Graham Gellie (left), a dejected Malcolm Blight leaves the MCG after tasting defeat in the 1992 grand final. (Newspix.)

THE COACH, PART II

end I don't reckon there's a player I wouldn't go up to now and say hello. In the heat of the moment you do stuff: guilty as charged. But once it was said and done, when you had to train again or play again, how else do you get better if you don't put it behind you? I don't hold grudges. Maybe that's a Barassi thing.

'I got better with that aggression as I got older. Sometimes it still got me, but stewing on things didn't help. I used to do it playing for Barass and I went into my shell. It was much better getting it out there and moving on, but when the fuse was gone it was hard to stop.'

Wells sometimes lightheartedly chided Blight, calling him 'Son of Ron', a Barassi reference that Blight does not shy away from. Even more than Barassi, however, the Geelong coach developed varying ways to win you back.

'We all copped sprays, that was the thing,' Billy Brownless said. 'Back then it was all part and parcel, you just took it on the chin. Honestly, you know, you would hate him; you would hate his guts. But he was great by Monday. We would have our chat and he used to love telling a few stories, then he would say things like, "Oh Bill, mate, you're a great player, that's why you're here. And we really need you for this week." He had this ability get you back on side straightaway. You would nearly want to hug him at those team meetings.'

In what would become a trademark characteristic, Blight had developed a rhythm to his coaching week. 'If you asked my kids what Dad did when they were young, they'd probably say, "Watch TV, drink port and smoke",' Blight chuckled, referring to his post-match analysis of each and every game, especially after a defeat.

139

'I could never give it away. Even if we went out after a game I'd come home and sit until two or three in the morning trying to figure out why we lost. It wasn't always with alcohol; that was just a friend at the time. It was all about, "What did I do wrong?" People don't see that side. I burnt myself out. Everyone thought I was relaxed and casual, but deep down you want to win.

'When I got to the club on Monday I had so many notes … sometimes I realised I was picking on something too much. By the time I revised them I had picked out the points that were really relevant. I'd write eight to ten pages of notes but the players might only see a half-page or a three-minute video. But I'd smash myself doing it, physically and mentally. Every game I could have done something better, but I think I nearly always found the answer to that game. Not to solving footy, but that game.'

Blight had stolen a line from legendary rugby league coach Jack Gibson: 'Winning Starts Monday'. He was passionate about bringing a renewed energy into the Geelong group during the match review. 'One of his key strengths was, irrespective of the result, when Monday started it was about preparing to win,' noted Neeld. 'A positive attitude began straightaway. He had an amazing ability to create positivity on a Monday regardless of what had happened on the weekend.'

The players and coach were growing to enjoy the review process. It helped when you were winning, as the Cats did frequently during the second half of 1989, and a trend was developing that would continue for much of Blight's tenure at Kardinia Park: berate, forgive, move on.

'I'd speak to Malcolm four days out of five during the week,' general manager Ken Gannon said. 'He'd blow up at match time, give someone a spray, you'd talk to him on the phone and he realised he'd gone off the deep end. He had this great honesty. "I'll just have to front up on Monday," he'd say. He'd apologise if he thought it was justified, or put it in context. But if it was serious he'd invite people from the board down so everyone knew where he stood. Malcolm had a great capacity to put things in context and bring everyone in behind him, and start off another week. I think the players grew to understand it.'

If nothing else, it gave the week a fulcrum around which to revolve. While Blight could be unpredictable, his men knew one thing: the Monday review would far more often be cast forward than back. Neeld has put that in place in his own coaching as an assistant at Collingwood. 'If you look back, make sure there is a reason for it, and it should be educating.'

'I loved Monday nights,' Blight enthused. 'I reckon it set the tone for the week. At some stage of the week you've got to start winning again. Every Monday night there was a theme. Play video, play games, it didn't matter, just something to get the group back together again, and start focusing forward.'

Ultimately, the strategy was about avoiding the fundamental reality that struck Blight about a football season. 'Footy becomes hard work. Drudgery. So I often went the other way,' he said. 'Sometimes when they got belted, really played poorly, I'd think, well, I yelled at them last week and it didn't work, let's go the other way. Bugger it, I'm sick of yelling. Let's start again.'

* * *

The Cats were flying by the midpoint of 1989. If Brownless and Exell were Blight's primary targets in attack, supplemented by the polish of Barry Stoneham, Robert Scott, Dwayne Russell and Bruce Lindner, the coach understood his absolute advantage was the quality of his midfield. Couch was en route to a Brownlow Medal–winning season. Both Lindner and Russell ranged up the ground, while Bairstow was a rugged, quality runner. Then he had emerging rover Garry Hocking, and the established Bews. Ruckmen Damian Bourke and Darren Flanigan rounded out a midfield that perfectly aligned with Blight's goal of 'first hands on the ball'. Finally, there was a versatile player named Ablett, who wandered from the wing to the goal square and back while managing to kick 87 goals that season.

Goals were coming from everywhere at a history-making rate. I did some numbers, which tell me that in the late 1980s and early 1990s we found ourselves at the apex of goalkicking peaks in the history of the League. In the decade after the introduction of the twenty-two-game home and away season in 1970, the benchmark aggregate for highly attacking teams was about 350 goals. Carlton broke through the 400-goal mark in 1979, with 402, and teams often breached that barrier—six clubs managed it before 1989, with Sydney's 419 goals in 1987 being the high-tide mark.

In 1989, Geelong kicked 425. By 1992, that figure had climbed to 453, comfortably the all-time high. (Through to the close of the 2010 season, only one other team, Essendon in 2000, had bettered 400 since that 1992 season. For the record, only three teams that surpassed that mark won the premiership in the same year: the 1985 and 2000 Bombers, plus the 1988 Hawks.)

THE COACH, PART II

Blight was not fussed about making history, just winning games of football. He rarely if ever tagged opposition players, choosing instead to back his men in an open field battle. 'Every time it went back to the middle, we had a plan to win the ball,' he said. 'Not stop the ball; win the ball. No matter who kicked the last goal, the only way you were going to go forward again was to win the ball in the middle. If that's the premise, I'm saying we're going to win it, it's going to go our way. Once the ball was in play, other things took place, maybe some negative things to stop certain blokes. But at the centre bounce we always tried to win the footy first.'

Geelong won ten of its final thirteen games of the 1989 home and away season. Impressive, but the Cats' 16–6 mark was good enough only for third place behind Essendon (17–5) and the League-leading Hawks, who produced a 19–3 record and a thumping percentage of 153.1. It created an opening finals match-up with the Bombers. As the Cats prepared that week, Blight realised that only three of his players—Neville Bruns, Mark Bos and Mark Yeates—had played finals football, and that experience dated back to 1980–81. He could sense the tension within the group, and decided to do something different on the bus trip to the MCG on match-day morning.

The coach instructed the bus driver to turn off the Geelong Highway before reaching the Westgate Bridge, just fifteen minutes from the ground. Stopping at a local oval he then grabbed a bag of footballs from under the bus and 'told the boys to go and have a kick'.

'The message was, "Remember when you were growing up as a kid? You would have loved this. We'll just have a kick around here, a bit of fun",' Wells said. The Blight message was that regardless of the scenario confronting his players, it's just a game. Play it to enjoy it. Which is the exact opposite of what happened for the next twenty minutes.'

'We got out there, we weren't even taped up and we started doing end to end drills and crisscross handballs on an uneven ground with sandshoes on,' Bairstow said. 'It was quite comical really.'

'And it was as bloody blowy as anything,' Couch added. 'We were nervous as kittens, fairly intimidated being in that first final. So we find ourselves out in the middle of some ground in Laverton, it was the hockey oval, and the ball was blowing everywhere and we were kicking it shithouse. I think our confidence was pretty well shot before we got to the G.'

Blight remembers standing there with a sinking feeling. 'I shouldn't have done it,' he said. 'I was standing there watching the ball flying around, thinking to myself, "You idiot".'

Brownless shared the sentiment. 'The problem was that the ground had a few holes in it and it was a bit dodgy, and, mate, it was really windy. We were kicking them fucking everywhere.'

Essendon never trailed, and we won by 76 points. My defining memory of that game is that Geelong was timid and completely overawed. The bus story made sense in contributing to their performance, but they really just didn't look mentally equipped for finals football.

As Blight headed for the bus, he collared Wells. 'We won't be doing that again,' he said. The coach threw his car keys at Wells and asked him to take his car, then he clambered onto the bus.

THE COACH, PART II

It would prove to be an eventful ride. Blight demanded the bus driver again stop, this time near Werribee. There would be no kicking of the footballs. Instead, they grabbed several slabs of beer.

'So Malcolm sat up the back and had a few beers,' Wells said. 'I think Mick Schulze set the record from Pilkington's [the glass plant in North Geelong] to the club with four cans. Just like that, Blighty won them back. Very much like he could bake the buggery out of them and it could get personal, but by Monday they were all eating out of his hand again. Well, by the time they got to the ground everyone had relaxed again.'

Their strong season finish had earned a double chance; they already knew they would be facing Melbourne the following week, and Blight had two plans in mind. The first involved Couch and Bairstow, and had been formulated as the final minutes of the Essendon shellacking wound down. 'We had made the night grand final that year against Melbourne and [Demons coach] John Northey tagged Couch and Bairstow. We lost by a few kicks. Then during the year the same thing happened. So, during the last quarter of the Essendon game we decided, these two blokes will be looking for Couch and Bairstow at the bounce. Well, they're not going to be there. Cop that.'

That was Plan A: the two best midfielders in the club would start on the bench.

Blight told Couch of his idea during the bus trip back to Geelong. 'But we were not going to tell Mark until Thursday,' Couch added. 'Mark was a very proud bloke and Blighty didn't want to upset him early in the week.'

145

Plan B required the assistance of football manager Gary Fletcher, who was dispatched to Bellarine Peninsula club Portarlington (the local Demons) to grab some training jumpers.

'For some reason we'd lost our aggression. I reckon the occasion got to them against Essendon,' Blight said. 'That week was the hardest training of the year; it was very competitive. I wanted Melbourne jumpers just for effect and Gary came back with the scungiest-looking red and blue jumpers you've ever seen. One on one, the 'us against them' exercise probably only went for seven or eight minutes. I didn't want to kill anyone but it made them puff a bit and livened everyone up.'

On the Thursday night after training, Blight revealed his plan to Bairstow over a meal of fish and chips. Couch had already accepted his fate, even welcoming the chance for a pressure release. Bairstow expressed his displeasure, at which point his coach produced a newspaper clipping noting the goal Blight had missed after the siren—when he had been awarded with another kick—against Hawthorn back in 1977. 'I know how you feel right now; this [gesturing to the clipping] was the low point of my career,' Blight said across the table. If it was an odd peace offering, it was missed on Bairstow.

'Smoke was coming out of Toby's ears,' Blight said. 'I wouldn't have been happy if I was them. It was a tough call. I tried to explain it to them, that we were taking some heat off them and their two [opposition] blokes would run around wondering what to do next. It was that same thing as always: if it's not working, change it.

'Anyway, we were a goal up and those two hadn't even been on the ground. They were angry young men, and they reacted the way I hoped they would.'

THE COACH, PART II

Both Couch and Bairstow had 21 touches despite a long period on the bench. The Cats demolished Melbourne by 63 points, and found themselves in a preliminary final.

Two weeks earlier, Essendon had exploited a team full of vulnerable, inexperienced finals debutants who were not helped by their unconventional warm-up on a Laverton hockey field. The result belied the recent history between the teams—Geelong had beaten us four consecutive times before that game, including a 9-goal thrashing at the MCG in Round 11 and a 10-goal hiding the previous year at Windy Hill. Better settled, and with the confidence of a finals win behind them, they trounced us this time at Waverley in the preliminary final. Ablett kicked 8 goals from a half-forward flank in a 170-point turnaround from a fortnight earlier. Bairstow, Hocking and Couch controlled the ball in the midfield, and Brownless kicked four.

This time we were the ones who looked shell-shocked. Geelong by 94 points. The man in whom the board had placed its faith had taken the club to its first grand final in twenty-two years.

10

ONE BRUTAL AFTERNOON

It remains the most rehashed moment from one of the most evocative games of football in the history of the game. Just two, maybe three seconds into the 1989 grand final, Geelong defender Mark Yeates charged off his wing and ironed out Hawthorn forward Dermott Brereton. There was no elbow or fist. It was all hip and shoulder. And it was all pre-planned.

'We had played Hawthorn in Round 9 at Princes Park, the game they ran over us,' Cats assistant Greg Wells recalled. 'Brereton ran through Yeates at two boundary throw-ins. Jumped into him with his knees, into Yeatsy's ribs, just picked him off.'

Yeates had been carried off the ground on a stretcher, accompanied all the way by Brereton, who was letting him know what he thought of his mental toughness. 'Dermott was going around pinging off blokes, it was legitimate in those days,' Malcolm Blight said. 'Dermott said he just used to run in, but in the grand final I thought he'd come for Couchy.'

Paul Couch had earlier that week won the Brownlow Medal. Some see it as a curse for the medallist to have to play the grand final later that week, an impossible distraction. Blight, of course, had experienced it in 1978. 'When you win the Brownlow you think you have to be the best player and you're usually not,' Couch said. 'We were at a function that week and Blighty and I were driving home together. I said, "I really feel like I'm a good player but still feel like I don't deserve it." He said, "Don't worry about that. You won that because of the twenty games you played in 1989. What happens on Saturday is entirely different. I've been through it, too. All you can do is do your best." The way he coached that week it was obvious he had been there. He didn't try and do anything different.'

Which did not solve the potential problem of the Hawks' number 23.

Brereton would years later say he was not conscious of his targets: 'just a Geelong jumper' would attract his crosshairs. But the Cats were wary of their gun centreman being targeted in the opening seconds of a grand final, so they decided to fight fire with fire. And Yeates was more than happy to set the fuse.

Two weeks earlier, Dermott had cleaned up Paul Van Der Haar during Essendon's semi-final against the Hawks at Waverley. 'VanDer' was a sizeable target who could normally look after himself, but Brereton had flattened him during a contested play on the half-forward flank. We were dirty on him, too, but that was footy. And it highlighted the danger that lurked for the Cats' midfielders.

'Honestly, it's one of those things I wish I didn't do, but ink's hard to rub out,' Blight now conceded. 'Maybe on the Tuesday of that week, we were thinking about the teams and what we were going to do. Mark had the darks on Brereton for cleaning him up because he missed a state game, and he was really proud about playing state footy. So he didn't take any convincing. He was going to pay Dermott a visit.'

This would be no state secret: Blight revealed his plan to his players the night before. Couch recalls the first option was for Michael Schulze to try to block Brereton coming into the square, but if he got past Schulze … 'Blighty was going through the positions and he said, "Right, one more thing. Yeatsy. Schultzy. You've got to stop Dermott from running into the centre square. Yeatsy, you're going to come off the line and nail him for us because you owe him one. And we are going to stamp our authority on the game".'

Yeates took instruction well. During half-time of the reserves on grand final day, as the players milled on the ground to get a sniff of the atmosphere, Blight drew a cross on the ground with his foot, telling Yeates where he wanted him to launch the assault from: 'If we are going this way, here's the mark,' he said.

It is a part of the game's lore that when the ball was bounced, Andrew Bews gathered the first clean possession and kicked long to the Geelong goal square, where Gary Ablett stormed out of the goal square and marked. He kicked truly. A dream Geelong start.

No eyes remained in the centre square, except those of the coach. Watching the replay, Yeates looks out of sync with every other player. They are all heading towards the ball, but Yeates has ignored his man and is cutting diagonally across the top of the screen until he disappears to the left. His intent was clear, and he collected Brereton with force. The Hawk enforcer spied the incoming missile at the last moment but had no time to protect himself. By the time all eyes had returned to the middle, Brereton was writhing on the ground.

Wells had been busy both watching the ball and moving magnets on the game board. He turned to Blight as the ball was being returned to the centre.

'How did it go?'

Blight took a long drag on his cigarette, then paused. 'Perfect,' he replied.

'I had said to Mark, "It's only an insurance policy",' Blight explained, asking Yeates to complete his task if it seemed Brereton was heading Couch's way. '"If you raise an elbow or a fist or anything, other than just meeting him with your body, I'll rip you straight off and you won't play another minute." To Mark's credit, he just used his hip and shoulder. It was a pretty sickening blow.'

Brereton was seriously hurt. He was told to come off the ground by trainer John Kilpatrick and physio Barry Gavin. From their position in the Geelong box, the Cats' coaching staff could hear Hawthorn coach Allan Jeans roaring, 'Get him off. Get him off!' Team doctor Terry Gay then arrived at the stricken footballer and insisted he head to the bench.

But Brereton could take as he received, and was about to write his name in legend. 'I only saw him with a metre to go [before contact],' he later said of Yeates. 'He made good contact all right, broke a couple of ribs and scans showed a half a centimetre tear in my kidneys. But you're identified, whether it's your best or worst moment, for what happens on grand final day ... [I thought] "It cannot end here. This has got to be the most important two hours of my life." I wouldn't mentally let it end there.'

Brereton stayed on the ground, vomiting and gripped by nausea as he headed deep into the forward line to recover as best he could. Shortly afterwards, he marked over Steve Hocking and kicked a goal. Teammate Robert DiPierdomenico calls that act 'the most thrilling thing I've ever seen'. The Hawks were away.

'I was a bit surprised when he got up, then keeled over again, then crunched over again,' Blight said. 'I just thought Yeates ran into him and that was that. But for whatever reason we never touched the footy after that. The most amazing thing about the game is that we were always five or six goals down, and they set that up with the next twelve to fifteen minutes of play with their kicking—it was unbelievable. They just kept the footy. We gave away some silly frees and things like that, but we just couldn't get the footy. Their kicking was perfect.'

By quarter-time, Hawthorn led 8.4 to 2.0. After Brereton headed to the forward line rather than the bench, the Hawks had twelve scoring shots to one, effectively setting up their match-winning advantage. Utility Gary Ayres remembers that his team was prepared for a physical contest. 'We had heard that there could be an opportunity early, that it could be very, very physical, and Allan Jeans had actually heard this as well,' Ayres said. 'His instructions were, "Whatever happens, just play the ball. Let the football do the talking. Don't concentrate on the man".'

They proved to be match-winning instructions as the game developed into a gripping mix of violent incidents and breathtaking scoring. 'It was more spiteful than violent', Ayres said. 'For Dermott to get up and go to the pocket and take a mark over Hocking, then to go back and kick a goal, it was a surge of adrenalin and excitement that very few people would ever get to experience. We knew that it was "on". In a way it probably shook us up a little bit, too, because we had never really been physically challenged like that for a long time, because we were so dominant.'

DiPierdomenico had his ribs broken and suffered a punctured lung when Ablett cannoned into him from behind late in the first quarter. He played the game out in extreme pain, but ensured every contest was a physical challenge. 'Dipper was the one to get them going,' Wells said. 'The one who would never, ever, flinch, no matter what.' Rover John Platten was heavily concussed after a first-quarter clash with Garry Hocking, while Michael Tuck, Scott Maginness and Darrin Pritchard were also hurt but played on.

Ayres does not judge Yeates, or Hocking, or any of the Cats that day. In fact, he conceded that twelve months earlier the Hawks had taken similar contingency plans into their grand final against Melbourne. '[Then-coach] Alan Joyce had actually identified three players because Melbourne had been playing reasonably aggressive footy,' he said. 'If there was anything to happen in the back line it was my role to basically become the protector. If it was going to be in the middle it was Dipper. And if it was going to be in the forward line the man who was to serve as protector was Dermott.

It was probably the first time I can ever think a coach had given us a licence that if anything was to happen you were to finish it. From that point on, in relation to grand finals, that made me more aware of ... you do what you have to, to win this game.'

Couch simply called the 1989 grand final 'vicious'. 'The most brutal game I have ever been involved in. It was like carnage out there. I think there were thirteen or fourteen injuries in the game. We had about six or seven and so did they.'

The Cats persisted, but still trailed by 37 points at half-time, and had shaved just a point off that margin by the final change. As commentator Bruce McAvaney pointed out, 'Even when Hawthorn was six goals in front it always felt like the scores were level. That was the quality of football. Retrospect is a beautiful thing, but even at the time it felt like something special'.

Contributing to that mood was Ablett, who was en route to kicking a grand final record 9 goals. So enthralling was the nature of the game—the wrestling, the drama and the pure sense of conflict—that Ablett's masterpiece seemed to grow organically, as if on a different plane from the match itself. It remains one of the game's finest cameos, and it inspired Geelong to claw within a single kick when they ran out of time.

The defining image of the result is a News Limited picture of Ablett and his opponent, Chris Langford. Ablett has his head in his hands, the very essence of anguish. Langford has his head bowed but arms clenched in salute, as much a picture of relief and exhaustion as jubilation. It perfectly sums up the teams and the day, an inspired Ablett cameo unable to run down the brilliant but ailing Hawks.

Hawk rover Platten was heavily concussed during the game and today remembers nothing of the game and its aftermath. The Cats can only wish for such luxury: most have spent years trying to clear the mental pain of coming so close. 'That was one we should have won,' president Ron Hovey said, echoing the broader feeling of his football club.

Hawthorn were premiers, again.

'If you ask Malcolm why we lost, he'll tell you we just ran out of time,' Wells said. 'In the coaches' box we thought we were going to get them. Five minutes into the last quarter [assistant coach] Dennis Davey said, "I reckon we're going to get these pricks." But we were rooted. The last bit of play was going down the Southern Stand wing and Couchy was in front and his feet went from under him. Which means he was rooted, because he didn't fall over, he wasn't gutless and he was terrific on his feet. And that is when I thought, "Oooh, trouble".'

Had the Cats salvaged a draw, both teams would have been forced to make multiple changes the following week. Geelong would probably be missing at least its skipper, Bourke, while Couch tore a thigh muscle and both Hockings would have been doubtful. However, the Cats would have had one distinct advantage—its reserves featured on grand final day, giving the club a match-fit edge in depth had a replay been required. For the record, both Cats sides fell that day, by 6 (the seniors) and 2 (the reserves) points.

The post-match mood in the rooms, which more resembled a triage cubicle, was sombre. One man grappling with the outcome was Mark Bairstow, who had 15 touches and kicked a goal but felt Blight had contributed to his side's downfall. Bairstow started on a wing; Couch was spending time at half-forward. 'This is the thing that I didn't understand in that game,' Bairstow said. 'We had played with basically attacking flair all year and then in the grand final [Blight] made a lot of moves, a lot of changes in the biggest game of the year. To me that was a bit strange. In my opinion I thought we made mistakes, worrying about knocking bloody Brereton over, worrying about players playing in different areas. Let them worry about us and let us go. We might have been down but we certainly wouldn't have been 43 points down. It's bloody hard to come back from that far down, almost impossible.

'It was very unlike the rest of the year. That year we had really played the ball. Run the ball. Basically took the opposition on at all times. Even when we were behind we used to take them on and we would score goals quickly ... that was probably our greatest asset. And then to turn around in the grand final and to basically try and be the aggressor not so much at the ball but at the man? I thought that cost us early and it cost us badly.'

Blight, Bairstow, Couch and the remainder of the Cats could not, of course, wind those two hours back. Yet they had all played their roles, albeit losing ones, in a modern football classic.

'Blighty and Allan Jeans were two different men,' McAvaney said, 'but the two of them came together and produced a masterpiece.'

11

'ME, BIG CHIEF MALCOLM'

JUST WHEN YOU think you have the game in your grasp, football hands you a lesson. Malcolm Blight received a long-lasting one in the off-season that followed that epic 1989 grand final. The Cats were nursing a sore and sorry list after that grand final loss to Hawthorn, one that required a carefully considered rehabilitation. It was the first of a long list of priorities that derailed that summer.

Paul Couch, for instance, seriously injured his knee during the grand final. 'I didn't realise I had done anything until I had been on the piss for two days and my bloody knee had blown up,' he said. 'That's how high we were, I couldn't walk but I didn't care.'

It typified an off-season that was contradictory to Blight's policy of running his men hard before Christmas. He insists the Cats did not fall for a 'near enough was good enough' trap; rather, they did not devote themselves to be adequately prepared for season 1990, the year in which, notably, the *Victorian* Football League became the *Australian* Football League. 'We started too late. We didn't celebrate, but there was a trip away, some blokes should have had operations, our preparation was all wrong,' Blight said. 'Even during that year things were strange. I collapsed at the Perth airport in 1990. I had a virus, so for four or five weeks I was really crook. By the time the season ended it felt like we all needed a break.'

Adding to an out-of-kilter preparation was a handful of significant absences that depleted the ranks of experience and team balance. After 195 games and two best and fairest awards, Mark Bos stunned the club by announcing his retirement. The captain of the previous three seasons, ruckman Damian Bourke, missed the entire season with a knee injury. And, in a move that took the football world by surprise, Mark Bairstow decided to return to the family farm at Lake Grace, Western Australia.

'He tried to talk me out of it, but I really had to get back there. I was happy to play and coach locally,' said Bairstow, who was just twenty-six when he returned to the west. 'Blighty kept in constant contact throughout the year, because he always used to say a lot of players seemed to play better when I was there. I had a pretty good rapport with Couchy and seemed to be able to get him going a bit.'

Blight, president Ron Hovey and Ken Gannon all stayed close to Bairstow, who would return the following season. His departure was another dent in an off-season that had Blight concerned, and the season opener provided the coach with the supporting evidence that his men were not ready. A replay against Hawthorn offered the chance of grand final revenge, however diluted the stage. Instead, the Hawks bludgeoned Geelong by 115 points, kicking 11.6 to 4 behinds in the final term. Jason Dunstall kicked 12 goals, further highlighting the Cats' perceived weakness in key defensive positions. In some respects, they never recovered. Only two players, Billy Brownless and Steve Hocking, managed twenty-two games that season. Gary Ablett missed a month with injury, and was battling personal issues—he and his wife, Sue, had separated in January. Andrew Bews, Bruce Lindner, Mark Yeates, Mick Schulze, Dwayne Russell and David Cameron—all grand final players from the previous year—did not manage to chalk up ten games as injury ate into the roster.

The Cats fell to Melbourne by 6 goals in Round 2, and alarm bells were ringing. But a kind schedule saw them play three straight games against teams that had not played finals the previous year, then Essendon, which they narrowly defeated, so by weight of talent alone Blight's team was 4–2 when Richmond visited Kardinia Park in Round 7. This would routinely be chalked down as a win in this era—the Tigers had lost ten of their last eleven against the Cats, and had not won in Geelong in eight seasons. Blight thought it was as good a time as any to try something different; he sensed the season was precariously balanced, and a lack of unity lay at the heart of his concerns. Some might have attempted an Allen Aylett–style rev-up in front of the players. Not Blight; instead, the Indian Chief legend was born.

When the players entered the rooms prior to the Tigers game, a whiteboard carried a message: 'No one get changed. No one get strapped.' Blight came in about two hours before the game and told every player to 'grab a towel and follow me'. He led his players out of the change rooms and through the bemused crowd to the car park, where they boarded a bus.

'The supporters are all asking, "Where are you going?" and we had no idea', Billy Brownless said. 'We were just following Blighty.'

Inside ten minutes, the players found themselves at the house of Peter Burnett, a long-time club supporter and popular Geelong hotelier. They were led to the rear of the house, where a swimming pool sat waiting. 'We were thinking he was going to make us swim up and down the pool just to get us up and going before the big game,' Paul Couch said. 'It was a freezing cold day in Geelong, so he decides against that and we go into this big room just beside the pool.'

The players were asked to wrap their heads with their towels, like Native Americans. 'He had this stick with him; we had to pretend to smoke a peace pipe', Couch continued. '"Me Big Chief Malcolm," he said. I'm thinking, "What the friggin' hell is going on here?"'

Blight laughs about the story now, but says the gathering was designed to bring a struggling team closer together. 'Everyone was sitting around on their rugs, and I was the Big Chief. And I just went around the players ... when the braves go out there, if we all do it together we'll be okay. If you go out there on your own, the cowboys will get you. If we stick together and care about each other, we might win the battle. Now, before you speak, just pretend to smoke the peace pipe.

'I told them they were half expecting to lose today, "Just as you came here and were half expecting to jump into the water. You reckon I'm going to make you freeze your balls off an hour before you have to play a game of footy? Just go out there and play, do what you should be doing, and don't worry about anything else".'

Couch provides the punchline: 'We got flogged'. In truth, Richmond won by 14 points thanks to errant Geelong kicking, but it was a humiliating end to an unusual day. Adding to the pain, the captain, Andrew Bews, tore up his knee that afternoon and did not play again in 1990.

By Round 13, the Cats were 6–7 and facing Hawthorn at Waverley. Their sole wins since that Richmond defeat had been narrow, unconvincing escapes against Footscray and St Kilda, and the rematch with the reigning premier shaped as a critical waypoint in the season. Their percentage was poor, and another big defeat would make for an uphill grind to make the finals. The wind blew hard to the outer pocket that afternoon, giving Blight the idea to waste the first quarter by defending to the 'dead' side of the ground. He even instituted the tactic as a 'rule' to reinforce how serious he was, insisting the Cats send the ball to the outer wing on every occasion. 'At the twenty-one-minute mark, it was 1.4 to two points their way, in an absolute howler. We were flying because we were frustrating them. We were even kicking it backwards to get to that side of the ground—people just didn't do those things in those days,' Blight said.

Geelong defender Austin McCrabb then took possession deep in the back line and, contrary to Blight's instructions, kicked it to the grandstand side. Not far from where he kicked the ball, there was a Geelong player on the ground being attended to by several trainers ... plus two Hawthorn players, who gleefully accepted McCrabb's offering. 'Bang. Hawthorn goal,' Blight recalled.

Greg Wells, seated in the coach's box, detailed the coach's response: 'Malcolm has just gone absolutely off his cruet. "Fuck! I can't kill him quick enough. Get him, I want to kill him," he was screaming. Then he rang the runner, Dean Schultz. "You fucking tell him from me that is the dumbest thing I've ever seen." Deano came back and was sent straight back out. "Go and tell him …" He kept sending him and sending him.

'We said, "Hang on, Malcolm, you are losing sight of what's going on." And Blighty said, "Don't start on me. I'll tell you what's going to happen now, they'll kick four in a row." And they did.'

At quarter-time, the Hawks led 7.4 to 2 behinds.

'The footy gods got us, you only needed one leak and the Hawks were away,' Blight said. 'The wall of the dam opened up. Game over.'

Blight stormed down onto the ground at quarter-time and made a beeline for McCrabb. He excluded the defender from the players' huddle. 'Don't even think about coming in here! Don't! Stay out there. Don't even think about it,' he screamed.

So, during the quarter-time break, McCrabb stood near the umpires in the middle of the ground, a lonely figure as Blight continued to yell at him from a distance. 'You didn't want to physically manhandle a player so I told him to go and stand with the umpires because he wasn't one of us,' Blight explained, before easing out a sigh. 'Poor bugger.'

Before the break ended, Wells had walked away from the group, uncomfortable with the treatment Blight had meted out. McCrabb's was hardly a rookie mistake—this was his twenty-fifth game since joining the Cats in 1987—but Wells felt the punishment far exceeded the crime. 'I walked away up the stairs, yeah,' he admitted. 'Maybe I was a bit soft, though; Malcolm was 100 per cent right. Austin had broken the bloody rule so I'm sure the exclusion and the bake was for everyone else's benefit too. If we are going have rules there are consequences to breaking them.'

Bairstow was not present but he was disbelieving when Couch related the story to him. 'If Blighty was going to spray him then, yeah, fair enough, but spray him when the group's there. To leave him out in the middle of the MCG on his own, I thought that was a bit harsh.'

The Hawks won by 68 points. Geelong won two more games all year, sliding to tenth place by season's end.

If there were positives in the year, they were hard to find. One was Ken Hinkley, who had been unsettled since his cross from Fitzroy after season 1988; due to injury, he'd managed just two senior games in 1988–89 and was ready to head home to the Victorian country in 1990. Blight convinced him to give League football one more try. Used predominantly as a half-forward, he kicked 27 goals in his first twelve games but in effect had little impact on a team that was haemorrhaging. Then dropped to the reserves, he felt his career slipping away when Blight told reserves coach Dennis Davey to send Hinkley to the back line.

'The message came just before half-time, "Go to half-back",' Hinkley said. 'I was staring at the runner: "You've got the wrong bloke, I don't play down there. I've never been there in my life." But Blighty encouraged me to use my skills and ability to read the play and use the attacking side of me from the back line. In the last three games of 1990 I was into the firsts and named at half-back.

I got almost 90 possessions, which was a lot of touches back then, and came away from that season thinking I could play a bit.'

Within twelve months, Ken Hinkley would be named an All-Australian half-back. A year later, he not only earned a second All-Australian guersney, but came within three votes of winning a Brownlow Medal.

Hinkley would become a Blight favourite. For now, though, the coach was fuming about a wasted season. He was also tired and unwell, still struggling with his virus, as the season ground to a difficult close.

* * *

As season 1991 dawned, Malcolm Blight continued to juggle a handful of issues. He had been buoyed by the news that Mark Bairstow was returning from his self-imposed exile at Lake Grace. The pair would form a bond that would lead to Bairstow not only becoming captain the following year, but also becoming a regular sounding board during difficult times for his coach.

Some Cats felt 1990 to be an aberration. Blight was busy with his full-time job, but confident he could manage the increasing demands of career and coaching. He then sent a message to the squad early in pre-season training via a misguided teenager on the list. A local recruit from St Joseph's, Michael Mansfield had played five games in 1990, a rookie season of promise due to his talent and versatility. He also was a tennis fan, and in mid-January had secured tickets to the Australian Open.

'Malcolm, I've got a chance to go to the tennis Wednesday night,' Mansfield said to his coach.

'Michael, we're training. But if you want to go, that's fine. You can go to the tennis.'

Mansfield went to Flinders Park that evening. Blight did not play him until Round 6.

'We were training at Deakin University and Blighty went right off,' Bairstow said. 'I don't know how he went off with Mike, but when he went to training that night he made a big thing of how Michael had made the decision to go to the tennis rather than train.'

Having returned to robust health, Blight seemed to be back to his confident best. What happened shortly after the Mansfield issue, however, rocked a coach, a football club and a town. And probably even a competition. In late January, Gary Ablett sidled up to Blight after training at the Deakin University grounds. They crossed paths in a doorway when Ablett caught his coach's eye.

'Malcolm,' he said, 'I think I'm going to retire.'

Ablett was twenty-nine, but was arguably still in his prime. He had come third in the best and fairest in 1990 despite missing five games, and had kicked 75 goals.

'There was not one inkling of this,' Blight recalled. 'I said, "Gary? Is that right? Have you thought long and hard about this?" One of the things I was pretty certain of is that talking players into playing is not on my agenda, so I just said, "Gary, I'm sorry to hear that, I'll get Ken to come and have a chat to you".'

'Once he'd made his decision, and it was final, what do I do? Put a nappy on him? If you don't want to play, off you go. The club was very good, we kept in contact and of course he was still on the list. It was raised in the match committee every now and then although I was certainly not going to beg him to come back. But the door was kept open.'

Blight sold the news to the playing group. For some, it drew a curtain on a niggling issue. Indeed, Blight was conscious of—and denies—accusations that he favoured certain players, and sometimes pandered to Ablett. 'There were definitely a couple of players who hated the idea that Gary got some sort of special treatment,' Wells said. 'But I think that Malcolm just realised Gary had a different nature. You don't have to have one rule for everyone, but you've got to be able to manage all these people, and [Ablett] was a bit different. Malcolm wasn't dazzled by his footy ability—in fact Malcolm was critical of a lot of aspects of Gary's footy. He kicked nine in that grand final but Blighty reckons he also cost us five. Malcolm thought Gary, like a lot of forwards, was a different player when he was going for the ball rather than chasing a man.'

Bairstow defends Blight's handling of the unique package that was Ablett. He felt Ablett was deferred to prior to Blight's arrival; in contrast, Blight understood how to get the best out of him, and accepted the occasional compromise. 'Malcolm handled Gary a lot better than John Devine did,' Bairstow said. 'John tried to make him one of us, which he never, ever was. And I know this is bordering on making excuses for one and not others, but Gary was an exception. And Blighty told the group on a number of occasions, if Gaz keeps kicking five, six, seven, eight goals then he can make exceptions. He brought that up a number of times at team meetings.'

In 1993, Blight ordered the bus to be stopped a kilometre from the Sydney Cricket Ground. He asked the players to get off and walk to the ground as a unit. Ablett refused. He kicked 7.6 that afternoon in a 25-point win.

Then there was the 'Mental Mile', an activity Blight incorporated at the end of each training session. 'Rain, hail or shine, he would line you up on the boundary and you would do two hard laps,' Bairstow said. 'Blighty used to call them the Mental Mile, "because this will get you to the line", he would say. Gary would go at about two kilometres an hour. He wouldn't put any effort into it at all. Gary used to say he should be in the Golden Slipper, not the Melbourne Cup. And Blighty looked the other way.'

The topic of Blight's favouritism for certain players pervaded his coaching career. 'I've heard it: "Blighty's pretty good with the good players",' Blight said. 'Well, that can't happen in a footy club. Hell, I liked trying to make the good ones really, really good. It's not like you walked past a bloke and didn't talk to him, but circumstances mean you could only do so much. Did I spend as much time with player number 38 as number 1, 2, 3 or 4? The system didn't allow it.'

Billy Brownless was a cross between class clown and Blight disciple, and for both reasons his talent is sometimes overlooked. He believes his coach was drawn to character as much as performance. 'He obviously liked you playing well, but he also liked a bit of personality,' he said. 'Those with personality and those who were a bit outgoing, I think he liked that. Not too outgoing that you would take him on, but if you kept the place interesting you'd be in his good books. Obviously you had to be getting a kick, too.'

It's an interesting observation from Brownless, whom Blight had considered trading in the off-season. 'He said, "I'm thinking of getting rid of you",' Brownless said. 'I was going away for the weekend and I was up in Brisbane and had a chat with the Brisbane Bears, with [new coach] Robert Walls. It was on the footy trip so it was after the season, and then about a week later he [Blight] rang and said, "Let's have a coffee." That's when he told me, "Nah, we've decided to keep you." Maybe he was just giving me a rocket.'

Blight typically had his seniors and reserves training together as a group. 'But you have to spend more time with the twenty you're about to play in the ones, of course you do,' he said. 'Let's be honest, as soon as you pick the first team of the year, there'll be five who don't like you straightaway. That's just part of coaching.'

Blight put himself above the criticism. There were football games to be won, even if the star player wasn't around to help win them. Blight's attitude was definitive: if Ablett did not want to be a part of the team, so be it. Others, such as Brownless, had a keen short-term sense of loss: 'Well, it was shocking news, no one saw it coming,' he said. 'But Blighty never played it up, never mentioned it.'

Even without Ablett, the Cats started the 1991 season sharply, winning their first four matches before running into a hot West Coast team at Waverley (the Eagles won their first twelve games that season). Inexplicably, Geelong then lost four out of five, culminating with an embarrassing loss to Fitzroy at Princes Park—the Lions' first win of the season. It took until Round 12 for the Cats to make a stand, a 40-point win over Hawthorn at Princes Park. Bairstow was outstanding, contributing 36 possessions and 6 goals. Brownless kicked 4 goals, taking his season tally to 41 and providing the goalkicking the Cats had feared they would miss through Ablett's departure.

That game took place on Monday 11 June. On the same day, with as much warning as that of his retirement—as in, none at all—Ablett announced he was coming out of retirement. It was a stark turnaround. Ablett has since admitted that he was 'suffering from depression very badly' through this stretch, and, privately, Geelong officials did not expect to see him on the playing field again. But he returned in Round 13, kicking 2 goals in a 5-goal win over Melbourne that elevated the Cats to fourth. His return was an unexpected bonus. 'And Gary was really easy to get to peak physical fitness,' Wells said. 'If you're talking a six- or eight-week bracket for normal people in the pre-season, we could get Gary super fit in three weeks. He was just an amazing specimen.'

Geelong started to separate itself from the ruck of lower-placed finals contenders. It was not simply Ablett's return—he would return a modest 28 goals in twelve matches in 1991—but the stellar form of Bairstow, Garry Hocking, Hinkley and Brownless that was carrying Blight's team. In Round 21, they visited the WACA to play a West Coast team that had won sixteen of its eighteen matches (the 1991 season featured multiple byes). West Coast outlasted Blight's men by a point, but the Cats had proven they belonged in the contenders' conversation.

They closed the home and away season with three straight wins to construct a 16–6 record. Geelong was going back to September.

* * *

The first final provided the victory over St Kilda that had prompted Blight's half-time outburst, so memorably recounted by Couch. Blight remembers this game for two reasons: 'It was the Lockett–Brownless show, that was a great game', he said. 'But Gary was terrible. In the last quarter of an exciting game, Gary was on the bench, he couldn't get a kick. He was just way too underdone in a match fitness sense.'

Brownless kicked eight, Lockett booted nine; the Cats won by 7 points. But Ablett had just 6 disposals that afternoon, a rare finals misfire for a player who had made his reputation in September. 'Gary was actually quite an intelligent football brain,' Blight said. 'It often didn't expose itself until finals time, because it was only then that he got up on his toes and was verbally noticeable in the group. He was generally pretty quiet, which didn't bother me, but he could spark up in big games. We made him captain for one big game and he played a blinder, he was up and about. I've never seen a guy murder more games; in ten minutes he would annihilate a team.'

Just not on this day, nor in the fortnight that followed. Out of form and legs, Ablett did not play again in 1991 after the first round of the finals.

In the second semi-final against—who else?—Hawthorn, the Cats overcame a withering if inaccurate Hawks opening term (3.11 to 2.1) to edge a single point ahead at three-quarter time. In time-on of the final term, trailing by 3 points, they had three chances to pinch a berth in the grand final. A long Bairstow shot fell short, then Michael Mansfield's left-foot snap off the pack slewed across the goal face. With less than a minute on the clock, Trevor Poole streamed forward in space, but his shot on the run from 55 metres was knocked through by the experienced Hawk defence. Siren. Geelong had fallen 2 points short. They were back at Waverley seven days later to confront West Coast in the preliminary final. After a tardy start, Geelong was never closer than the 15-point final margin. Again, they had chances, but a final term that returned 3.9 proved a frustrating way to finish the season.

Some, like Couch, believe 1991 was the Blight era's best chance of a premiership. This might be seen as an unusual belief given they had reached the grand final in three other seasons, but the Hawks were ageing, though their experience saw them rout West Coast in the grand final seven days later (played at Waverley as the MCG was being refurbished). The Eagles looked not quite ready for that stage; they had just 1298 senior games to their name in their grand final team, whereas Hawthorn had 2331. As that first final Essendon played against Geelong in 1989 showed, sometimes the finals stage can prove overwhelming.

Worn out and depressed by falling at the penultimate hurdle, Blight had reached a turning point in his life. Earlier that season his son, Adam, had been knocked down by a car while exiting a tram on his way home from school. Patsy had called Malcolm and told him his son was in hospital. Adam was fine, just a little shaken up.

'It actually made me stop and think, "Jesus, I've missed half his life." That's about when I decided to go full-time coaching. A family thing so often triggers these things. Can't keep doing this. Not that I saw him that much more, because he was going to school, but you feel as though you're available.'

So, after that preliminary final loss, Blight went to club president Ron Hovey and declared his hand. It was time to stop splitting priorities, and he was content to walk away from his professional life outside football to concentrate solely on the Cats. Blight had been juggling both careers, and a family, and he felt stretched to his maximum. 'I quite often drove back from

Tullamarine [airport] the long way on a Wednesday to give me some think time. I'd get home at three o'clock, then race down the highway. I think we were always prepared, we had a theme ready and a program was up on the board. But on February 17, 1992, I ended full-time work. I remember it because it was my wedding anniversary. I was happy to do some consultancy, but thought, "Let's give this a fair dinkum crack".'

12

THE EAGLES

YOU CAN ANALYSE football until you are blue in the face. Or, in Malcolm Blight's case, until it is 3 am, the tape is still running, and the bottle of port and packet of cigarettes are both half empty. Sometimes there is an easier, more logical conclusion than the angle of the entry to the forward fifty, the match-ups in your backline or the timing of your rotations. 'Sometimes the other team is just too good,' Blight said.

It's an uneasy conclusion to draw for a man whose confidence seemed capable of overcoming most obstacles placed in his path. He would back his preparation and football nous against anyone. But the talent of his Kardinia Park teams never quite withstood scrutiny against two of the all-time great combinations in the history of the game: Hawthorn, Blight's conqueror in the 1989 grand final and 1991 preliminary final, and the emerging force from the other side of the country, the West Coast Eagles.

'When people have rated players before the game and after the game, even five and ten years later, Geelong was always rated 10 or 15 per cent lower than those teams,' Blight said. 'In some ways to make the grand final was quite an achievement, but the biggest frustration of my whole football life was that when I got to a grand final, playing or coaching, I never started favourite. We could never go in with that sort of confidence.'

His sidekick and long-time ally, Greg Wells, agreed. 'If you picked the best side out of the thirty-six players when we played Hawthorn or West Coast in all of those finals, we would be out-numbered. Put the two eighteens together and pick one side, we might get six or maybe seven of the final eighteen or twenty.'

Billy Brownless endorses that belief. 'There is no doubt that we weren't good enough, it was Blighty's coaching that got us as far as we did,' he said. 'Certainly we had some really good players at the top end but, geez, we dropped away. We really dropped away. Our bottom ten players were okay but against those teams we sometimes weren't up to it.'

This argument, of course, is being presented in retrospect. When season 1992 opened, Malcolm Blight had every reason to feel positive that Geelong would make another strong run to the finals, and contend for a premiership. In the off-season, the Cats had recruited defender Tim McGrath from North Melbourne, seeing some polish in the red-headed defender that the Kangaroos had missed. Mobile ruckman John Barnes was signed from Essendon; after a decade at Geelong, backup ruckman Darren Flanigan had been cut loose—he played a final season with St Kilda—and Barnes added speed and youth to the ruck depth. The once-banished

Michael Mansfield was sent to the back line after a decent 1991 season finish, while a rookie called Peter Riccardi had emerged from the Under-19s and shown promise. Plus, Gary Ablett was now fit; he had produced a pre-season that indicated he could return as a goalkicking presence. For a final change, Bairstow was elevated to captain.

And then no change at all: in Round 1, Hawthorn overcame a 28-point half-time deficit to defeat the Cats by 20 points at Waverley. Hawk spearhead Jason Dunstall continued to torment Blight by kicking 12 goals; in his glittering fourteen-season career between 1985 and 1998, Dunstall averaged 6 goals per game against Geelong and played a strong part in a 14–4 win–loss record against the Cats. Adding insult to injury, former captain Damian Bourke again hurt his knee that day, and would not return until Round 11. The hope of the pre-season seemed to dissipate in a single afternoon.

Ken Hinkley recalls the review of that Hawthorn game with horror. 'We had a video review, and there was a bit of talk going around, a murmuring that someone was in the gun,' Hinkley said. 'Blighty had put an iso-camera on me for the whole quarter. And he reviewed that thirty minutes of tape in front of the whole team. He didn't refer to me by name, called me "number 29" for the best part of thirty minutes. I thought, "Who is this arsehole, treating me like this in front of people?"

'The next week I played terribly and the following Monday he came up and said, "That didn't work, did it son? Just go back down the back and enjoy yourself." I won the best and fairest that year. He just tried something. If it didn't work, he tried something else.'

A Round 2 loss to Melbourne did not help Blight's mood, so by Round 3 the Cats were being hounded by their now full-time coach. And they took it out on Richmond. In a throwback to the freewheeling days of 1989, Geelong booted 29 goals to demolish the Tigers by 126 points. Robert Scott kicked 7 goals, and full-back Tim Darcy was given some respite by being sent forward, where he booted 6. It seemed to ease the burden, as Blight once again promoted an all-out attack.

Next stop, Subiaco and the Eagles. This became the Gary Ablett show; he was a one-man wrecking ball that Sunday afternoon, churning out 27 kicks, 9 marks and 9 handballs from his half-forward flank. He kicked 5 goals, and the visitors never trailed after half-time to win by 24 points.

The Cats were up and running: in a similar stretch to that fearsome month of 1989, they destroyed Fitzroy by 98 points, then ventured to Carrara and handed Brisbane the sixth-largest hiding in the game's history, a 164-point thrashing. Ablett kicked nine (for trivia buffs, John Hutton kicked 8 of the Bears' 11 goals). A week later, Adelaide copped a 123-point dismantling at Kardinia Park behind 7 goals from Brownless and 6 more for Ablett. Andrew Bews said the mood mirrored what the Cats had caught in 1989. 'The entire group was very, very strong and physically fit and really in a good headspace,' he said. 'Because we had guidelines and rules … the aim was to kick goals quickly and really get stuck into the opposition as physically as possible. Although Blighty hated people being reported. He pulled me aside one day and said, "You'll be history if you get reported at Geelong".'

By Round 15, the Cats sat on top of the ladder and hosted

second-place Footscray. A 9-point Geelong win followed, but then guess who came calling? J Dunstall. Nine more Dunstall goals, and the Hawks won by 19 points in a Kardinia Park upset. Three weeks later, the Eagles came to Kardinia Park and won by the same margin. When this season is analysed impartially, those two home losses underlined that Geelong was a contender, but hardly a favourite.

In Round 22—the third-last round in that season's restructured draw—a moment came that tested the Cats' discipline. Brisbane came to Kardinia Park, and the Cats were comfortably in control at half-time, leading by 40 points. Early in the third term a stoppage on the grandstand wing changed the mood of a game that already had a sense of niggle. With players stationary, Bears utility Peter Worsfold struck Hinkley, an off-the-ball incident that incited the crowd. Hinkley was not unconscious, but he was 'pretty groggy'. He left the ground and did not take further part in the game. 'The only thing I remember was a boundary throw-in, then "whack",' Hinkley said. 'It was an unusual game, quite physical, with quite a bit of off-the-ball stuff going on. I was one of the blokes who copped one.' Rather than retaliate, the Cats reverted to their biggest weapon: attack. They punished Robert Walls' men, piling on 14 more goals to win by 93 points.

Hinkley had been in great form that afternoon, collecting 14 touches and largely doing as he liked. Blight believes the incident cost Hinkley his shot at a Brownlow Medal—he lost by three votes—arguing that he lost any chance of votes that day and was not right the following week. But, as his players knew, Blight was not one for recrimination. 'It wasn't Blighty's go, not at all,' Hinkley said. 'He expected you to play hard and do the best you can, but not do anything silly. He coached footballers to play football.'

Only, sometimes, with a twist. The coach decided to shake things up at half-time of the second-last home and away game. Perhaps it was his Adelaide upbringing, but players sensed that Blight reserved a special place for match-ups with the Crows after they came into the competition in 1991. On this day, the Cats were visiting Football Park for the first time. Geelong was on top, Adelaide was ninth, but the Crows flogged Blight's men. Trailing by 12 goals at half-time, the coach lost his temper.

As the players entered the rooms at half-time and sought a drink, Blight walked in. 'Get 'em in!' the coach yelled. Greg Wells tried to explain that the medical staff had to tend to several players, and drinks were required. Blight just repeated himself, only louder. *'Get 'em in!'*

At Football Park, a tiny coach's room sat to one side of the main change room. Blight squeezed every player into it, and approached the whiteboard on its wall.

'This is what we were going to do,' he said, pointing at the diagrams. 'This is how we were going to do it. This is where we were today.' His volume was increasing and he continued. 'This is what we are doing! *It's not worth a pinch of shit, you fucking blokes!'*

Then he reached over and turned off the lights.

'It wasn't just dark, it was pitch black,' said Mark Bairstow. 'He started moving around the room, and he was roaring, but you couldn't see a thing. He basically went through the whole team.'

Brownless was one of the few who avoided a spray, having kicked 3 of the side's 4 goals to half-time. 'It was a tiny room with a fucking madman at the front,' he recalled. 'Mate, there were twenty of us sitting there and he would yell out in the dark, *"Argh!"* Which was scary enough, but then he would stop and you would think, "Oh, fuck, where is he?"'

For effect, Blight smashed the whiteboard with his fist, breaking his watch in the process. 'Honestly, you couldn't see a thing, then, *"Bang!"'* Wells said. 'You hear *"Smash!"* and his watch bursts, it goes flying off into the crowd somewhere. Then he turned the lights back on. The look on their faces was unbelievable.'

To a man, players laugh about the 'lights out' episode at Football Park. To a man, they were not laughing at the time.

Blight says his histrionics were not pre-meditated. 'We were getting beaten again so I tried something,' he said, chuckling at the memory of the stunned gallery of faces when he turned the lights back on. 'There weren't a lot of smiles in the room. I don't reckon anyone breathed for a couple of minutes; I was just trying to get their attention.'

Wells took the team for its warm-up before the second half; in reality he was trying to calm the team down after Blight's rant. 'They were trying to get their breath back,' he said. 'See if you could get your heart rate down below 140.' The now-infamous Blight spray didn't work: Adelaide won by 93 points, but a decent hit-out against Essendon in the final round secured the minor premiership for the only time in Blight's tenure at Geelong.

In their first final, Brownless kicked 9 goals in an MCG 10-goal thumping of the Dogs. The Eagles, however, lay in wait, and dispensed a 35-point second semi-final lesson to Blight's men. Geelong had started strongly and led by 16 points halfway through the second quarter. A knee injury to Eagles utility Karl Langdon further strengthened the Cats' hopes, but—in an extension of the spearhead trend—they could not contain West Coast full-forward Peter Sumich. Sumich kicked 8 goals, while wingman Peter Matera had 30 kicks that day—he would prove to be an ongoing thorn in the Cats' side.

The football gods provided for Blight that season: earlier in the finals, Dunstall and his teammates had been bundled out by the Eagles, and the by-now shattered Bulldogs had no counter for Geelong's running strength in the preliminary final. The margin, again, was significant, a 64-point Geelong waltz into the grand final, where the Eagles were preparing to make their own slice of history.

* * *

Late in the second quarter of the 1992 grand final, Geelong was bucking the mood of the experts, who had tipped West Coast as a strong favourite to claim its first AFL premiership. The Cats were ahead by 17 points at quarter-time, led by Paul Couch, who was easily evading his opponent, Craig Turley. Four goals to the good by late in the second term, veteran Neville Bruns—playing in the final game of his fifteen-season career—ran back with the flight of the ball in the forward line. He dropped a difficult chance; in some ways, the Cats' premiership hopes spilled with the ball. 'Bruns holds a chest mark and kicks a goal and we would have led by five, although he was running backwards and it was a difficult mark,' Blight said. 'Then they kicked the last two goals before half-time and it was a very down mood at half-time; I was very disappointed. It was a disconsolate room. I think our group feared them.'

Rather than roast his men, the coach sensed it was time to regroup. 'I went the other way and tried to be nice,' he said. 'In fact, of all the games, that annoys me the most, that one. I reckon it got away.'

Hinkley concurs. 'You could sense they were coming, maybe that attitude got into our team,' he said. 'We got put on the back foot by a great side, and we didn't recover from that.'

Ablett kicked the first goal after the long break, which should have been enough to eradicate the uncertainty Blight had sensed in the group. But the Eagles played as if they had destiny on their side. Brett Heady went to Couch and not only quietened the centre-man, but became a prolific ball-winner. Unheralded runner Tony Evans got off the leash, as did Dean Kemp. And then there was Peter Matera.

All week, Blight had fretted about Matera's influence. He had been sublime against the Cats in the earlier final, his mix of pace, endurance and penetrating kicking making him a handful off a wing. Such was the Matera presence that some clubs had 'Matera specialists': at Richmond, for instance, Nathan Bower's speed saw him earmarked on a wing every time the Eagles appeared on the schedule. For this contest, Blight had decided his captain would take the responsibility.

'That was a very late decision', Bairstow explained. 'I think he asked me in front of the group whether I was willing to take him on and I said, "Yep, I know that he is a bit quicker than me but I certainly will." But I hadn't played on the wing all year, or though my career, basically. I mean, if you are put into that situation in front of everybody and he says, "You're captain of the club.

How do you feel about doing it?" of course you are going to say yes. You go out there and do your best, don't you.'

'The thing I didn't understand was why, in the biggest game of the year, why would you take a ruck-rover or centreman to a wing?'

Bairstow had another thing going against him. Early on grand final morning, he prepared for the game, as he often did, by wandering down to check on his horses. Bairstow was training a small team; as he took his best horse out of the stall to check him, he received a solid kick on the knee. 'It was quite a strong kick,' he said. 'I was actually going to pull out because I wasn't right.'

He did not get the chance. 'You know what it's like when you are in front of your teammates and peers ... it is hard to say, "No, I can't be out there." I probably lacked a yard of pace on him anyway and then to have a crook knee as well ...'

Blight had tried rookie Riccardi on Matera earlier in the season. Matera had not been dominant in either home and away meeting, averaging 15 disposals and kicking a single goal. Blight had gone with Riccardi again in the first final, 'and it was a bit too much for him,' the coach said. 'Mark [Bairstow] had played a bit in state games and as a youngster as a wingman, so we thought it was worth trying.'

Not knowing about the kick from the horse—and with his captain resolute not to make excuses—Blight backed Bairstow to win the ball and hurt the Eagles by kicking goals himself. Bairstow had kicked 32 goals that season, so the plan had some foundation. 'Look, I reckon our captain taking on their best in-form player makes a statement. And at half-time, our best player was Mark Bairstow. The sad thing was, Matera ended up kicking five,

Bairstow kicked two points and missed another one from thirty metres out; he shanked it. He'd normally kick two of those, he was reliable, a 3.1 sort of kick. People ask, "Why didn't you move him?" Well, I thought he was our best chance to kick a goal. It didn't happen, we ran out of steam.'

Bairstow knew he had wasted his chance. 'I kicked a couple of points and could have actually put a bit of pressure back on them,' he said, 'because Matera never really paid much attention to me.'

The Eagles wingman was too busy putting on a memorable clinic of his own. 'In that third quarter,' Blight said, 'it felt like Matera kicked twenty-three goals from eighty metres out, after carrying the ball fifty metres each time.'

And it looked like it. Matera won the Norm Smith Medal for best afield that day, sparking 5 straight goals from the Eagles in the third term. West Coast led by 17 points at the final change. Geelong was spent. When the siren sounded, the Eagles led by 28 points, becoming the first non-Victorian team to claim the premiership. Blight noted as much after the game, unconsciously also touching on his lack of timing in his coaching career: 'We're finally in an AFL competition now,' he said, before adding somewhat sardonically: 'Great, isn't it?'

He spoke to the press but not his players in the aftermath of that defeat. Blight did not address them as a group until the best and fairest dinner, and his sombre mood still showed. This one hurt, and he finally conceded that his aggressive policy of all-out attack might be flawed. 'I was really dark after that, really dark,' he said. 'We all needed a bit of space. Let's take this all in. Everyone at the club needed a bit of space. Some thought it was too long, but I hadn't cooled down. Once I'd spoken to the group it was all right, but we had to make changes. We couldn't keep getting twenty goals kicked against us.'

That was essentially the theme of 1993. Malcolm Blight thought it was time for some changes. Problem was, his old dogs, or in this case Cats, had no new tricks up their sleeves.

*   *   *

Of his six seasons at Kardinia Park, it is obvious that 1993 was the most testing for Malcolm Blight. It's evident in what he says. Evident in his team's record. And evident in the response from his players, who all but rebelled that year against a man they grew to understand—and like—less and less.

Blight had decided that he needed to make changes. 'We had a number of players who could read the play forward, not back,' he said. 'When you keep getting caught at the hurdle you have to make adjustments. We tried to make them, add a wing to it, if you like … but the wing didn't start flapping.'

This cut to the core of the Blight coaching philosophy. Sending players to the back line in a bid to teach them to defend only made for an unhappy playing group. And losing exacerbated the problem. West Coast came to Kardinia Park in Round 7. The Cats led by 11 points at the final change, but lost by 8, dropping their record to 3–4. They remained around that .500 win–loss mark for the weeks that followed, unable to build any momentum. Blight was frustrated; so were his players. 'It was becoming obvious that it was too hard and too late in some blokes' careers to change them. We tried, and we lost a lot of games.'

One change, however, not only worked, but changed the face of football in the short term. Until the end of season 1992, Gary Ablett had been seen as the very essence of a utility player. He could dominate teams from a wing, or go forward and kick multiple goals from half-forward. Blight had seen signs in 1992 that, while Ablett remained a handful for the opposition, at thirty-one he was getting no faster or fitter.

So Ablett became a full-forward.

'We pushed him down the goal square,' Blight said of the 1993 move. 'He was reluctant. I remember him saying, "I'm not a full-forward, Malcolm," and I had empathy for him, because he could do all these tricks up the ground and full-forward can make you feel a bit inhibited. I suppose I went through a bit of that later in my career.'

With a high-scoring target up forward, Blight felt it took the pressure off his midfielders to push forward and score. And with Billy Brownless and Barry Stoneham both missing large parts of the season with injury, the Ablett decision proved doubly effective. 'Gary was not great defensively. Some people have only ever played back pocket or half-back flank their whole life, and they annoy the hell out of me when they say someone is not defensive enough. They don't understand how much energy it takes to constantly be going after the footy to win it. The effort you expend with someone up your bum all day. But I could sense they were starting to run off him a bit too much.

'For Gary's longevity and for the team structure it was better he went closer to goal. He wasn't quite tall enough in real terms, but his strength was enormous and he was such a lovely kick.'

Ablett missed three of the first five games. In his two appearances, he kicked 15 goals. Then the Cats met Essendon in Round 6, a game that has been righty immortalised as a football classic. Ablett kicked 14.7. Funnily enough, in a team meeting before the game we agreed that keeping Ablett to five goals was a reasonable outcome … not five goals for every player who matched up on him!

At the other end of the ground, Paul Salmon kicked 10.6. In the very definition of a shootout, Geelong surrendered a lead midway through the final term and fell by 4 goals. I wasn't lucky enough to play that day, but even as a spectator it was a memorable experience.

His opponents during that afternoon proved what a difficult matchup challenge he could be when played out of the goal square in space. Chris Daniher started on him. Ablett had four by quarter-time. Wingman Derek Kickett was then shifted to Ablett—the first time the ball came in, he out-marked Kickett despite Daniher flying in from the side to help out. At the next two centre bounces, first Liam Pickering then Garry Hocking earned a quick clearing kick in Ablett's direction. Two more goals.

After half-time, a young stripling called James Hird was handed the Ablett task. Twice he bodied Hird out of position; another time he sat back, allowing Hird to lead him to the ball. It bounced straight over Hird's head, and Ablett casually kicked a checkside goal from 40 metres. One of those days. By now the Bombers were sending two men back to try to help, but Ablett's sense of timing and space meant Hird time and again got caught one out.

In the fourth quarter, the Cats star flew over a pack to take the mark of the day with a now-greasy ball. His catch set up his fourteenth goal—he kicked a dozen of them from marks—and put his side in front by 3 points with eleven and a half minutes to play. But despite Salmon leaving the ground with injury, neither Geelong nor Ablett could sustain the onslaught.

Greg Wells was Blight's runner that day. He recalls the phone on the interchange bench buzzing, and Blight telling him to 'get a pencil'. 'Which meant there were going to be a lot of moves,' Wells said. 'The game was like pinball that day, table tennis, call it what you like. Anyway, in the middle of reading out what he wanted me to do, he went silent. I looked up, and Ablett was in position to take another mark, which he did. I could hear Blight laughing down the phone. "Shit, how good is this bloke going?" Blighty said. He obviously thoroughly enjoyed the day, except for the losing part.'

Wells was showering after the match when he spotted Ablett. 'He's over in the bath, and I'm in the shower,' he said. 'I know we lost, but I said to him, "That was pretty special." Gary said, "Oh, thanks, thanks Wellsy. Do you know what gets me going? When they start ganging up on me".'

Ablett had kicked 14 before, against Richmond at the MCG the day he changed from wing to forward pocket. He would do it again the following season against Sydney. But this was the day his bona fides as a full-forward seemed to be settled. Four more times in 1993, he kicked double-figure tallies. In seventeen games that season, he totalled 124 goals. Remarkably, the second leading goalkicker on the Cats 1993 squad was small forward-come-rover Robert Scott, with just 27. So, ultimately, while Ablett was dazzling, the Brownless and Stoneham injuries would prove damaging beyond repair, and the inconsistency of the team's performance was frustrating no end to the coach. On the back of a grand final defeat, Blight felt lost.

'I think that 92 [grand final] loss stuck in his guts,' Bairstow noted. 'He seemed to really get angry with different players and wanted to change everything. But he had forgotten the way he got there, which was by using the strength that we had, and that was our attacking ability, letting players be what they could be. We got the best out of them by letting them play footy, rather than trying to be something they weren't. All of a sudden we were struggling. I think he was very down on himself.'

There was unhappiness in the camp, which was not helped by Blight's distance. 'Malcolm sort of went into his shell for six or seven weeks,' said Bairstow, who as captain felt obliged to play the intermediary. 'It was like a nervous breakdown ... it wasn't, but that's how it came across. A bloke that went completely introverted.'

When St Kilda handed the Cats a 71-point thrashing at Waverley in Round 16, the relationship threatened to break. The Saints were twelfth entering that game; Geelong was a game and percentage out of the top six, with a 7–7 record. It was a crippling blow to their chances of returning to the finals, and irrefutable proof that tinkering with the game plan had brought a football club undone. 'In the end, it was not working,' Blight said. 'I got the senior players in and admitted something was wrong. Whether I was listening or not listening, whatever the reason was, something was not working. I said, "Mark, you're captain, you go first. Whatever it is, let's get it out there. You're not enjoying it, and I'm not enjoying it. Either we fix it here, or I'm out the gate".' It was effectively a precursor to the leadership group model of twenty-first-century football: the 'honesty session' that has driven club values in the modern game.

The players, in Blight's words, 'did not miss' their target. 'A lot of it was personal things I'd said, changes of plans,' he said. 'I was grumpy, constantly shouting. If that was the feeling of the group, whether I believe it or not, at some stage something has to give. Some things were still not negotiable, but anyway it was more about the way I operated rather than what I said. I still wanted to coach, so what was the plan?'

Later that week, Blight threw in a bit of his own man management. 'We thought we were in for a big training run,' Bairstow said. 'Blighty said, "Bring your boots, we're having a full training." We got to training and he said, "Put your runners on," and we jogged down to Darren Flanigan and Bruce Lindner's pub. We had a couple of beers and played pool, then went home—that was a big turning point. Everybody was getting changed thinking, "Shit, we're going to be doing a full two hours' training," and instead we jogged down to the pub.

'You could tell he had lightened back up again in his attitude and then from then on he was really positive. Consequently, things started to turn around pretty quickly.'

Geelong won its last five games of the season. In the final game, a visit to the WACA ground to play the Eagles, their finals hopes were still alive. Perhaps it was the venue, which is better known for hosting cricket than Australian Rules, but Blight started referring to his men as a cricket team. 'Everybody was batting for Australia,' Bairstow said. 'We were going to go out to bat … he went on through the whole team, and based it on a batting line-up. The ruckman and the ruck-rover, you are going to be the opening batsman. Billy [Brownless] was going to be the big hitter, etcetera.'

Geelong kicked 6 goals to 2 in the final term to win by 20 points. It was not enough to extend their season: in the final game of the home and away season, Adelaide defeated Collingwood to pinch the final available spot in the six. The Cats missed out by 4.2 per cent. In an even season in which Essendon's 'Baby Bombers' pinched the premiership, every one of the top six clubs breathed a sigh of relief that the red-hot Cats had fallen short. Honestly, they were playing as well as anyone, and their finals experience would have made them a handful that September. So would Ablett, who was probably in career-best form.

Geelong's season was over, but at least the Cats had their coach back.

13

THE EAGLES, AGAIN

As the cats prepared for season 1994, they had an interesting addition to the coaching panel. Gary Ayres had long been a Geelong nemesis; as a member of the seemingly invincible Hawthorn teams of recent years, he seemed an unlikely candidate to take the vacancy left by departing assistant Graeme Gellie.

But Ayres had in some respects fallen out with the club to whom he gave sixteen years of exemplary service. Captain in 1993, he had a year remaining on his contract when the club summoned him to the boardroom. 'Hawthorn was in a lot of trouble financially and I think they were trying to protect their bank balance in relation to the players they felt were not really going to be there for a hell of a lot longer,' Ayres explained.

'I sat in the boardroom at Hawthorn and was told that if I was to play on for next year … if I played every game I would be getting about $30,000 a year. If you can imagine, after playing fifteen years at the club, it was a real smack in the face.'

Disgusted, and disappointed, Ayres walked. He had verbally accepted a playing role with Frankston when Geelong recruiter Stephen Wells—brother of Greg—called him. Wells was keen to sound out Ayres about the assistant and reserves coach role that Gellie had left. Ayres agreed to visit Blight's East Malvern house to discuss the job.

'Malcolm and I had a terrific chat for a couple of hours,' said Ayres, who sought advice—and received encouragement—from his former coach, Allan Jeans. 'Blighty just laid out his philosophies and beliefs about footy. And, basically, because I was just out of the game he pretty much said, "You're in the job. See how you go." So I said all right.'

Part of Blight's conversation with his new assistant centred on the Cats' strategy for the coming season. The lows of 1993 were behind him—he felt mentally refreshed: 'After 93, I thought, we've got strengths, let's play to them'.

It was a rocky beginning to 1994, however; Geelong opened another season in disastrous fashion. In Round 4, when they travelled to Football Park to play Adelaide—where he had switched off the lights the previous year—he decided to mix things up before the bounce. 'He finished his [pre-match] speech and said, "I want you to line up outside the Adelaide race",' said Paul Couch. 'We were going, "What the hell?" He said, "We're going to play it like a grand final. We're going to stand in a line there, side by side, and watch these guys come out and scare them".'

THE EAGLES, AGAIN

Heading out on the ground early, the Cats bizarrely took up position at the head of the Adelaide players' race. Mark Bairstow recalls Blight even suggesting they clap the Crows onto the ground. 'We had obviously been losing so he tried something different,' Greg Wells said. 'Well, I'm up one end with Couchy and Kenny Hinkley, the two calm guys. Malcolm is down the other end. "Line up. Face the front."'

Paul Couch might have looked calm, but he was mortified. He decided to concentrate on the dancing girls to distract himself, 'because I did not want to focus on Adelaide coming out because I was so embarrassed. It wasn't good'.

By this stage, the crowd had well and truly noticed. So had the Crows. While the crowd heckled, Adelaide sought to avoid a potential psychological ambush by seeking an alternative path onto the ground. 'We could see down the race,' Wells said. 'You could see [Adelaide coach] Graham Cornes, his face was like, "What are they fucking doing?"'

So the minutes—and embarrassment—dragged on. Finally, the Crows emerged from their race. Geelong players were asked to eyeball the opposition; most stared at their boots. And Adelaide defender Nigel Smart made a game of it, pulling faces and rolling his eyes back in his head as he ran onto the ground.

The ploy almost worked. Geelong led by 7 points at three-quarter time, only to be overrun by 27 points.

'I said to Malcolm in the debrief, "Do you think that worked?"' Ayres recalled.

'What do you mean?' Blight said.

'Well we obviously didn't win the game. It didn't unsettle [Adelaide].'

'Yeah, but what did we lose by? Do you know the average losing margin that we have had here before? About 50 or 55 points.'

Improved losing margin or not, it was a defeat. Geelong was 1–3, though they had recovered to 5–4 when Brisbane came to Kardinia Park. The Bears were not a basket case—they had beaten second-placed North Melbourne at the Gabba the previous week. But they had never won in Geelong, and few tipped them to do so on this occasion. Their last four trips to the ground had resulted in four losses, by an average of 98 points.

Ablett kicked six, but had little help as the home side conceded 7 goals in the last quarter to lose by 25 points. In Round 12, again at home, they fell by 3 points against St Kilda, who had won just three games for the season. And in Rounds 14 and 15, the club's two closest rivals came calling. The fortnight threatened to define the season: West Coast flew home from Kardinia Park with the four premiership points, and then Hawthorn produced a 10-goal second half to sink the Cats at Waverley.

Geelong simply could not get on track.

The coach felt some experienced members of the playing group were not showing the hunger he wanted. 'Blighty knew I had paid my house off so he got me and said, "Listen, I want you to go and mortgage yourself up again, because you're playing too comfortable. You're not extending yourself",' said Paul Couch, amused by the absurdity of the request but understanding the message. 'So I had to go and buy something [laughs]. Yeah, he wanted you to be on edge all of the time.'

It was not the only time the coach had pushed into people's territory away from football, but it was rare. 'I definitely didn't try to delve into their personal life, but occasionally a quip like that got them thinking,' he said. 'It was harmless without being derogatory but there's a half-truth in there. And Couchy knew that.'

And acknowledged it. 'Another time I was sick,' Couch said, 'although I had been playing pretty well over about four or five weeks. I rang up and I said, "I can't make it [to training] tonight." He said, "What are you doing, taking pressure off yourself, are you?" He could see me easing back into that comfort zone. He could picture it, and he was probably right.'

Meanwhile, Ayres was grappling with a starkly new environment and, in his reserves role, the concept of losing. 'It was totally different,' he said, comparing the Geelong and Hawthorn experience: most notably, the chasm between the homespun Allan Jeans and left-field Malcolm Blight philosophies. Jeans was famous for his handling of different teams: 'They're like sausages—you can boil them, grill them or curry them, but ultimately they're still sausages'.

Those Hawthorn teams had a certain aloofness that set them apart from the competition. Even on state representative trips, they tended to stick together. It wasn't arrogance as much as protecting the shell in which they operated—don't be friends with the enemy—so during our playing days we just didn't fraternise. Jeans had them almost programmed to be silent killers projecting this family image.

Whereas Blight, well ...

'You would hear Allan talk about the "sausages" and then Malcolm's Indian campfire, having towels over their heads,' Ayres said. 'And his persona and his style. Allan said virtually nothing. It was just a complete contrast of two different types, albeit that there was an age difference, but even to the point I don't think I had heard Allan Jeans swear in the whole time I knew him, ten years. It was enlightening also. What Malcolm was doing with that particular group was getting them to a point. It was a great learning curve for me because I went through a point where I had lost my first seven games as [reserves] coach. And I said to Malcolm, "I'm not used to this. Losing is not in my vocabulary." Hawthorn's winning ratio was something like 72 per cent over the time I was there.'

Blight's response was telling. 'He just said, "Just coach to coach the player",' Ayres recalled. '"Don't coach as if you're that player because that player can't do what you did."'

This awareness strikes at what made Blight the enigma he was. I always thought average players made better coaches, because they had to work harder to understand the game when they played it. For the naturally gifted, the game just came to them. While his comment to Ayres might support that theory, Blight disputes the contention. Maybe Barassi's treatment of him instilled the long-term benefit of the value of hard work and persistence, rather than cruising on talent. Plus, I'm sure Malcolm learned a huge amount about player management during his years at Woodville. In coaching, losing can be a bigger teacher than winning ... you just have to outlast it.

Ayres did. He recovered the reserves season, getting them back to 11–11 for the season with a strong second half of the year. The seniors, however, seemed to have their work cut out.

* * *

If Malcolm Blight had credits—if not an air of invincibility—among the Geelong faithful, it seemed they had dried up by Round 16. Melbourne came to Kardinia Park with a 7–7 record; Geelong was 6–7. A loss would surely condemn the home side's season, and when the Demons rattled off 6 goals in the third quarter to earn an 8-point lead, the crowd turned.

Blight had his own way of dealing with fans. At Waverley that season, he'd been heading to the ground at quarter-time when a Cats fan seated on the aisle got stuck into him. 'He gave it to Malcolm as we walked down through the aisle,' Ayres recalled. 'Malcolm turned to me and said, "Wait until three-quarter time." Just as we went down at three-quarter time Malcolm approached this gentleman, who had his back to us. Blighty leaned in to his ear and went *"Boo!"* And the guy jumped about ten feet in the air, it was one of the funniest things I have ever seen.

'We went down and addressed the players. On the way back the guy put his hand out and said, "Oh, that was a good one, Malcolm".'

Blight had also been heckled by the Geelong crowd earlier in the year during the narrow win over St Kilda. Down by 26 points at three-quarter time, he'd walked down through the crowd with Ayres in tow and the jeering started. 'It felt like the punters have seen enough of me, this was year six of me there,' Blight said. 'As I walked out on the ground, and the crowd's booing, I turned to Ayres and joked, "They hate Hawthorn people here".'

His Cats kicked 7 fourth-quarter goals that day, to win by 3 points. But on this occasion, against Melbourne at Kardinia Park, Geelong fans clearly thought it would not happen again. The booing had an edge that the players and coaching staff could not miss. 'It was pretty poor by the Geelong crowd,' Couch said. 'We were disappointed in that. He didn't deserve that.'

Being booed as the head coach makes for a lonely walk through the crowd. Even when you can't hear the specific abuse, and you usually can, it feels like a horribly personal confrontation. Think of another workplace in which that happens. As a player, you can tend to hide in numbers. Even as an assistant coach, you know it's the boss copping the heat—as Barassi said (leaving the expletive aside), it was 'his head on the chopping block'.

Ayres believes that afternoon might have eaten away at Blight's desire to coach, but it also provided the coach and players with a spark. 'We know that they are paying members and have a right to voice their opinion but it was extremely disconcerting when that came out. We actually got up and won the game. There was the famous picture of Barry Stoneham sticking the two fingers up to the crowd and that was more or less to say, "That's what I think of that." That was the turning point in that year.'

Though he had previously dealt with the jeering by deflecting it with humour, Blight seemed disconcerted by that afternoon's barrage. 'I remember putting my hand on him and I said, "Well we'll get this game",' Ayres said. 'It was really a time for me to see physically how much pressure a coach can be under. And Malcolm had been in the game for a long, long time, don't forget.'

The Cats responded. Indeed, they got motoring, winning six of their final eight to finish the home and away season in fourth place. In the final game, Brownless took advantage of Ablett's absence for a week to kick 8 goals from 8 kicks. This suggested he was running into form after an injury-depleted year, a season in which his coach had sent him to a health farm at mid-season to restore not only his body, but also his mind. Though Stoneham was again hurt, and would miss the finals, a fit Brownless and Ablett would stretch any back line.

Which, of course, they did.

Pitted against Footscray in a Friday night qualifying final at the MCG, the Cats flew out of the gates with an 8-goal first quarter. The Bulldogs, however, ground away, narrowing a 13-point half-time deficit to just 2 points at the final change. Geelong had been missing Michael Mansfield, who was injured in the opening minutes, while ever-reliable defender Ken Hinkley found himself on the bench in the final term with an ankle problem.

And still the Dogs came. Inside the final minute, a penetrating Rohan Smith kick to the goal square was spoiled by Cat pair Adrian Hickmott and Paul Brown. But Brown's opponent, 220-game veteran Richard Osborne, stayed down, crumbed the pack and put Footscray a point in front. When the clock stopped, there were twenty-six seconds remaining.

Garry Hocking then provided the most crucial clearance of the evening. The man known as 'Buddha' was by now the premier player in the Cats' midfield, and was shortly to claim his third best and fairest award of the past four seasons. He had been quiet that night, held to just 13 possessions and clearly hampered by injury. But of the 611 disposals he gathered in 1994, none held the importance of that kick to half-forward.

Standing in front, David Mensch marked and turned quickly. Brownless led out of the square, and Mensch's weighted kick into space was perfect, allowing Brownless to run onto the ball and mark uncontested. There were eight seconds remaining. As Brownless measured his kick, the siren went. Without pause, Brownless slotted the goal. 'Billy,' roared commentator Sandy Roberts, *'you're the king of Geelong.'*

The 5-point win earned a semi-final berth against Carlton. When historians look back at the score, this game would seem to be a formality: Geelong led all afternoon at Waverley, winning by 33 points. But the circumstances behind this result were extraordinary.

On the eve of the game, Greg Wells looked grey when he left the medical room after the final, light training session. Approaching the coach, he knew there was only one way to break the injury news. And there was plenty of it.

'There's no Mansfield,' he said.

'We knew that', Blight replied.

'Well, Buddha [Hocking] and Toby [Bairstow] are out, too.'

'Shit,' said Blight. 'That wasn't in the script.'

Wells cringed. 'There's more… Couchy's not playing. He's tweaked a groin.'

'Oh, Jesus,' Blight exhaled.

Wells tried some Blight logic on his coach, who he says was rattled for the only time in their six-year relationship. 'Oh well,' he said. 'We'll still have eighteen on the ground, you know.'

Blight stared at him. 'Yeah. Shit,' was all he could manage, then he headed to the showers. Bairstow and Couch were the club's two most experienced midfielders, and Hocking the best. Mansfield had developed into a reliable, attacking half-back who could be a dangerous forward option in a pinch.

THE EAGLES, AGAIN

'Blighty was in the showers for ten minutes at the most,' Wells said. 'He would have showered and looked at the floor, and kept thinking. By the time he returned, that confidence was back, and he asked the players to gather around.'

Blight had the four injured players sit on one side of the room, and their replacements on the other. The balance of the team sat in the middle. He started speaking. 'Wow, what an opportunity,' he said. 'This is history-making stuff. Whenever the Geelong Football Club history is written, there will be a sentence or paragraph on this game if we win it. You can't say that about a lot of games.'

'By the time he came back, he was totally in control. He was in brilliant nick, he looked and sounded confident,' Wells said. 'Then he got the mood light, going through the Carlton side and cracking jokes about them. The players were completely relaxed by the time he had finished.'

Aaron Lord, Liam Pickering, Shayne Breuer and Steve Hocking all pulled their midfield weight that afternoon. Ablett kicked 6 goals, while Mensch added three. John Barnes was outstanding, almost the prototype mobile ruckman as he gathered 20 possessions and took 9 marks. The Cats survived, and knew all four of those absentees would be returning for the preliminary final against North Melbourne on the following Saturday, the match that would become known as the 'Hand of God' game.

North started the preliminary final well, leading by 3 goals at quarter-time. Blight was understandably unhappy at the break, targeting first Peter Riccardi—he picked him up by the shoulders of his jumper—and Garry Hocking in the huddle. Hocking responded, his 16-touch second term sparking a 7-goal term for the Cats to establish a commanding 24-point advantage. The scoreboard did not tell the entire tale: North's appalling conversion rate, having kicked 5.13 in the first half, was undoing the fact that it had a good share of possession.

The Roos' imperious centre half-forward, Wayne Carey, then lifted his side despite a nagging calf strain. Carey kicked 4 goals in the term; Blight had no choice but to banish his opponent, Tim McGrath, to the bench as Carey single-handedly lifted his side back into the contest. The margin at the final change was still 18 points, but North seemed to have momentum.

And they stormed home in the final quarter. With Bairstow groggy after a heavy third-quarter clash, and lingering question marks over the key midfield Cats, Geelong appeared to be running out of legs. North's Brett Allison tied the scores with minutes to go; Riccardi gathered on the outer wing and stormed forward, kicking to a forward pocket. The ball spilled from Brownless's hands and into the path of Leigh Tudor, who snapped a floating left-foot kick to the goal square.

North full-back Mick Martyn had played it perfectly. A cult figure at Arden Street, Martyn was tough, reliable and a better player than people gave him credit for. On this day, he did precisely the right thing, positioning himself in front of Gary Ablett to avoid giving away the cheap kick. But Tudor's kick wobbled and floated over his outstretched arms. Ablett put his right hand—the 'Hand of God'—into the air and claimed the mark. Just metres from goal, he could not miss.

There were two seconds remaining.

Then, siren. Any score would secure a grand final berth.

Above: Mark Bickley, Malcolm Blight and Darren Jarman celebrate the Adelaide Crows' 1997 grand final victory. (Getty Images.)

Right: In one of his more infamous Adelaide moments, Malcolm Blight and football manager John Reid walk around the Football Park boundary line before the siren against Richmond in 1998. (Newspix/Sarah Reed.)

Above: Malcolm Blight famously joins his Adelaide players in their celebration huddle minutes after the final siren of their 1998 grand final triumph. (Newspix.)

Right: The Crows enjoy the spoils of back-to-back premierships—Malcolm Blight and Adelaide captain Mark Bickley raise the 1998 premiership cup. (Newspix/John Feder.)

Flanked by Crows officials Bill Sanders (left) and Bob Hammond, a clearly relieved Blight breaks the news that 1999 would be his final season in charge of Adelaide. (Newspix/Russell Millard.)

New Saints coach Malcolm Blight on the late January day in 2001 when he announced new captain Robert Harvey (centre) and vice-captain Andrew Thompson (right). (Getty Images/Sarah Morton.)

A coach's frustration boils over: Malcolm Blight addresses his St Kilda players on the ground—literally—after their disappointing Round 10, 2001 loss to Melbourne. The Demons kicked 10 goals in the final term to win by 31 points. (Newspix/Damien Horan.)

Above: With his sacking as St Kilda coach made official the previous day, Malcolm Blight faces the media outside his house in July of 2001. (Newspix/Kelly Barnes.)

Right: July 19, 2001—Malcolm Blight departs the football club offices after being sacked by St Kilda, having had 'no inkling whatsoever' of the decision. (Newspix/Peter Ward.)

Left: Partnered by (from left) the Channel Ten team of Stephen Quartermain, Anthony Hudson and Michael Voss, Malcolm Blight shares his wisdom from the commentary box during a 2007 home and away contest. (Newspix/Matthew Vasilescu.)

Below: Relaxed and tanned, Malcolm Blight enjoys life after coaching during a 2005 swim in his Palm Cove pool. (Newspix/Wayne Ludley.)

Malcolm and Patsy Blight pictured at the 2007 Magarey Medal count in Adelaide. Though her ill health was a contributing factor to his 1999 decision to leave the Crows, Patsy was a strong ally throughout Malcolm's coaching years. (Newspix/Matt Turner.)

Brownless sidled up to Ablett before he took his kick. 'I told him not to kick into the man on the mark and not to play on,' Brownless said. 'He didn't say anything, he just gave me a funny look.'

As Martyn slumped to one knee, devastated, Ablett kicked a goal. For the second time in three finals, the Cats had won courtesy of a kick after the siren. If the Hand of God was telling, Blight's football gods also had a role to play. 'The footy gods looked after us in spades that September,' he said. 'It was like the Miracle at Kardinia Park, three times in a row. Billy's kick, winning against Carlton with those blokes out, then Leigh Tudor's kick to Gary.'

On the other side of the draw, the Eagles waited, having disposed of Melbourne in the other preliminary final. This was the first season in which two preliminary finals were played, the AFL having expanded the finals format to eight teams. West Coast had waltzed past the Demons by 65 points, and, having finished the home and away season as minor premiers, they were—once again—favourites to claim a second flag in three years.

But Blight was confident. 'I always thought it was your turn when you have won more finals than lost,' he said. 'And this was the first time [we had won more than we lost]. We went there 8–6. Before that finals series we were 5–6, so after winning three I thought this was set up for us.'

That Monday after beating North, club president Ron Hovey popped his head through the coach's door. His statement summed up the incredulous events of the previous three weeks. 'We're in another grand final,' Hovey said, a look of pleasure but near bewilderment on his face. 'Can you believe it?'

* * *

When the Cats had turned up for training in the first week of the finals, council trucks were out on the Kardinia Park surface. Displeased, Blight headed for the office of football manager Gary Fletcher. 'What's going on?' he demanded.

Fletcher's response beggared belief: 'There's a women's cricket match coming up and the council is top-dressing the ground.'

To this day Blight finds it difficult to accept the timing of the council work. 'We could only train on half the ground. Then we came back Wednesday night and the ground was fully covered. We couldn't train on it at all,' he said.

The Cats moved training to the oval used by local club St Joseph's, which is literally next door to the ground—technically, still in Kardinia Park, which takes in the Geelong ground. 'That was week one. Next week, still sand everywhere. I am seething at this point,' conceded Blight, who was keen not to let the players become aware of his anger. 'Let's just say I was very cross with a lot of people.

'After we got through North Melbourne I thought, well, St Joey's had been fine but I wanted to get back on our own ground. I made the decision to go back there on the Wednesday night for our major training session. And I've got a funny idea I might have lost the game right there. On top of everything else about being up for three weeks ... that circumstance put me in a situation I should have avoided.'

As he relates the story now, Blight is still clearly upset by his decision. He had wandered out onto the ground and tested the surface himself. But some rain that day, combined with the lingering layer of sand, made the ground heavy under foot.

He had, of course, wanted the players to enjoy the grand final week experience of their own ground—and with their surrounding fans. 'I'm really sorry it happened,' he said. 'And I'm sorry that we, as a club, couldn't stop it. Whether we would have won or not, who'd know. But when I think of all the years at Geelong, that incident hurts as much as any. As the game went on, we were flat as tacks.'

The Cats led by a point at quarter-time, a remarkable effort given West Coast had kicked the first 4 goals and seemed a class above Blight's men. Then Eagles defender John Worsfold clipped Garry Hocking in a collision; Hocking would return and be serviceable, but the incident stole the momentum of the game. 'When Worsfold collected Buddha, it was like the entire place fell apart; every bit of luck deserted us,' Blight said. 'It was pretty embarrassing to lose by that much. We had unfit blokes everywhere, and the Eagles were impenetrable.' West Coast walloped Geelong by 80 points, riding an 8-goal-to-1 final quarter against a lacklustre opponent. Ablett rarely saw the ball, kicking a single goal to close a stunning season with 129 majors.

As Blight sat there in the coach's box in the final term, his men unable to counter the onslaught, he knew his time was up. But he could not cleanse himself of his decision to train on Kardinia Park. 'That lived in my body for four weeks, I couldn't get rid of it,' he said. 'I still had a year to go [in his contract], but I was finished. Would it have changed my life to win it? Yes, it would have. Now that I've won one I know how good it feels.'

It was a sour taste after six memorable years at Kardinia Park. Ultimately, the football gods could not grant Malcolm Blight's wish. But on reflection, others considered his return at Geelong—three grand finals in six years without the maximum reward—a fair reflection on the coach and his playing list.

A stalwart throughout was Paul Couch. The following words perhaps sum up the experience of playing for Malcolm Blight: 'I would think 90 per cent of his players would be happy with having played under Blighty. Some weren't, but that goes for every coach. He was brutal on a lot of blokes, and some couldn't cope with it. I once said to him, "What did you do different in Adelaide?" He said, "Well, I was probably too hard on you blokes. I probably got into you too much, probably two or three more times than I really should have"'.

Bairstow—his captain and sometime confidant—has the final word. 'He was a terrific coach in different patches,' he said. 'Blighty had highs and troughs at Geelong, I suppose, like players do. His highs were very high and his lows were very low.'

Finally, Gary Ayres would seem to be in a position to make an accurate assessment, having played against Blight's Cats teams, been his assistant for a season and then taken over as head coach when Blight walked away. 'Where he potentially fell down was the back line, which was just not one of the best back lines that was going around', said Ayres. 'It was short. Obviously Steve Hocking and Steven O'Reilly were there for a little while … Paul Brown played a little bit of footy there, so did Micky Mansfield. Ken Hinkley was more your attacking defender, lay off, zone off.

'I think the better teams could actually really kick holes in that defence when it mattered the most, and unfortunately that seemed to be when it got to finals time.'

14

CATCH-UP

EVEN AFTER MALCOLM Blight's course had steered down Geelong Road to Kardinia Park in 1989, John Reid stayed in touch, hoping that one day he would be in a position to reunite with his close friend on another football stage. That day arrived in October 1995, when Reid was appointed to the freshly minted position of general manager of football for the Adelaide Football Club. If it sounds unfathomable that the Crows did not already have such a role, in truth they were not alone. There was a wide variance in the state of financial health and infrastructure among AFL clubs; some interstate clubs boasted membership waiting lists and bulging coffers, while a club such as Fitzroy, whose equipment van was being driven unregistered and whose membership base was so small it was managed on Rolodex cards, lay writhing on its deathbed.

The Crows were stuck somewhere in between, still playing catch-up after their hastily induced 1991 birth, an inception conceived by Port Adelaide's audacious claim on an AFL licence in July the previous year. The Magpies' bid had forced the hand of the SANFL administration. Fuming, it launched a counter-bid, knowing that it retained the playing card most likely to earn the right to field the fifteenth AFL team: a viable stadium. Since 1973 the SANFL had owned and operated Football Park, the primary football venue in Adelaide with the capacity and facilities of AFL standard. A SANFL-driven franchise also drew from a far broader fan base than that of Port Adelaide, and was the logical inclusion in the AFL's expansion plans. Thus were born the Adelaide Crows.

Now to create a football team—playing list, coaching staff, administration, fan base and culture—in ninety days. 'We were chucked together in a matter of months', said Mark Bickley, one of about seventy SANFL-listed players invited to train for the inaugural Crows' squad. When Port Adelaide came in [the Magpies eventually joined the AFL in 1997] they had probably two years to prepare, same as Gold Coast and Greater Western Sydney these days. Our start felt completely rushed.'

Coach of the newcomers was Graham Cornes, a short-lived teammate of Blight at Arden Street. He was a giant of the South Australian game, having coached the Glenelg Tigers to five grand finals and two premierships in six seasons, and, importantly, coaching with astonishing success against Victoria in state-of-origin contests, winning six times in his eight meetings with the Vics. He was twice named All-Australian coach.

There seemed no more logical choice as the first coach of the

Crows. Cornes had long been dismissive of Victorians' self-asserted superiority of the VFL over all other competitions, so the chance to steer an Adelaide team in the Australian Football League suited his psychological profile to a tee. 'He certainly wouldn't admit this,' Bickley noted, 'but Graham almost had an inferiority complex about Victorians, it dictated his behaviour and the way we trained. In that first pre-season, a lot of Victorian clubs were doing 100 by 100 metre sprints, so we had to do 110 of them. Anything they were doing, we'd do more, or do it better. He made a point of it. He wasn't apologetic about it, in fact he made sure we knew exactly what we were doing and why.

'Training felt like a 40 to 50 per cent step up from the SANFL pre-season training levels, and I was surprised to survive. If you ranked the players on their standing in the SANFL I would have been in that 50–70 bracket from a talent perspective, but one of the things I always had going for me was that I was very durable. We were training thirteen days out of fourteen, every second Sunday we had off. Because of that, and the age profile of the group being maybe in the twenty-four to twenty-seven range—a lot of those guys succumbed to injury or just exhaustion.'

While the environment under Cornes' control was steeped in football culture, and sat amid a football town, there was a problem: none of that culture belonged to the Adelaide Crows. Rather, the SANFL clubs and their diversity of culture imbued the original playing list. 'The impression I had was that we were a bunch of misfits that had to be gathered from around the state, not knowing what our charter was as a collective group,' recalled Andrew Jarman, one of the standout talents in the Crows' early years.

'We had some senior players in terms of Chris McDermott and Tony McGuinness and two or three others, then a bunch of young lads, deer-in-headlights sort of kids.'

The inaugural captain, McDermott put the conflict caused by club origin even more bluntly: 'It probably took us two years, at least, to bury those differences. The first couple of years were extremely difficult. While you might have had the message it took a long time for blokes to understand it and for it to sink in'.

CEO Bill Sanders calls those opening months 'an exciting blur', but he vividly remembers the challenge of building an identity within the group. 'The club was a potpourri of players from all over South Australia,' he said. 'While footy cultures are essentially the same, when you get a mix of guys like that we had to try to manufacture something that was inherently Adelaide Crows. But most of the players retained their club allegiances. They'd finish training with us and go back to their own clubs for a drink sometimes … trying to engender spirit and camaraderie is not simple.'

The fans and insiders put such matters aside when the new-comers belied that 'misfits' tag to thump the Hawks in Adelaide's AFL debut. The ageing Hawks were still the benchmark in the game, having won three premierships in four years prior to 1990, when they slipped to fifth. This 86-point Football Park thrashing shook the competition to its core. Not only had the goalposts been shifted, but a power shift in the game seemed imminent, as the Crows were taking shape as an imposing state-of-origin team.

Jarman, who claimed three Brownlow Medal votes in that stunning opener, knew better, particularly that life on the road would be a brutal teacher. 'My expectations were only to survive, knowing that our group physically and mentally was not going to be strong enough to go and play every second week away,' he said. 'And if we could win between four and six home games that might have been a reasonable result. Obviously we did surprise a few sides but I always felt we were a year behind. I thought that year we just had to throw it all out there and by about Round 8 or 9 they would start looking for players for 92. That first year for me, as a senior player, was to keep the energy up and try to set a good example for the younger players. Survive and not get embarrassed. But I thought in our away games we were totally embarrassed with our inept performances.'

The Crows' 1991 return was an honest ninth place with ten wins from twenty-two games. Jarman was right—they were awful in some road games, especially at Victoria's remaining suburban grounds. In Round 3, Essendon coach Kevin Sheedy reportedly tied the windsock on the outer school end to its mast so the visiting Crows had no sense of the preferred end; Adelaide lost by 7 goals. They tasted 20-goal thrashings at Moorabbin and Victoria Park, and an 84-point hiding at Geelong. Yet they won in Sydney, against Richmond at the MCG and at Princes Park over the immensely proud Blues.

In 1992, they improved by a single win but again finished ninth; however, there was a discernible difference in competitiveness: the Crows' for–against percentage was 101.4, an encouraging increase on the 89.4 of their inaugural season. They won five of the final six home and away games, and the emergence of a handful of new talent, notably promising ruckman Shaun Rehn, defender

Ben Hart and a spring-heeled forward named Tony Modra, suggested this Crows team had improvement to come.

By their third year, the fitness base and talent combined to make the Crows a formidable force feared across the border to their east. In 1993, Adelaide turned over forty players in search of their best twenty: when Cornes found the right combination, the Crows were not just highly competitive; they were a contender. They remained fragile on the road, winning just three times, but their 9–1 home record (only Hawthorn that year won at Football Park) was an AFL-best. And they had Tony Modra. Incumbent spearhead Scott Hodges was hurt early in 1993, allowing Modra, a mature-age recruit from West Adelaide who had played eight games the previous season, his turn in the goal square. Modra kicked 10 goals in Round 1 against Richmond (and, for the record, 13 more against the Tigers in Round 16). A star was born. High-flying, athletic and mercurial, if a little unpredictable, Modra was a free spirit in a team crying out for structure and discipline. It would be churlish to suggest he lived on talent alone, but his God-given gifts—judgement, leap and an accurate kicking boot—saw him boot 129 goals in 1993.

They finished fifth, and prepared to taste finals for the first time. Their elimination final opponent, Hawthorn, would take some beating. Two weeks earlier, in their Round 20 meeting, the Hawks had led 8.6 to 0.1 at quarter-time before an easy victory, which makes the final that followed even more remarkable: Cornes' men won by 15 points at the MCG. 'That was just an amazing moment, three years into a program and we were playing finals football and playing well—you had to pinch yourself,' Jarman said.

'You would have a look around and think, "Geez, we've fast-tracked pretty well and Graham's got us at a good level at the moment." We got a lot of confidence out of that game. I recall the excitement after the game, some guys were tearing up.'

Inaccuracy hurt them dearly against Carlton in the semi-final that followed, though the oddities of the final six allowed Adelaide another shot at making the grand final via a preliminary final date with Essendon. This time there were more tears, but of the anguished kind. Adelaide was leading by a seemingly insurmountable 42 points at half-time, and fans began to prepare for a trip to Melbourne for the grand final. The players' minds must have been making the same journey. 'We did some dumb things in that prelim final,' McDermott conceded. 'If you could have your time again you would've done A, B, C and D. I thought that we had a really good team; it was a wasted chance.'

At three-quarter time, a number of Crows were seated in their huddle, exhausted. The Bombers noted their flagging opposition; it was all the motivation they needed. Essendon stormed home, kicking 5.1 to 1.2 in the final term to win by 11 points. Against the one-way traffic, Jarman missed from just 15 metres out, 'and I never will forget that. You know, I practised those goals every evening at training with my eyes closed. That was the moment and that's where you're judged,' he said. 'And that is something I will have to live with for the rest of my life I suppose.

'In front of eighty thousand at the MCG, playing against one of the great footy sides and you are 42 points up at half-time,' Jarman continued. 'And you are two quarters away, an hour away from playing in a grand final … I think we lost our way at half-time when we went into the rooms. Something didn't feel right, and, yeah, I don't think we were ready for a grand final. That is the inexperience we had as a group and a coaching staff.'

The best and fairest winner that season, Tony McGuinness, believed that MCG afternoon set the club back significantly. 'We had been pulling guys out of ten SANFL clubs, and basically most of them had probably hated each other for the previous years,' noted McGuinness, who became Crows captain in 1995. 'Then we found ourselves with a chance to make the grand final. The shame of it is that the 93 preliminary final was probably the sticking point in the whole development of the club.'

Defeat or not, that contest was the high-water mark for the Cornes years. After an appearance in the pre-season cup grand final in 1994 and a 4–2 home and away season start, the Crows badly fell away. A Round 17 win over competition leader and (eventual premier) West Coast breathed late life into their finals hopes, but seven days later the last-placed Sydney came to Football Park and extinguished those chances.

'They had a board meeting and the captain, vice-captain and deputy vice-captain were asked to come in and give their view,' recalled McGuinness, who was vice-captain under McDermott that season. 'My view on Cornes was that 94 had been a tough year and he didn't coach particularly well, but given that we had made a preliminary final the year before and really should have won the game, I thought that there were enough reasons to reappoint him. That's what I told them. Quote, unquote.'

It was not enough.

'We completely lost our way in 94, on and off the field,' McDermott assessed. 'We just dropped the ball and then we were

CATCH-UP

in a panic. A new sort of club with new administration, plus there was always this undercurrent of thought that we needed to have a Victorian coach, that we would never be successful until we had a hard-nosed Victorian coach and Graham didn't know what it was like.'

Jarman also sensed the vibe midway through the year. 'Graham worked bloody hard to develop a real strong football side but I felt we had lost our way. I felt that in about Round 18, if I recall, we lost about three in a row. I reckon he was gone then. [Club management] didn't think we were tough enough for Victorian football because of our away results. And if you look at our away games they were bloody embarrassing.'

Away from Adelaide, the Crows won twelve out of thirty under Cornes from 1991 to 1994. They played finals once, but finished no better than ninth in the other three seasons under his command. His goose was cooked.

*   *   *

Across in Melbourne, the Fitzroy Football Club was barely registering a pulse on the national league landscape. The Lions had played finals four times in the 1980s, but were suffering a nomadic existence, having being evicted from the Junction Oval after season 1984. Their membership was dwindling, and the very effort of getting a competitive team on the ground was proving exhausting for coach Robert Shaw. For four seasons he had been in charge, and a 1994 finish of fourteenth, with just five wins, was enough to convince him to vacate the least-coveted seat in the game. Then the phone rang.

215

'My time had finished [at Fitzroy],' Shaw said. 'Once I made that announcement, Bill Sanders rang me and approached me, and contrary to media perception it was certainly after I had resigned and it was also after they had made the decision on Cornesy … Fitzroy was one of the great and enjoyable things of my life but it was really draining and really tough.'

Shaw was admired through the football world for his commitment to what was externally perceived as a basket case. With limited resources, he had fashioned a team that was never to be taken lightly. It struck a nerve with Sanders and his board, who were looking for an uncompromising Victorian approach to take the Crows to the next level.

Ironically, Shaw was not Victorian, but a Tasmanian transplant into the VFL/AFL world. He played fifty-one games for Essendon across eight seasons, the weight of nagging injuries finally derailing a promising career after season 1981. He cut his coaching teeth with Clarence in his native Tasmania, before returning to Windy Hill as an assistant to Kevin Sheedy for three years. Two years as Lions reserves coach followed before he assumed the head role.

In truth, Fitzroy's 'have-nots' status in fan support and facilities ensured Shaw was rarely under the spotlight, despite finishing no better than tenth in four seasons. It could hardly have been a worse preparation for the job with the Adelaide Crows. 'Obviously I was really excited, so there was no trepidation about coming in as an "outsider",' Shaw said. 'I didn't read the writing on the wall because I'd built up very good relationships with the media in Melbourne and rather naively thought that's how everyone worked. But going from ten teams in one town to one … I wasn't prepared, and that's the honest truth. And going from the traditional clubs like Essendon and Fitzroy to a four-year-old club in Adelaide, with the benefit of hindsight I'd like to have been a lot older and a lot wiser.'

If he thought the Lions' job had been a challenge, he was in for a rude shock when he crossed the border. It did not help that he lost reigning best and fairest and All-Australian ruckman Shaun Rehn just three games into the season, for the first of Rehn's three knee reconstructions. Fitzroy's Round 7 trip to Football Park did not help his cause; his former team, perhaps with a point to prove, recorded just its second win for the year. And a 96-point thrashing from Collingwood in Round 13 saw the Crows tumble out of the eight, never to return that season. By now, the decision to do away with Cornes—*their* man—for an outsider was being widely questioned, especially in the electronic media. Remember, this is a town that produced *The Crows Show*, a weekly thirty-minute production on the fortunes of Adelaide, and filled countless other hours each week with a focus on one football team.

'The honeymoon period lasted three and a half minutes,' Shaw said of the scrutiny. 'Not the hardcore, day-to-day media, but certainly the support acts and the celebrity specialist writers, they were very quick to pounce. I felt that the normal, day-to-day, hardcore football journalists were quite prepared to give me an opportunity and they wrote it [their copy] in a very positive frame.'

For all the disenchantment in the group, the Crows started season 1996 in scintillating form. A pre-season grand final appearance suggested a more promising horizon. They won their first four games of the home and away season, after which their percentage was a staggering 199.3, and sported a 6–2 record by Round 8. But five consecutive losses brought their momentum to a halt, and the bitterness in the playing group bubbled to the surface. 'There was never any harmony and it was a ... well, disaster is a harsh word, but probably a good word that described it,' McDermott said.

Rehn's wretched luck continued—in Round 3 he suffered another injury requiring a season-ending knee reconstruction—but the Crows' hot start had captain Tony McGuinness in a positive frame of mind. 'From there you don't have to win too many more to make the eight, so at that particular point of time, everyone's expectations were very high,' McGuinness said. 'Then it just went completely pear-shaped, it just got worse and worse. Shaw really felt the pressure. Personally, I felt that the club didn't support Shawy to the level that perhaps it should have given that you had a Victorian coming to Adelaide for the first time. It was always going to be a tough gig.'

As interested observer Malcolm Blight said of the Shaw era, and the rising unhappiness with the outsider, 'Eggs on cars is no fun'.

Mark Bickley was McGuinness's vice-captain, and believes confidence in the coach fell away dramatically as 1996 dragged on. 'Players were certainly unhappy but the club was aware of the environment and how Robert was managing it. Dealing with the media, his persona with the fans, he was a square peg in a round hole. There was always going be a change at the end of 96. The situation was untenable.'

The club board commissioned John Reid to provide a comprehensive overview of a football club that had stalled after such a promising start in the AFL. 'They asked me to look at a range of things,' Reid recalled. 'Basically, I thought Shawy was not the right bloke to be coach and lot of blokes on the list needed to go. But also that the culture needed to change. The culture was about "me", not the club.'

Andrew Jarman reflects on 1995 and 1996 with equal parts horror and shame. 'As a group and as a football club we bombed out, we couldn't go any lower to be honest with you,' he said. 'Ninety-six was just a shit year that you want to forget quickly because, on and off the field … everyone was just blaming every-one and it was just a horrible atmosphere and it just stank, the place stank.'

A Jarman selection incident was the low point for most. Though he kicked 2 goals against Melbourne in Round 13, Jarman knew his body was struggling, with sciatic nerve problems inhibit-ing his training and match-day performance. He was typical of the playing group—unhappy, out of form and disgruntled. Eight points up at half-time, the Crows fell to Melbourne by 51 points that Sunday afternoon (only the Demons' fourth win in thirteen weeks). Though they were just a game and percentage out of the finals, morale was sinking fast.

'Shawy called me in on the Monday and sat me down and said, "Mate we just want to give you a week off. We know that you have been sore." And I'm like, "Yeah, no worries." I had a week off and pulled up pretty well and then we were playing Carlton the following week at Princes Park. So I turned up to training that week and trained as well as I've trained for a while … [but] all week no one spoke to me about my role playing Carlton.'

On Thursday nights, Crows senior players were typically handed an envelope with a travel itinerary schedule for the coming weekend. Confident of a return to the seniors, Jarman opened his when he got home. 'I opened it up and there is the letter: "Jars, this week you are playing for Norwood against Port Adelaide on Sunday, report at two, blah, blah, blah." I was thinking, "What the fuck's this?" I don't care that I had to play for Norwood but just tell me. Give me some sort of indication of what was going on. So I was filthy.'

Jarman rang his close mate Chris McDermott, who suggested he ring Shaw, but the coach did not answer his phone. 'So then I went to work and I get a call from Johnny Reid at about ten-thirty,' Jarman continued. 'He said, "I'm just letting you know that there has been an emergency and you are playing because someone has pulled out." And I said, "What do you mean I'm an emergency? Why wasn't I told this on Monday?"'

The veteran of nine SANFL seasons and six AFL campaigns then made a snap decision that essentially ended his career at the top level. 'I said to Reidy, "I've been told I have to play Sunday for Norwood, so I'm playing for Norwood." Shaw should have told me Monday at training, "Mate this week you are probably going to be an emergency against Carlton but no doubt just keep fit and stay healthy." That's all I needed to hear.

'Because I didn't play it was just massive. I let the club down and I pissed on the group. Well, there might have been a bit of that but I was also standing up for our younger players about this whole thing, which had to change. That's the lack of communication by a senior coach and football manager.'

The issue escalated to Sanders' office, and the CEO rang club captain Tony McGuinness to see if a peer could change Jarman's thinking. Only a handful of people were aware of the problem, and management was keen to nip it in the bud. 'I believed it was the coach's or the chairman of selectors' responsibility,' McGuinness argued. 'My position was, why was I ringing Jars to convince him? Just tell him to get his bags together and get to the airport and tell him to play. They said, "Well they've already done that and he is refusing".'

McGuinness insisted they call him back and deliver the ultimatum, but Jarman would not be moved. He played for Norwood in a decision that understandably marked his card.

McGuinness described it as symptomatic of a season that had started with promise but quickly came off the rails. 'I don't think [management or coaches] had lost their authority,' he said. 'But the deck of cards was just continuing to fall down on the back of the massive expectations—when you are six and two, I think logically most people are going to think that you are going to finish in the top three. It just went all pear-shaped. People were just all over the shop.'

While Bickley refers to Shaw's tenure as 'lost years' in his career, he does credit the fallen coach for bringing through the talent bed that drove later success. 'Recruiting Kane Johnson, Tyson Edwards, Andrew McLeod, Simon Goodwin, those sorts of guys, in some respects the club gained the grounds for those premierships once they had a sniff of senior football. But it was Blighty who really had the ability to engineer something.'

* * *

In August of 1996, Malcolm Blight's father Jack died. While he had suffered a bad case of malaria during World War II, Jack had stayed active until complications began to slow him down in his seventies. Still, his death was sudden, and it called Malcolm home.

'In August, at my dad's funeral, there had been some talk that Robert Shaw was going to finish. It had got out,' Blight said. 'A couple of blokes came up to me at Dad's funeral, people like [former Woodville teammate] Lindsay Heaven and Ralph Sewer, and they said, "You wouldn't coach the Crows, would you?" To be honest, I hadn't thought about it.'

John Reid had. The former Blight assistant was fresh off submitting his report that recommended Shaw was not long for the coaching world. The shortlist of replacements numbered one name: Malcolm Blight. Reid tracked his mate down: Blight was in town for a media commitment. Reid sensed Blight was interested, and a brief series of meetings unfolded. Each party was familiar with the other, as chairman Bob Hammond, CEO Sanders and football manager Reid met with a man they had known and respected for many years. 'Not long after his dad's funeral I said to Bob Hammond and Bill Sanders, "I reckon Malcolm's hot to trot, go sort out the figures with him",' Reid said. 'They organised it very, very quickly. Compared to what they'd been paying it was more, but it should have been. Bill knew him from Woodville, Bob rated him highly, and they were the two key players.'

On 22 August, the *Adelaide Advertiser's* Michelangelo Rucci confirmed that Blight was the club's preferred candidate, and that he had been formally approached the previous day, within hours of Robert's Shaw's resignation. In truth, of course, the conversation with Blight had been in play for some months.

As Sanders noted in the Crows' yearbook twelve months later, they needed convincing on only one matter before making an offer:

> We had to be convinced that Malcolm had the fire in the belly, and desire to take on the challenge, having been out of the game. Although closely involved, he was removed from the smell of the liniment for a couple of years ... and I think in most people's eyes he appeared to be very comfortable in the media. Certainly he is highly regarded in his media role. So in discussions with Malcolm, we had to be convinced that, one, we wanted him. And that if he said yes, it was for the right reasons.

Both Sydney and Hawthorn had inquired about Blight's interest in coaching after he stepped away from Geelong. The timing had been poor: the first time, his son Adam was finishing his schooling. Up until 1995, his daughter Melanie was doing the same. Now, in 1996, both children were tackling university in Melbourne, somewhat freeing up his family commitments. Blight was convinced; there was nothing to do but sign.

Having quickly come to commercial terms for the coaching role, Blight and Reid met at the former's holiday house at Blairgowrie, on Victoria's Mornington Peninsula. Their agenda for three days was Reid's report, which made for disturbing reading for the incoming coach. 'John had only been there for a year, but I reckon he saw things were done differently to what he thought football should be,' Blight said. 'How people operate when they're there, that's their business, not mine. But he knew that wasn't me, so this was the way we were going to do it.

'We'd been through five unbelievable years at Woodville. I'd been through the Geelong experience, and he was at South

Adelaide. His morals and ideas were the same as mine. So there were hard decisions to make but we were on the same page, which is all that mattered.'

Of all the issues in the report, Blight was most disbelieving about not only the Andrew Jarman selection incident, but also the club's response: remarkably, after doing his penance in the reserves until Round 19, Jarman returned to play the final four games of the year.

'They won eight games in 1996. In that environment, if Andrew Jarman decides after being selected for duty ...' said Blight, whose voice trailed off in incredulity. 'Then he's played thereafter? Morally there was something in the club that needed a good look at. I don't understand how that happens. Blaming the player is easy. Sometimes you need to look behind all that and ask how that could happen. How could he still be at the club with no penalty at all? Internally, there were a lot of angry people but not a lot seemed to happen. As an outsider, I thought, "Not on my watch. Something's wrong".'

By the time Reid and Blight had completed their Blairgowrie lock-in, they believed they faced a three- to five-year process in rejuvenating the internal process, pride and culture of a fallen football club. In many respects, the fragmentation in the Crows' camp was worse than in the first months after the club's establishment. Then, there had been an excuse; by the end of 1996, however, player interests, a shaky football department and on-field problems had brought them to their knees.

Things needed to change.

15

THE BIG FOUR

MALCOLM BLIGHT CAN recall the first time he drew a line through a player's name. Not long after being installed as captain-coach of North Melbourne, in the pre-season of 1981, the Kangaroos had begun to make cuts to their list. 'To put it mildly, I was wet behind the ears,' Blight recalled. 'After all the pre-season training we had to start shortening the list, so for the first time I had to sit in front of a player and tell him, "It's not working for you, we're going to move you on".'

Thus, the first player was sought as the long, unenviable task of reducing numbers commenced. His name? Ricky Aylett.

There was a certain poignancy about the decision. Ricky's father, Allen, was a giant of not only North Melbourne but the game. A Tassie Medallist winner for being best player at the 1958 national carnival, he won the first of three consecutive Kangaroos best and fairest awards in the same year. He also captained the club for four seasons. Yet he was more than simply a famous playing name—as president of North Melbourne in the 1970s, Aylett had steered the club's path to its first two premierships via bold, aggressive leadership. A key aspect was his relentless, ruthless approach to recruiting talent from across the nation—including a young South Australian called Malcolm Blight.

'That process was never easy, but ... the son of the president and a great family friend, I had to tell him he wasn't going to be at North Melbourne,' Blight said. 'Ricky was a half-back, medium-sized player; he tried his guts out every time he trained and played. He just didn't quite have "it". But he was a fantastic bloke, and ended up being CEO of the club and having a wonderful life.

'It was almost like the footy gods put it in front of me to test me at the start. Trust me, I did a lot since ... it never got easier.'

It's true. Sacking, de-listing, not extending a contract ... call it what you like, but ending a player's football dream can be devastating. It doesn't seem to matter how experienced they are, either—they rarely seem to see it coming, and just as rarely agree with the decision. You fulfil their dream by handing them a jumper; just as quickly you strip it away.

If that sounds melodramatic, it's not. I once drove for two hours to spend time with a young recruit we had let go from St Kilda. He had not been drafted, but had been a decent Under-18s player who we gave a shot. This teenager was so traumatised by his release that he had considered taking his own life, and it took a lot of TLC to bring him back from his despair.

And just as Blight had to deal with releasing Ricky Aylett, I was forced to make a decision on Luke Beveridge. Luke's father,

THE BIG FOUR

John, was (and still is) the recruiting manager at St Kilda, and he's a magnificent person—which made it doubly difficult to end his son's League football career. But it is a fact of football life.

When Blight and John Reid concluded their three-day live-in analysis of the Adelaide Crows, it was clear the men agreed on a re-shaping of the playing list. It would not be as dramatic as the mass culling of their first year at Woodville together, when more than half the list was shown the door. But in many ways—when considering the names on Blight's list of departures—it would be equally, if not more, significant.

Incumbent captain Tony McGuinness would go. So too would his predecessor, Chris McDermott. Andrew Jarman and Greg Anderson were also on the list, along with veterans Wayne Weidemann and Scott Hodges. Even though Blight and Reid knew it was the right thing to do, they were equally aware that the departure of the first four names—McGuinness, McDermott, Jarman and Anderson—would generate headlines. Each, in his own way, was a sacred cow.

McDermott had been Crows captain from 1991 to 1994. A state-of-origin regular, he was a logical choice as the Crows' inaugural leader, for he was a tough and uncompromising utility from Glenelg who had won three consecutive best and fairest awards for the Tigers in the mid-1980s. There were few if any more respected names in South Australian football. During his days of kick-to-kick as a kid, he had proudly sported a jumper rarely seen in his schoolyard. 'I was always one of the few blokes who kicked the footy in South Australia wearing a Woodville jumper,' McDermott smiled. 'He was a childhood hero, Blighty. I followed

MALCOLM BLIGHT

him when he went to North Melbourne out of interest, and then I happened to play with him in state football. Out of all the blokes that I have played with or against, he had an enormous mark, or probably the biggest. They talk about Carey, I guess, and Ablett ... but Blight was incredible.'

Such was Blight's status in South Australia that when McDermott and Blight both represented the state against Western Australia in 1985, McDermott was reluctant to approach his team-mate. 'It was almost a "Mr Blight" thing. That was my first state game and I remember he was having a gasper at the team meeting on Friday night,' McDermott recalled. 'Then he went out and kicked five or six in one of the great state games. Honestly, I could not remember saying one word to him during that time. That was in the old days when the old blokes ruled the roost and the young blokes shut up and they knew their spot.'

If he deferred to his seniors at the time, it didn't take long for McDermott to assume the role of an elder statesman of the game. His marriage of talent and hard work saw him develop into an elite player at AFL level—in 1992, his best and fairest year, the then–twenty-eight-year-old averaged better than 32 touches a week, a League high; Robert Harvey's 28.7 was a distant second. McDermott continued to churn out big numbers under Graham Cornes, but the arrival of new coach Robert Shaw heralded a change in leadership on the ground. Shaw replaced McDermott with the latter's close friend Tony McGuinness. In some ways, it was simply another brick crumbling in the Crows' wall; others, however, such as Andrew Jarman, believe it had long-ranging consequences for player and club.

228

'The biggest mistake Robert Shaw made was to strip Chris of the captaincy and give it to Tony McGuinness,' Jarman said. 'Chris McDermott was the heart and soul of our group and I think that he lost Chris straightaway after that. If you look at Chris's last two years at the Adelaide Crows it was horrible for him.'

McDermott's output fell away dramatically under Shaw. In 1995, his production fell by more than 40 per cent in the twenty games he played. McDermott has a simple explanation for it. 'Shaw didn't think I could play, so he didn't play me. I spent a fair bit of time back in the local comp [SANFL] in 96.' With injury also eroding his effectiveness, McDermott managed just nine AFL games in 1996. Midway through the season, when it was apparent Shaw would not be returning, he harboured hopes of extending his career under a new coach. But thanks to three days in Blairgowrie, he was never on the agenda.

*   *   *

By the time Tony McGuinness took over the captaincy from Chris McDermott in 1995, he too was an established star of the game at the national level. He had stamped his arrival on the SANFL by winning a Magarey Medal at age eighteen; in his last game with the Tigers he engineered a premiership for his club before heading across the border to join Footscray for the 1986 VFL season. He was a natural choice for the Crows when they started their AFL life—at twenty-six, he was at his prime. Remarkably, McGuinness claimed best and fairest awards at all three clubs, Glenelg, Footscray and Adelaide.

A long-kicking left-foot rover, McGuinness suffered injuries in 1995, missing much of the middle third of the year and the final handful of games. Still battling manfully to get fit the following year, he played every game in the second half of the season but was hardly the force he had been. As skipper, there was little he was enjoying about his football.

'Given the turmoil around the club I remember vividly being in a compromising position, being asked to do things that perhaps normally captains wouldn't be asked to do because of all the turmoil around the place', McGuinness said, referring to being dragged into the Andrew Jarman's 'play or not play' controversy. 'It was sort of like a deck of cards falling down and it was hard to concentrate on just playing, let alone all the other stuff. I didn't have a good year and I had come off the back of a knee injury the year before. The irony of the whole thing is that in hindsight I probably was finished.'

Jarman is arguably the most intriguing of those on Blight and Reid's list. Gifted of hand and foot, and blessed with the capacity to continually find the football, in some ways Jarman mirrored the timing of McDermott and McGuinness by arguably playing his best football in the 1980s. Though only twenty-five when making his debut for the Crows—he teamed with McDermott and McGuinness to down the Hawks in their 1991 AFL debut—his record prior to that season was stunning: the 1987 Magarey Medal, two best and fairest awards for North Adelaide and All-Australian honours in 1986 and 1987.

The national stage didn't know what had hit it. Here was a balding, long-sleeved and not particularly fast midfielder giving cheek to the establishment. Be it blowing away the opposition or blowing kisses to opposition supporters, Jarman quickly became public enemy number one for Victorian clubs already paranoid about the cross-border rivals. 'What I tried to do was bring a lot of tension and focus towards me to take a bit of heat off the younger players,' Jarman explained. 'If I could niggle and rattle and abuse the opposition to a degree but still maintain my performance, that just gave our guys a bit of breathing space. So I probably changed my role slightly that first year. Playing with a bit of arrogance and giving the Vics a bit of grief.'

Jarman looks back on the Shaw seasons with mixed feelings. 'The mentality in those days was, "Why is a Victorian coming over here to coach South Australia?" Look at the resistance that Malthouse had at the Eagles initially, although he was building a brilliant football side at the time so their results were okay. Whereas we just wandered out ... there were no really big names coming home, no big signatures on a bit of paper to get excited about. I mean in 95 or 96 there was no Wayne Carey coming home, no Stephen Kernahan or Craig Bradley signed for the Adelaide Crows. No one wanted to come back to South Australia and play for the Crows.'

For all of that, Jarman became a highly effective contributor, be it through the midfield or slipping forward to kick 52 goals in his final two seasons. If he was anything, however, he was a smart footballer. And he was smart enough to know that, after his decision to play for Norwood rather than the Crows on that fateful 1996 weekend, he was not coming back. 'I was dead in the water regardless of who they chose to coach,' he said.

Of the four primary names on the Crows' chopping block after season 1996, Greg Anderson seemed to go most quietly. There was acceptance that his best days were behind him—he had won his Magarey Medal a full decade earlier, and had managed just thirty-seven games in his last three seasons for Adelaide.

A utility who could 'play big', Anderson stood out in any competition because of his trademark flowing blond hair. He had been among the favourites for the 1990 Brownlow Medal, having joined Essendon in 1988, and his high point with the Crows was All Australian honours in 1993, his first season back home after his five-year stint with the Bombers. Those final Adelaide seasons were largely spent playing for SANFL club Port Adelaide—the club he had originally debuted with as a strapping seventeen year old in 1983—and helping secure the 1995 and 1996 premierships. He did not have the state icon status of McDermott, the pedigree of McGuinness or the eye-catching love–hate qualities of Jarman. But, just the same, he had been a major talent.

He, too, was on Blight and Reid's list.

Blight outlined his plans to Bill Sanders. 'In doing the job, there are some players I would want to move on,' he said, before naming his list. 'If that happens, what would be your position?'

Sanders knew things needed to change; he didn't pause. 'We'll back you all the way.'

*　*　*

The final months of season 1996 were difficult for the coaches, players and administration of the Adelaide Crows. Robert Shaw knew he was departing. A narrow loss to North Melbourne in

Round 20 then sealed the team's fate—they would not be playing finals football. And the administration knew it needed a new coach. It was not a good time to be sporting the navy blue, red and gold.

'The playing group was high maintenance over those two years with Robert Shaw,' Chris McDermott explained. 'Really high maintenance. It was volatile. There was a lot of ... he seemed to embrace a couple of players and ignore others. Right at the end Shawy walked off at the training track ... he just disappeared. Walked off. You know, halfway through a drill I looked around and he wasn't there. So we had to stop it and bring it in and speak to the group and explain to them what was going on.' Shaw had essentially checked out, if not mentally then physically, leaving training early in his disenchantment. 'Yes, it was a bizarre place to be around for a couple of years,' McDermott concluded.

Which makes McDermott's departure fitting. As in, bizarre. John Reid believed the former skipper was about to retire and that when McDermott arrived for his post-season review meetings for uncontracted players his retirement would be finalised. Instead, the player himself arrived with an open mind about his future. It just happened that McDermott, Andrew Jarman and Tony McGuinness all had their reviews back-to-back on the day after the traditional 'Mad Monday' post-season drink: Tuesday 3 September, 1996.

McDermott can laugh now about the procession in and out of Reid's office, though it took a number of years for him to emotionally reconcile his departure. 'Reidy said, "We think you've had your time, time to move away. There's nothing here at the club for you." I had parted mentally with the footy club, and probably needed to move away. So with a fair bit of hindsight it was the best thing that I could've done and best thing for the club. At the time, though, looking at the player list, I thought I had twelve months at least. Now, it's hard to argue with the decision.'

McDermott left the room, stunned, walking straight past Jarman on his exit. Though Jarman knew he faced the axe, he wanted to hear it from the new coach. 'I wanted to be told by Blighty, the incoming senior coach', Jarman said. 'I wanted to hear, "Andrew, no mate. What you did is not good".'

Instead, Jarman entered a room occupied only by Reid. 'Why aren't I talking to Blighty?' he demanded.

'Well, he's not here. I'm just letting you know it's all over,' Reid responded.

'Geez Reidy … is that it? Right, see you later.'

Just like that, another door closed.

'I would have loved to have sat down with Malcolm and found out why I was cut,' Jarman reflected, though he has conceded the Norwood fiasco lay at the heart of it. 'And am I a dickhead? Am I a troublemaker? I would like to know that. Because that is how you learn when you are told the honest truth. But I never got the opportunity.'

As Jarman departed the room that day, McGuinness was walking in. 'Did you get a new contract?' he asked his by-then former teammate.

Jarman just shook his head and kept walking, joining McDermott in the bar.

'There was a procession of players going in and coming out very quickly. I was the last one to go in,' McGuinness said. 'I had

THE BIG FOUR

been sitting there for two or three hours, thinking that we were going to be talking about a new contract because I was keen to play. Then John Reid opened with, "Have you considered retirement? Do you reckon you've had enough?"'

McGuinness was shocked. After the to and fro on a decision McGuinness increasingly suspected had already been made, it was agreed that the captain would have several days to reconsider his position. 'By this stage,' McGuinness recollected, 'all the media were sitting outside the club because seven players had gone in and come out before me and been fired. The next forty-eight hours was just complete turmoil.'

When McGuinness joined McDermott and Jarman in the bar—along with South Australian football legend Russell Ebert, who happened to be at the club that day—he had a shocked look on his face. 'He was white,' McDermott recalled.

'Tony was mortified that he had been cut,' Jarman said. 'He clearly didn't see it coming.'

The fourth member of the quartet, Anderson, still had a season remaining on his contract. Quietly, later in the week, Reid came to a settlement to end a career that had effectively stalled.

The Adelaide media fast sank its teeth into the biggest football story since the inception of the Crows. But it was the Melbourne television production, *The Footy Show*, that fuelled the fire as the week unfolded.

'*The Footy Show* rang and wanted me and Chris and Andrew to come on the show on the Thursday night,' McGuinness said. 'We were all happy to do that. In hindsight I probably shouldn't have because my future was still in limbo ... although you could argue

235

it had been decided by the club, just not publicly. So we arranged very late Thursday afternoon to catch a flight to Melbourne to go on *The Footy Show*.

'The club was pissed off because obviously the slant was not going to be positive. So John Reid very quickly got hold of me and said, "Well, look if you are going to be in Melbourne you probably should catch up with Malcolm." So Malcolm and I had breakfast on Friday morning for an hour or so.'

The pair met at an Exhibition Street hotel. Not surprisingly, the meeting did not go well for McGuinness, who argued that the extenuating circumstances of injury and the club turmoil had challenged his 1996 season. Blight was blunt in his assessment of the coming year, referring back to his Geelong coaching days as good enough reason to promote change.

'We're making some changes and I'm honestly telling you that I think you're finished ... my advice to you is to finish up,' Blight said.

While McGuinness sought to at least join pre-season training to prove his worth, Blight had clearly drawn a line through his name. The former headed to Tullamarine airport and caught a soul-searching flight home ... only to be again confronted by the media. His statement at the time said it all: '[Blight] thinks I'm finished and I should retire. So I guess I'm retired'.

McGuinness toyed briefly with a trade to Sydney. The Swans had reached the 1996 grand final and he looked like the ideal style of 'top-up' player to add run and experience to a midfield. The thinking remains even today—if Sydney had squeezed a single season out of him, the short-sightedness of the decision would

THE BIG FOUR

have been justified by a premiership. But his failing body denied him even that chance.

'I'm torn between wondering about, had I stayed under a very good coach and a team that performed well, whether I would have had a place in the side,' he conceded. 'Or would I have been the twenty-sixth player every week and ended up playing the whole year in Glenelg? I've got no hard feelings about it. Having coached at Glenelg and Port Adelaide, you learn you have to make tough decisions. In the end, the coach is the coach.'

*   *   *

Fifteen years later, there is no less fascination with that September week in 1996 that changed the fortunes of a football club. The general perception is that Malcolm Blight rode into town and sacked the four biggest names on the list; Blight laughs at the contention. 'The premise was that they were all sacked—that's not right,' he said. 'One [Anderson] was paid some money, the other three were out of contract. What irks me is this: every time it comes up, what gets overlooked is that they were all sensational players. The fact that you've finished, and how and where you've finished, is sometimes out of your control, we all know that. But it doesn't take away from their playing days.

'I thought Chris McDermott had retired. If he hadn't, he should have. We all have a use-by date. Tony was the hard one, a really hard call. He was still playing okay. I just thought the way he developed as a player towards the end of his career, he'd get the dinky handball and kick it long. I don't like playing that way.

237

So hopefully I was honest with him. If he wanted to go to another club that was fine—the Swans nearly picked him up. But the way I was going to play, no. Was he getting the maximum out of himself? Could he get any better? I'm not sure. All those issues counted.

'And the Adelaide Football Club had made the right decision on Andrew Jarman; all I did was confirm it.'

Like Blight, Reid believes too much is made of not only the departures, but also the delivery of the news ('It was just bang, bang, *bang!*' as McDermott later said of the meetings). Both had considered who would best drop the hammer; it was decided that Reid, as the incumbent club official, would be best to clean up the existing list, and Blight would make a fresh start. 'It was pretty clinical but there's no nice way to do it,' Reid said. 'If you're finishing up you're finishing up. It's a five-minute conversation, and most people want to get out of there anyway. For instance, the meeting with McDermott was quick because he'd technically retired. He'd run himself ragged to the finish line, given everything. I think he still wanted to stay involved and Malcolm said no.'

McDermott had been carried off Waverley Park after his last game, the Crows' Round 22 loss to St Kilda (and their fifth straight defeat to close the year). If there was finality about his departure and not that of McGuinness and Jarman, all now three believe it was a necessary evil for a football club lacking direction.

'People were sympathetic about our departure but that disappeared pretty quickly because there was great excitement when Blight was announced publicly as coach,' McDermott said. 'It was enormous news in Adelaide that he was coming back, the biggest thing in town for a long time.'

THE BIG FOUR

Blight was formally announced as coach on 2 September, having inked a three-year deal reported at $1.2 million. Expectations were high—'Only the finals will do', read a headline on an opinion piece. The following day, his face beamed from the front page of the *Adelaide Advertiser*. In his press conference, he memorably responded to a question about being the Crows' Messiah: 'I can't spell the word, but I know what happened to the last guy they called the Messiah'.

His next line proved to be a portent for the senior talent: 'The fact the club had finished twelfth is not just the coach. The players will cop the brunt of what's happened to the Adelaide Football Club'.

That statement highlighted Blight's mandate to make the difficult decisions on his senior group. An Adelaide native, football commentator (and later a media colleague of Blight) Bruce McAvaney recognised there were few men with the combination of conviction and reputation that could have swung the axe so brutally. 'Malcolm had the confidence internally but also the external status that allowed him to do that,' McAvaney said. 'He could have come back and changed government and we would have let him. He really was the Messiah. Maybe a legendary Victorian coach could have done it, but no other South Australian could have, it was a massive thing to do. For him to turn the club inside out, only he could have had the internal arrogance to do it—and it's an endearing quality—and he had the reputation.'

Football clubs move on. As McDermott noted, the excitement of Blight's return quickly overwhelmed the public disbelief at the roster cleanout of the top end. For their part, Jarman and

McGuinness insist their annoyance with the decision was not focused on their careers, but more the wellbeing of the football club.

'We were senior players who were trying to build an organisation that didn't have a real culture, we didn't have any real mantra about how we wanted to be perceived as a footy club,' Jarman said. 'We wanted to be like an SANFL unit playing like a Carlton but we were a bunch of misfits who were thrown into the bloody deep end without any life jackets. That's what it was like.'

Jarman then laughed, revealing his underlying disappointment surrounding his departure. 'I didn't care if I was coming off the bench. I just wanted to play for Blighty,' he said. 'But he made his decision, mate. Blight is ruthless and he planned it out, that start-again type attitude that mattered. Looking back, it was probably the best thing he did.'

Equally, McGuinness seemed to bemoan the timing of his departure. He recalled a meeting in Bill Sanders' office the day after Robert Shaw informed the club that he would not be returning in 1997. 'Bill said to me, "Wait for next year, it's going to be great, you're going to love the new coach." So obviously they were a reasonable way down the track [with signing Blight]. I was thinking, "Yeah, yeah. Yeah." So the news was like a sledgehammer.

'I don't have any negativity, despite public perception and [the perception] of those inside the Adelaide Footy Club about me being hard done by. There are a couple of reasons for that. First, in hindsight, I may well have been done anyway. And the second one is, having coached, the coach makes these difficult calls. The only thing is it could have been handled a hell of a lot better and maybe it's not anybody's fault. Maybe it was just a difficult situation that got out of control.

'But we were a young club trying to build a culture, trying to build a Past Players group. A smart operator would have gone the other way, so I could have said, "Well I got the chance to meet Blight and Blight told me that I'm done." If anything it adds more credibility to it. Nothing more than a man telling you that you've finished up and I would like to see you at the games and all the best. I'm not sure which player would have argued. They would have shaken hands and asked for his autograph.'

Which perhaps drills to the core of the issue.

Jarman confessed he would have loved to have played for Malcolm Blight.

McGuinness—a Woodville fan like his mate, Chris McDermott —simply wanted to meet Malcolm Blight and shake his hand, and have his retirement properly managed by a man he had idolised— 'Long sideburns and massive torpedo punts'—as a child.

And McDermott even today admits he is in thrall of the man whose jumper he wore as a boy. 'He's fascinating. You can sit there for hours and hours and listen to the stories. I mean, I've had a conversation with [former Australian test cricket captain] Ian Chappell, sort of another childhood hero. And to speak to Blighty, that just reminded me they had very similar characters. Fascinating blokes. Strong leaders. Good on the lip but an enormous presence.'

That turbulent week in September 1996 ended four great Australian Rules careers. For all their admiration for Malcolm Blight, they just weren't in the plans of the new Adelaide coach.

16

THE MESSIAH
STRIKES

OVER THE SUMMER of 2010, Malcolm Blight read a biography of revered horse trainer Bart Cummings. As Cummings divulged his secrets—or as much of them as he would allow—the management of his stable struck a specific chord with one particular reader. 'I loved Bart's book,' Blight enthused. 'There were similar things in there that I found in teaching and treating players. Occasionally you have to say hello to them, liven them up.'

So it was in a summer fourteen years earlier, when Blight arrived at the Crows amid much fanfare. He found an emotional attachment to the team came easily; Woodville connections through Bill Sanders and John Reid gave him a natural level of comfort, and as a South Australian he thought of the organisation as 'my state team'. And it did not take much to win the team over.

'Everyone in Adelaide had a soft spot for Blighty and in some

THE MESSIAH STRIKES

ways even for Geelong,' Mark Bickley said. 'They played such an exciting brand of footy and played in three grand finals; we were all disappointed they didn't get one. If you grew up in Adelaide and didn't really follow a VFL club, you'd usually pick the underdog in the grand final. But because of Blighty everyone followed *his* team. He was such an iconic person and player.

'When the players started hearing his name connected to the Crows it was pretty exciting because he had an actual track record. Obviously because of who he is, but really because he had been to the grand final a few times and understood what it took.'

That very awareness of standards made Blight wary of the playing group he was inheriting. He knew it had been fractured by two unhappy years under Shaw and a fundamental lack of success since that high point of 1993 preliminary final day. Yet his coaching experience at Woodville and Geelong prepared him well for the first player gathering. 'His first meeting with the players wasn't even an introductory sort of thing—he outlined his game plan entirely,' John Reid said. 'He had a whiteboard and he explained his thinking and his philosophy. Trainers were included; everyone was in the room. He hit a mark straightaway because he was very clear and decisive, even uncomplicated, but a big difference to what they had been used to. The respect from the group was immediate.

'You could see it on their faces: "This is Malcolm Blight saying this, shit, he's dinkum about it". These kids were looking at him. He's just a normal bloke, but they were looking at him like a god.'

Simon Goodwin sat in that room, captivated. Taken eighteenth overall in the 1996 pre-season draft, Goodwin was a product of South Adelaide Football Club; he brought height and mobility that would make him one of the club's all-time great players across

275 games, plus respect that would earn him the captaincy late in his career. In 1997, Goodwin was green, but he was immediately attracted to the uncomplicated Blight style. 'In the first two weeks you certainly knew straightaway you were going back to the basics of football,' he said. 'The fundamentals, all the things you sort of take for granted. Straightaway this focus was on those things, which was refreshing. He was a great teacher. The height of the drop punt, kick it a metre above the guy's head. Why you should wear your socks up, in case you got a sprig mark and it got infected. Everything had a reason, all those finer details of the skill of playing the game.'

With the departure of captain Tony McGuinness, Bickley was appointed skipper. Like younger teammate Goodwin, he sensed a buzz around the rooms from day one of the Blight tenure. 'From that first session it was apparent things were different,' Bickley said. 'There were his rules, he was essentially saying, "I've got a tried and tested game plan, I know it works. If you follow it, I guarantee you'll have success." The players were crying out for something to attach themselves to in a united front, because it had been a bit fractured in the past few years. We instantly warmed to that notion.

'Plus, he mixed really well with the players and was relaxed with any sort of person. Patsy was fantastic about getting the partners to socialise … Cornes and Shaw were teetotallers, not particularly social people, but now the club was probably functioning as well socially as it ever had. And that makes a difference.'

Before footballs, there was running. Just as Blight had implemented a gruelling pre-season on his arrival at Kardinia Park, a decade later he did the same thing at Adelaide. Assisting him this time was Neil Craig, a 321-game veteran from Norwood, Sturt and North Adelaide and a South Australian state-of-origin captain. Craig—who would later become Adelaide head coach, in 2004—had coached the Redlegs from 1991 to 1995; importantly, he had compiled more than fifteen years in sports science with elite athletes, including Australian Olympic teams. As Blight said, 'Neil added expertise to my gut feel. He put numbers to it'.

Both men agreed on one thing: get miles into the players' legs. Somewhere, Bart Cummings was nodding.

'The time trials, the five one-Ks, we transported all that from Geelong,' said Blight, a self-confessed 'B-grade trainer who did enough to get through'.

'Neil added his flavour; it was all about getting them fit, running them hard early. The balls come out when they're fit. When you start kicking footies early in the pre-season, and there is chasing the footy, blokes get thighs and groins [injuries]. You chase the footy honestly, that's what you do, and that's when you get hurt because you're not prepared. So get miles in your legs first.'

As the pre-season unfolded, Blight began to recognise something in himself. A handful of years out of the game had not only re-energised him, but might have even mellowed the man. Not long after the squad commenced kicking drills, five or six players had forgotten to bring their boots for a session. Once upon a time such an oversight would have solicited a Blight tirade about discipline. Now, he thought more carefully about his response.

The entire playing group that night closed training with a stint of 'air cycling'—essentially lying on your back circling your legs as if riding an imaginary bicycle upside down. Blight started tapping players on the shoulder, allowing them blessed relief from an exercise that deadens the legs. In rapid succession he released about thirty-three players to the showers, and it was quickly apparent that only those in runners, not boots, continued those painful arcs in the air. 'Then I said to Neil, "Everyone else has gone in, these blokes are doing better than anyone. I reckon they should do a bit more." Their legs were getting pretty heavy now, even with sandshoes on. I didn't mention boots or runners, not a word. Eventually we stopped them, but we never had a problem with boots again. I reckon ten years earlier I would have screamed hell out of them. What a waste of energy.'

The coach set about determining the level of talent at his disposal. There was the exposed form of the veterans: Bickley was a deserving leader; Tony Modra was coming off a 75-goal season; Darren Jarman was a sublime, experienced talent. Shaun Rehn would return from a knee reconstruction early in that 1997 season, while Nigel Smart and Ben Hart were defenders with 100 games behind them, around whom Blight could anchor his back line.

One of the coach's pre-season tasks was to take Bickley for a stroll along the River Torrens to discuss the captaincy. Blight believed Bickley was 'a good citizen', a logical replacement for Tony McGuinness and an ally in the playing group if he needed one. 'Mark was the sort of person we needed,' the coach explained. 'He didn't make excuses; if he played poorly he played poorly. If a teammate came to him about what the coach was doing, he'd say, "Well, go talk to the coach or do something about it".'

As he walked the Torrens banks, Bickley considered the path he had taken. The last player included on the Crows' original 1991

THE MESSIAH STRIKES

list—he was the fifty-second selected—was now chosen to lead the team. 'I wasn't the best player in the team, but maybe the most sensible, solid and consistent,' he reflected. 'Malcolm was big on consistency. I was pretty calm about it, but inside I was stoked, that *Malcolm Blight* thought enough of me to make me his first captain at Adelaide. It was the start of a really strong relationship that we had.

'Blighty pointed out that the most important thing was to remain what you are, keep leading by example. He had no expectations other than that. No pressure to be a great player, it was just everything that Malcolm put in place, especially those team rules; I was always trying to police them as best I could on and off the ground.'

By Round 1, the consensus in the group was that the Crows' identity had been restored. Even in his first months, the Blight charisma and Reid pragmatism provided cohesion in a unit that had lacked unity. 'To be honest, I don't think there were too many groups within the club that were happy, and we're talking about guys at very different stages of their career,' Bickley said. 'The older guys knew their time had come, guys like Andrew Jarman, [Wayne] Weidemann, all of those who left when Malcolm arrived. Then there was the middle-age group of players like me, we were seeing the years ticking away without success. And the younger guys hadn't been developed at all.'

If the Crows were going to succeed, said Blight, it was this younger group who would take them there.

*   *   *

247

The irony of Neil Craig now being an insider at the Adelaide Football Club did not escape a number of observers … even his senior coach. During his five years as head coach of Norwood, Craig had been a Crows antagonist, arguing against his club being partially used as a reserves team for the AFL organisation. Of course, every SANFL team confronted the same scenario, as AFL-listed players not included in the Crows' twenty-one had natural allegiances with their original local club, or were assigned one.

While SANFL clubs were gently nudged to utilise Crows-listed talent in a role to suit the AFL entity, teams like Norwood would go about their own business. If the issue frustrated Blight, he tried to ignore it, preferring to deal one-on-one with his players. 'What I told the lads was, "If you're going as hard as you can, I'll assess you. I don't have to assess anyone else out there, just you. You're my player." That's why I pick an Andrew Eccles out of the seconds at Sturt. I can't control where he played there, so I just assess what I see.'

In Round 1, 1997, the Crows hosted Brisbane. They kicked 20 goals and won by 36 points. Young midfielder Brett James played among his best games for the club, dishing out 26 handballs as he collected three Brownlow Medal votes. Teammate Tyson Edwards must have looked on longingly. 'Tyson was typical of a lot of players on that list, blokes who hadn't gone to the next level,' Blight said. 'I was chatting to him and he admitted he had never got three votes, ever, in a game of footy, from junior days to playing with West Adelaide. He was serious; I couldn't believe it. I couldn't teach him to kick or mark any better; he had beautiful skills. He had to believe in himself.'

THE MESSIAH STRIKES

Edwards played the first thirteen games of the 1997 season before returning to West Adelaide. He languished for seven weeks in the SANFL. 'Then in the paper he got three votes,' Blight said. 'I got it blown up and put in his locker: "T Edwards, three votes". I said, "You're in next week." He was off: he went on to play 300 great games.'

Blight laughed when recalling the story. 'If I'd known that earlier, I would have paid one of the journos to give him three votes.'

It was typical of a season in which an experienced coach searched for ways to make his new charges click both individually and as a team. Sometimes it worked. Sometimes, as he discovered in Round 2, it didn't.

The headline following the Crows' visit to the MCG in Round 2 should have focused on yet another disappointing effort away from Football Park. Richmond led all day to win by 28 points. Instead, the media post-match zeroed in on Blight's press conference, in which he labelled the efforts of ruckman David Pittman 'pathetic'.

Pittman was twenty-eight, and that Saturday afternoon was playing his seventy-seventh game. He was hardly a raw rookie, and his failure to register a statistic in the first quarter raised Blight's ire. He was injured not long after, and closed the game without touching the football—sum total for the afternoon: five hit-outs—and Blight let him have it. Twice.

'Straight after the game on the ground I did an interview with Neil Kerley,' he said, 'and I gave David a burst but I talked about the first quarter. When I did the press interview later I left out the bit about the first quarter … I really went too far.'

249

Looking on that day was Goodwin, who had badly torn a quadriceps muscle in Round 1 and would miss thirteen weeks. 'That was pretty confronting for David,' Goodwin said of the Blight criticism. 'For the rest of the team it was Blighty trying to push the right buttons. I don't think the players saw it as a negative; he was quite apologetic in the end, but it was such a public comment.'

Captain Bickley chose not to get involved. 'Pitto is a really strong character, we sort of knew he would be okay.'

The 'Pathetic Pittman' wash-up threatened to undo a lot of the goodwill Blight had established in the previous months. He made sure to chase the ruckman on the Monday following the game, the media having pounced on the issue that morning. 'David and I later sat down and had a really good chat,' Blight said.

Pittman presented a simple scenario to his coach. 'If that's what you really think, and right now in the cold light of day you think I'm pathetic, I'm happy to walk away because I don't want to waste my time here,' he said.

Blight was forced to backpedal, and was happy to do so. 'I apologised to David,' he said. 'It read as though he'd been no good for all that time, and that wasn't fair. From that day onwards, every time he went up in the ruck, he played as though his life depended on it. And because he could play key defender he became a super important player in our team. With Rehn coming back it meant we had a really good duo.'

The Crows blew a 17-point half-time lead against Carlton the following week, losing by 28 points at Princes Park. Just as they could be formidable at home, a malaise seemed to strike them down as they headed out Sir Donald Bradman Drive to the domestic airline terminal. From the day they lost that 1993 elimination final at the MCG to the late Sunday afternoon when they departed Princes Park after yet another away loss, the Crows had played 35 games away from Football Park. They had won five of them.

At 1–2, with two road losses, Blight did not like what he saw. It was not simply a difficulty in adjusting to life on the road— travel seemed to introduce unnecessary stress into the routine. 'But Blighty couldn't give a rat's,' football manager John Reid said. 'He just tried to make sure we went with the flow and it made a huge difference to the playing group. Previously there was almost this paranoia about coming across to play in Melbourne.'

As a seasoned domestic traveller, having held national roles for substantial transport companies, Blight was accustomed to the unpredictability of flying. Yes, he was amazed by the fuss. 'They made a big deal of travel,' he said. 'I spent half my life in a plane, flying around for work. If the plane is ten minutes late, what are we going to do about it? Walk? So I was big on getting people to relax and worry about controlling what you can control. It was all blown out of proportion: "The plane is late, it's a conspiracy by the Victorians!" My attitude? Who cares? If people around you are on edge all the time, eventually you get on edge, so it wasn't healthy.'

Having stumbled out of the gate in his first season with Adelaide, Blight had other things to worry about rather than flight schedules. Round 4, for instance. And Port Adelaide Power.

* * *

It did not help that the meeting between Adelaide and Port Adelaide was declared the Showdown, a brand bestowed on the local derby rivalry that remains today. But whatever label was placed on this game, it could not have hyped the contest any more than it already was.

Port Adelaide had endured a testing start to its inaugural AFL season. The Power had confronted the other Magpies, Collingwood, in Round 1 at the MCG and were humbled by 79 points. In their home debut against Essendon they fell by 33 points, but in Round 3 they broke through to beat Geelong by more than 6 goals. Blight recalls the atmosphere in Adelaide that week being akin to something far greater than a cross-town rivalry. This was war ... and it was one he refused to buy into.

'I used to barrack for Port Adelaide, so the hatred that the whole Crows camp had—and it was real—well, that just wasn't in me,' he said, to this day amazed by the enmity the Crows' front office had for their cross-town rivals. 'And I'm talking real hate—it was incessant all week. That week was as big as any grand final I've been in, and I've been in ten.'

The distraction was clearly proving overwhelming, and the coach knew it. 'If I had a diary, early in the week I would have written, "We're in trouble here".'

'The build-up was unbelievable,' added John Reid. 'Actually, half the supporters would *rather* win a Showdown than a grand final.'

The Power jumped Blight's men, but not before defender Rod Jameson jumped Port opponent Scott Cummings. As if the Football Park cauldron was not sufficiently aflame, Jameson and Cummings exchanged punches before the first bounce—it earned Jameson a three-week holiday courtesy of the tribunal, and sent the 47,256 fans into a frenzy. It also inspired Port Adelaide, who drew away as the Sunday afternoon wore on. The Power led by 3 goals at half-time and 33 points at the final change.

'We were terrible,' Blight said. 'At three-quarter time I was pretty rational. I like the ball to get to centre half-forward; going wide annoyed me. But we'd gone away from that. So Jason McCartney, I put him at centre half-forward and said, "You work in this area here: when we get the ball, don't go more than twenty-five metres either side of the middle. The rest of you, just start running, take them on".'

Adelaide kicked 6 goals to 2 in the final term. While Blight's charges came home strongly, the final margin of defeat, 11 points, was flattering. Bickley recalls the long, dejected walk across the turf. 'It was almost unfathomable that they beat us,' the captain said. 'Walking off the ground it felt like the world was caving in.'

As the final siren sounded, Crows CEO Bill Sanders was standing alongside his Power counterpart, Brian Cunningham. The pair parted ways, Cunningham to the winning presentation and Sanders to fight his way to the rooms. 'As I got to the race, people were converging on it, and I was thinking something was happening there,' he said. 'What was happening was me! I got abused like I'd kicked the winning goal for Port. "Hey Sanders, get Ben Hart out here, the weak so and so …" I looked up, and this joker spat through the wire at me. I went after him, the crowd parted like I was Moses, and this bloke took off. That gives you a sense of the feeling in that rivalry.'

Blight confirms there were tears in the room after the game, describing the aftermath as unlike anything he had ever seen. 'And that includes the rooms of losing grand finals.'

253

MALCOLM BLIGHT

When Bickley entered the rooms, he was expecting a Blight savaging. 'He had a lot of pride, and I thought it might have been pricked by what happened that day.'

Blight chose to focus on some positives of the last thirty minutes. 'Amongst all that, I praised Jason McCartney because we'd had a good last quarter,' he said. 'But when I look back at the tape, Jason did not touch the ball. All we did was kick it in his general area.'

Blight then hatched a plan. What he did in the next forty-eight hours would change the course of the Crows' destiny, and in some respects alter football history.

* * *

When the Adelaide Crows sat down for their review of the Showdown loss, they were uncertain what to expect. Their new coach was not yet present, and they noticed it was not simply players called into this meeting on the Monday afternoon. Some front office staff were present, as were several board members, plus club trainers and football manager John Reid.

Blight then walked in, deliberately late. Knowing he had the room's attention, he strolled to the whiteboard and drew the number eighteen on it. Nothing else. Then he turned to the group. 'What does this mean?' he said.

Silence.

Reid recalled what happened next. 'Malcolm just quietly and casually said, "Boys, there are eighteen games to go. Let's not get hung up over this one".'

To further break the ice, Blight showed a tape of Rod Jameson jumping over a pack 'like a swan dive, schoolboy stuff, to get at

254

Cummings,' Blight said. 'Rod got reported for swinging 100 times at Scotty Cummings. Everyone laughed at the tape, then we sent the boys out to train. The whole thing took three minutes. Trust me, I was ready to kill fifty-eight people and had a thousand notes on what went wrong but we had eighteen games to go. If I've done anything in football, I remember that for being a really pressured situation and what I did freed everyone up.'

The significance of that brief meeting is not lost on any of those who attended, or on those who were observing Adelaide from a distance. Commentator Bruce McAvaney's self-confessed fascination with Blight was then in an early but healthy state, and he had a strong sense of the crossroads the club had reached. 'The Crows were in disarray after the Showdown loss,' McAvaney said. 'It could have been a crippling loss because it's hard to describe what it meant to both clubs … It was a grand final in May. I thought, "That's the end of them," but he managed to pick them up.'

If morale had climbed up off the dressing-room floor, it did not seem likely to improve enough to resurrect a 1–3 season that now faced a trip to Princes Park to meet the Western Bulldogs. The Crows had lost eleven consecutive times at that venue; in the seasons that followed, they would not win there again until 2001. But this one afternoon in 1997 turned a season around. Adelaide roared to an entirely unexpected 50-point win, inspired by Bickley and Mark Ricciuto, plus an 8-goal performance from spearhead Tony Modra.

'God, we hadn't even won a game in Melbourne for two years,' Bickley said. 'Put it this way, not many people tipped us. But that day set us up, we were away.'

The Crows did not win a week later, but Blight extracted a lesson that proved invaluable as the season evolved. Visiting Collingwood's famous Victoria Park for only the Crows' sixth and final home and away match at the venue—the Magpies played just two games at their traditional home that season, and no more after 1999—Adelaide lost by a single point, but a key position defender was born.

Peter Caven had played fifty-six games in five seasons at Fitzroy and Sydney before Adelaide signed him in 1996. He played twenty games in his first year but had failed to lock down a role or a future. Then his new coach rolled the dice in search of a defensive option on Magpie forward Anthony Rocca. 'I looked around the room and thought, "Who can we play on Rocca?" who was a giant. We had all these injuries and the next best option was Peter,' Blight said. 'He'd been back and forth to Sturt [in the SANFL] and neither he nor I seemed to know where he fit. So I just said to him, "Someone's got to play on Rocca, Peter, I'm going to play you at centre half-back. Here's the rule: in general play, read the footy, but when there's a stationary situation—a ball-up, boundary throw-in, whatever—you play in front. If he takes mark of the year on you fifteen times, I don't care, you'll be playing again next week. But I'll bet out of the packs the ball will fall short." He did exactly what he needed to do.'

Rocca kicked a single goal and took two marks all day. Caven had 21 touches and ran off his man to kick a goal of his own. A simple act of faith in a player and a role had proven Blight's hunch worthwhile.

'I always thought it was one of the best coaching tools, telling a player he had a role and he would stay there no matter what,'

Blight said. 'I actually said to [Geelong forward] Barry Stoneham, "You're going to play centre half-forward for the next eight weeks because we need one. Get used to it." You know what you have to say to that bloke next time you see him? "G'day, Baz." That's all. Players don't need much, particularly at the bottom clubs, to get them going. "Lenny Hayes, you're going to be ruck-rover for the next month, I don't care how you go." They just want to know what they're doing.

'The thing with Peter was a bit of a fluke but that was necessity. From then on he was on the board every week, centre half-back was his. He was super fit and he and Ben Hart were running off their blokes. By halfway through the third quarter, the other blokes were tonguing.'

The Crows lost at Victoria Park by a single point, but the football gods then handed them a schedule that would allow Caven and his teammates to settle. A crushing home win over third-placed Essendon saw them sneak into the top eight, then four consecutive dates with teams out of the eight (including the bottom three teams) saw them string five straight wins together. After their 1–3 start, they were now 7–4, and the group were gaining confidence in themselves and their coach. Blight was at pains to reiterate to his men that it was a long season that constantly challenged. He claims credit for being the first coach to publicly compare the season to a marathon race rather than a sprint. 'And I've never seen the bloke run out of the stadium first win the marathon.'

'One of his great traits was that he knew which buttons to push for which players in the right environment to maximise their performance,' Goodwin said. 'He understood his players so well.

When to berate and challenge, whether it was a phone call, in the team meeting or half-time, he had a great feeling of how to maximise each individual.

'You knew what you could do and not do. For instance, you got the chance to kick a torpedo once a game. Stuff it up and put it away for the day. If you got the ball in the centre square you had to kick it forward. If you kick it sideways you might as well keep running to the bench, because you're coming off. And he was strict on that. And he certainly let you know if you went against some of the rules.'

Bickley concurred. 'On game day he was in your face,' the captain said. 'Non-negotiables: step outside those parameters and you copped a spray. But at the same time he always had the ability to win the players back. Quite often when we were doing our review after a poor performance he'd say, "That was a terrible weekend. You guys played poorly, as a coach I coached really poorly—I came in at half-time and didn't address what I needed to. Let's just look at the positive stuff and move on to next week".'

One player making more regular appearances was Shaun Rehn. After enduring back-to-back seasons of knee reconstructions, Rehn made his 1997 debut during that win at Princes Park over the Bulldogs, playing a handful of minutes off the bench. His value could not be overstated—an All-Australian in 1994, he was gradually increasing his game time as the season unfolded. 'And every week he got five per cent better,' Blight said. 'We used him pretty well, each week just a bit more. He was cherry ripe by the end.'

The Crows by now had momentum, though Blight was sensing an impasse of sorts with Modra. If Ablett was the enigmatic star

THE MESSIAH STRIKES

of his Geelong coaching days, Modra filled that role on a number of fronts in Adelaide, including having the undivided attention of a football-crazed city. 'When Tony was "on", he had some magic about him,' Blight said. 'His recovery wasn't great, but gee he could mark it. He was really exciting.' Modra that year had kicked 50 goals through to Round 11, but his form tapered to such an extent that he finished the season with 84 goals, including finals. The coach believes it was not form or injury but distraction that took the edge off his performance. 'Tony used to come into my office every Monday and we'd have a talk,' Blight said. 'Then something happened mid-season. He went to the club and said, "I want to be a one-club player, I want to sign for another three or four years." He still had eighteen months to go on his contract. The club chose to wait, so there was this frustration for him because he didn't get the offer he wanted.

'Look, he should have waited until the end of the year. He stopped coming into the office. He wasn't happy, and his form gradually petered out a bit.'

So, too, did the general form of the team.

From 7–4 and second place at the halfway mark of the season, they scrapped their way to a 13–9 home and away season end record, good enough for fourth but seemingly a long way behind the competition benchmarks, St Kilda and Geelong.

Their trip to Kardinia Park in Round 13 had done little to make them think they were in the league of the competition leaders. The Cats kicked 6.3 to 3 behinds in the first quarter, establishing a margin that rarely looked less than comfortable for the home team, and was just shy of 10 goals by the final siren. The afternoon was memorable for two reasons: when Blight crossed the ground en route to the coach's box for the first time, the grandstand stood as one and gave him a standing ovation. It seemed his time at Kardinia Park, and the excitement he'd brought to Geelong, had not been forgotten. And, later that day, defender Ben Hart received a promotion.

The Crows had stayed in Geelong the previous night, leaving them with a short bus ride to the ground. What took place in those minutes did not please the coach. 'Some people reckon you can judge a team by the mood in the rooms before the game, but usually I don't agree with that,' Blight said. 'On this day, though, I knew we weren't switched on. It was really noisy and almost frivolous in the bus on the way to the ground. There was just a spectrum of noise, laughs and giggles. We're going into battle; there needs to be more focus than that.

'We got badly beaten, and I'm sure a fair bit of paint came off the walls after the game. I wasn't happy. That bus trip [to the ground] had driven me nuts. So I made Ben Hart the Bus Monitor. This wasn't fussing over travel; this was about preparing for the game. When anyone came on the bus, he would read the rules to them. Any more of that on the bus again, and you'll be out. As a new player came into the team, "Ben, you sit on the bus with him. Tell him the rules".'

Bickley believed the chemistry in the playing group was far superior to that of twelve months earlier; winning helped, of course, but the passing of the leadership baton seemed to be valuable. The departure of Tony McGuinness, Chris McDermott and Andrew Jarman had forced that handover, perhaps even by design. 'Some

THE MESSIAH STRIKES

people thought Blighty was trying to assert his control over the team immediately by getting rid of the blokes who might have had the power in the locker room,' McAvaney said.

Those exits opened doors for others. 'In a lot of ways we had been really comfortable letting the older guys do all the work; we went along for the ride,' Bickley said of the 1995–96 Crows. 'Malcolm freshened up the entire group. Because I wasn't a standout player I felt my style had to be a bit more inclusive, so I brought in another five or six senior guys and said, "If we're going to be any good, we have to take responsibility for the group." We ended up having a really good working group. Rehn, Nigel Smart, Ricciuto, Pittman and Darren Jarman.'

In Round 22, the Crows squandered a 31-point half-time lead over Essendon at Princes Park. The defeat cost them third place, and Goodwin remembers the disappointment. 'All year, Blighty had been challenging us just to play finals, then we get in this great position and blow it,' he said.

But Blight's challenge had been met: after an absence of four years, Adelaide would play September football in 1997. The list hardly seemed prepared for it, having won only six of the last eleven games, but the coach reached into his positivity quiver. 'Well done, fellas,' he said. 'You're in the finals.'

He then set about explaining September, a conversation John Reid remembers well. 'Malcolm sat them down and said, "Boys, you can really get hung up on this stuff. It is exciting, we're playing finals, but you don't have to grow two heads, or an extra arm. You can cope with what you've got. The less fuss and bother we make about it, the better we'll be".'

261

17

SEPTEMBER 1997

IF MALCOLM BLIGHT had learned anything in his first home and away season coaching at Football Park, it was the ability to 'kill' games of football when he had to. If the Crows had to kick into the wind in the first quarter, they simply turned the game into a stalemate, burying the ball in the dead pocket and maintaining possession for as long as possible. It did not make for attractive football.

'We were very disciplined with it,' Blight said. 'Whenever we lost the toss we would do that.'

On the biggest day of the season to date, the coach changed his mind.

In round one of the finals, Adelaide would host a West Coast that had won an equal amount of games in the home and away season. They had met just once that year, on a Saturday night at Football Park in early July, and the Crows had handed out a

SEPTEMBER 1997

77-point thrashing. Blight, then, should have been confident, but he decided to deviate from what had worked that year.

'I don't know why I decided to do this against the Eagles, who I still had nightmares about because of my Geelong days, but I got Bickley and Nigel Smart together and said, "Listen boys, you know how, all year, if we lose the toss we push it wide? We're not going to do that today. If we lose the toss, we're going to take them on and kick goals into the wind".'

The game had been delayed from the previous night due to Diana, Princess of Wales' funeral. On this Sunday afternoon, Bickley recalls a 6- or 7-goal breeze was blowing, and now his coach was asking him to mix things up. 'Malcolm came up to me before the game and said, "I've got this feeling. Because we've had to wait an extra day, everyone will be toey." That was his thinking.'

The Eagles won the toss. Adelaide attacked. And the Crows led 4.4 to 3.1 at quarter-time. The match was a slog, but the visitors didn't threaten as Bickley's men won by 33 points in front of a rapturous Football Park sellout. The captain was a star, while the Rehn–Pittman ruck combination was overwhelming against a team whose ruck position was its glaring weakness. The absence of Mark Ricciuto through injury—he had broken down in Round 22—did not detract from the midfield as the Crows booked their berth in the semi-final round. It was here, recounted Goodwin, that the coach came into his own.

'I think the prominent thing for me in 97 was how relaxed he was throughout that whole campaign,' Goodwin said. 'He tried to keep himself relaxed to keep the playing group relaxed. It was a young group. And it helped that there didn't seem to be any expectation because I don't think our supporters genuinely thought we could win it.

'Malcolm was great about working through the finals. We'd win and have some fun with it, say, "We'll get another invitation from the AFL to play this week, it'll come on the fax machine on Monday".'

Sure enough, on the Monday, Blight was wielding the fax, waving it in front of his players. He laughs at the memory. 'I'd say, "Look at this, fellas, we've been invited back again",' he said. 'My point was that whether you're the top team or eighth team, you can only win one final in a row. And we had a saying: "Shh. We're schneakin' up on them".'

The truth is that each and every Adelaide player and official felt that by simply winning a final the Crows had overachieved. 'Deep down we probably thought we might not quite get to the grand final; each finals win was a bonus for that team,' Reid admitted.

An anomaly in the finals system of the time guaranteed the Crows a home final against Geelong the following week. The Cats were fuming—they had won two more home and away season games than Adelaide, but had fallen in the qualifying final to the reigning premiers, North Melbourne. As a result, they were forced to travel to Football Park, though for much of the contest it seemed not likely to matter: Geelong led early and were 2 goals up late in the third quarter when their versatile forward Leigh Colbert ran back to take a courageous mark with the flight of the ball.

Replays from any angle confirm it was a mark. With three-quarter time beckoning, Colbert would shoot from about 35 metres out to put his team 3 goals to the better in a low-scoring game.

SEPTEMBER 1997

But, caught out of position, umpire Grant Vernon did not pay the mark. It is a decision that grates Cats fans to this day. Blight's Crows ran over the top of Geelong in the final term, holding on by 8 points.

Rehn was superb, covering for an early injury to Pittman. In his 150th AFL game, Darren Jarman led his team in possessions in a game notable for incredibly low statistics, while Nigel Smart, Ben Hart and Rod Jameson continued to provide the defensive presence that had made the Crows' back line such a weapon. Crucially, for the second straight week the Crows had finished with more run in their legs. The drive of Blight and the science of fitness adviser Neil Craig were arguably now reaping their biggest rewards—a month from the finals, Craig had introduced an increased workload to 'top up' for September. 'The work he had done in training the mind through the conditioning work gave us that belief,' Goodwin said. 'Okay, we're doing extra running four weeks out from finals to give us that belief in September. Maybe it even had a placebo effect, tricked your mind. Whether there was any science behind it, I don't know, but we were running games out really well.'

That Monday, Blight waved another fax in front of his players. 'Guess what? We've been invited back!' he said gleefully.

This time, it would be a preliminary final.

'Every week of those finals, it seemed like, "Well, that was enough, we've done well to get this far," because our expectations just weren't that high,' said CEO Bill Sanders. 'But Malcolm kept pushing and pushing in his own way.'

*   *   *

When Simon Goodwin retired at the end of 2010, he reflected on his 275-game career and settled on the standout win of those fourteen seasons. It came on 20 September 1997. 'That was the one win you thought, "Wow". It was probably the best game I ever played in.'

By this stage of the season, Goodwin had considered that fate might be playing the Crows a strong hand. Getting two consecutive home finals and the Colbert mark not being paid had instilled a sense of destiny in the Adelaide playing group. But by half-time of his team's MCG preliminary final date with the Western Bulldogs, the feel-good story looked to have come to an end.

The Bulldogs looked too accomplished for the visitors. The margin was 31 points, although the Crows' inaccuracy (they kicked 0.7 in the first quarter) suggested they were getting plenty of the ball—they had simply squandered their chances. 'We knew we were in strife but they weren't hurting us on the scoreboard as much as they should have,' Reid said. 'The further the game went, the whole box felt we were in this game. They were burning their chances; ours would come. There was that period in the game they dominated and they couldn't put the score on the board.'

Still, the Crows had their issues. Modra tore up his knee in the opening quarter—he would not play again until Round 16 the following year. With Ricciuto gone for the season, it meant Adelaide was missing its two 1997 All-Australians. It was now that Blight played a card he had slipped up his sleeve all those years earlier when he was coaching Geelong. Call it a basic coaching tenet, but one that only experience can teach.

'Being involved in grand finals when you lost, it was not about mistakes, it was about learning,' he said. 'One of the issues in grand finals was when your midfielders didn't play well you had nowhere to go. No disrespect, but Couchy and Bairstow struggled at half-back, Buddha could play there a little bit, but then there was no one to then go and take their places. They couldn't go somewhere else except maybe a wing. They were all natural on-ballers.

'There was never going to be another on-baller I coached who couldn't play half-back or in defence. When they're not having a good day, you could do something else with them. Edwards, McLeod, Ricciuto, Goodwin, Bickley, all of those guys had to play half-back. I don't care if you're Chris Judd or Gary Ablett junior, I would never let a bloke play midfield for the whole of his career. Because, grand final day, if they play poorly what do you do with them? In Adelaide, the first day I spoke I said, "Look, I've been through three grand finals and lost. They were no player or individual's fault, probably my fault for not thinking of this earlier. If you're not happy with it, piss off". That was in front of the board, playing group, every staff member. From here on, don't think you're going to be a star in the midfield without playing on someone before you go in there.'

In essence, Blight was crystallising the depth of midfield rotation that typifies the modern game. He had tried to install the system in Geelong but believed that by the time he arrived the list was too mature—too much trying to teach old dogs new tricks. In Adelaide, he was working with a compliant playing group that revered their coach. 'I mean, Malcolm was my boyhood idol. Whatever he wanted, I did,' Bickley said.

Blight slipped Andrew McLeod into the centre square. At the same time, he moved Troy Bond into the centre, and a fortunate turn of events might have decided a football game. 'Because we were struggling, I put Bond onto the ball at the same time as McLeod', Blight said. 'Troy got a couple of kicks before Andrew got going, so they put [Bulldogs tagger Jose] Romero onto him. It freed up McLeod, who started to control the game. Jarman got going, good players were touching the ball and we were away.'

The football world knew Jarman's qualities: he had played for Hawthorn before coming to the Crows. Anyone east of Bordertown, however, was not as well acquainted with Andrew McLeod.

'It was the first time we'd played him there in public view, a big stage,' Blight said. 'I can't believe the opposition left McLeod pretty much alone at half-back. He sliced teams up with his run and kick, and we got away with it all year. A couple of times during the year we tried him on the ball for five or ten minutes and he could clearly do it, so we put it away for later. Because we were so far down we had to change the midfield. That was where we had a chance to change the game. That was the bonus I had up my sleeve. It was still up to the players, not me, but the team got some wheels on.'

McLeod simply kept getting first hands on the ball. Another standout that day was Kane Johnson, the maligned kid who had seemed unlikely to cut it when Blight arrived. Caven was a strong contributor, while defenders Smart and Jameson both slipped forward to kick 2 goals each. And, ultimately, Jarman's class in the forward line was making the difference on a day when neither side could finish. 'Having someone with such clinical finishing made you walk tall, made the work up the ground worthwhile,' Bickley said. 'At five goals down at half-time, there were enough of us still around from the 93 game that we knew there was still plenty of footy left to play. But that was an amazing half of footy.'

SEPTEMBER 1997

The Crows kicked 8.10 to 3.7 after half-time. Just as Adelaide had wasted its chances in the first quarter, the Dogs failed to take countless opportunities in the final term, kicking 6 behinds of their own. The last came in a goal square scramble in the final minute, Footscray teammates Chris Grant and Paul Hudson scrabbling for the same ball and Grant missing from short range, albeit under huge pressure. That moment haunts Dogs players and supporters to this day.

The team of destiny survived, if only just, squeezing past the Bulldogs by 2 points. 'Once the siren went, the sobering thought was that we had a grand final next week,' Blight recalled.

Equally sobering was the news that Modra would be missing from the grand final. While the coach had slightly fallen out of love with his star forward, century goalkickers were not easily replaced; Modra had kicked exactly 400 goals in his previous five seasons, at a highly respectable 4 goals per game. But Blight harked back to his final season at Woodville, after which management had briefly tried to convince him to return for one more year. He had kicked 126 goals, but believed anyone could succeed if the structure was in place, so he shuffled through the ranks for a Modra replacement.

Early in the week, he told his match committee that defender Shane Ellen would go to the attacking goal square. 'Were you going to get a Modra who could take a specky three storeys high? No,' Blight explained. 'But we would get a player who could lead a bit, take a mark and go back and kick a goal. There's always one of those somewhere. I'd seen Shane play full-forward for South Adelaide for about a quarter one day. It was windy, a terrible day. He had about four chances with the wind, and none against it.

269

But he led out twice, took his mark, and maybe kicked 1.1. We'd been trying to find a spot for Shane and decided he had a nice pair of hands.'

Blight approached Ellen at a light training session on the Monday night. 'You can lead a bit, take a mark?' he asked rhetorically. 'You can kick all right?'

Ellen nodded, uncertain where the conversation was headed.

The coach slapped him heartily on the shoulder. 'Good,' Blight said. 'You can play full-forward then.'

'Then he looked back and said, "So, you've got a game",' Ellen said. 'I was never a certainty in the Crows side. Leading into the grand final, just to know that I was getting a game and starting on the ground, plus the freedom of full-forward, I was pretty happy.'

The simplicity of the message was designed to underplay the stage the team was about to confront. Ellen's captain received similar instructions. 'Once we got to the grand final he said, "Don't think about winning a grand final",' Bickley recalled. '"It's about getting out there and competing. If anyone talks about winning, kick them up the arse."'

* * *

When the Crows were playing in Melbourne, tradition dictated that, after the team meeting on game eve, management and coaches would gather in a nearby hotel for a quick beer. On grand final eve, 1997, Malcolm Blight informed his CEO, Bill Sanders, that he saw no point in breaking with that routine. 'I just thought, "No chance, there will be Crows supporters crawling all over town",' said Sanders. 'That wouldn't have been a good look.'

SEPTEMBER 1997

The group wandered up to the room of club official Terry Moore. As they reflected on what lay ahead, Sanders glanced over to the window. Blight, cigarette in hand, was gazing out across Melbourne.

'You right, mate?' Sanders offered.

'Yep,' replied Blight. 'I'm just not sure how we're going to win this game tomorrow.'

Sanders was rocked by the response, but he had grown used to mentally deflecting such Blightisms. 'We'll keep that inside this room, shall we?'

The coach's pessimism was founded on three factors: the form of the grand final opposition, St Kilda, the journey his own men had trodden to get there, and the doubts he was having about his own ability to defeat the footy gods.

For a start the top-of-the-ladder Saints had earned the double chance and therefore the week off. In contrast, the Crows would be playing finals for a fourth straight week. St Kilda had won nine consecutive games and won its two finals by a combined 77 points; Adelaide had ground through the second half of the season and barely scraped through its last two finals.

There was a further complication—Blight's teammate and friend from Arden Street days, Stan Alves, was St Kilda coach, and had developed a deep, talented squad. 'Stan had them playing really well,' Blight said. 'It was difficult to know where to concentrate on beating them, because whenever you discount anyone he's usually the one that hurts you.'

Blight barely slept this game eve, those doubts making for a fitful night. Having been to the mountain three times as a coach

271

and lost all three, he did not suspect those footy gods were about to end his heartbreak. 'I really felt I was going into my fourth grand final as a coach with no hope of winning it,' he said. 'Your mind does a lot of things to you. My dreams included being beaten by 49 goals—that one stood out. Ultimately we'd made it to a grand final with thirteen wins, so on the day I woke up thinking, "This could be [loss] number four". Of all my chances I thought we were least likely to win that final. It was an ordinary night's sleep: a four-time loser of grand finals, there are not too many of those around. It was a bit scary, actually.'

Yet there were positive signs hidden in the mist. For instance, the last team to defeat the Saints had been Adelaide, prevailing in Round 15 at Football Park. During grand final week, Blight had shown his men footage of that game, instilling hope in the playing group.

Ironically, given the club's previous travel pains, being on the road was now seen as a benefit. Their home town was predictably suffering from Crows-mania: shop windows and houses were daubed blue, red and gold; the newspapers carried grand final supplements every day; plane, bus and train bookings were sold out in hours; while the ultimate prize, a ticket to the game, was almost priceless in a literal sense—anyone lucky enough to have one was highly unlikely to part with it, no matter the offer. The club therefore welcomed the chance to escape the madness.

Bickley awoke on grand final morning and was presented with a good omen. 'Adelaide was crazy that week, but once we came over Thursday night we became isolated—all the distractions went away,' he said. 'I can remember turning the TV on Saturday

SEPTEMBER 1997

morning. Channel 7 was doing a live cross to the house shared by Aussie [Austinn] Jones, Tony Brown and Joel Smith. Here I am in my pyjamas, taking it easy, and these guys are trying to eat breakfast with a camera crew in their kitchen. Then they crossed to David Sierakowski's house, and he was there with his dad [Brian, who played in the Saints' 1966 premiership]. We just didn't get caught up in any of that; it made me feel like we had an advantage.'

Blight set about making the day as normal as possible, while working around the unique setting of a grand final. Only one Crows player had earned a premiership medal—Darren Jarman was a triumphant Hawk in 1991, though he had been quiet that day as the Hawks closed out a historic, sustained era of success. The coach's pre-match address was straightforward and instructive. 'There was no pump-up speech—I suppose Blighty knew by then we didn't need any extra motivation,' Bickley said.

Blight then addressed the day itself, concocting a strategy to ensure his players were not overwhelmed by the notoriously challenging pre-match build-up. Referring to the twenty-minute stretch between running onto the arena and the first bounce, he told his men to take it all in—take in the atmosphere and appreciate the day for its carnival appeal. 'Go out there, look around, soak it up, even look for where your family is sitting,' Blight instructed. 'Get all of that out of the way.'

As Bickley recounted, his coach then created a metaphorical switch to set the day alight. 'Blighty just said, "After the toss, Mark will come back to your huddle and have a few words to you, then he'll look up to me in the coach's box and put his hand up. That'll be the signal for you guys to turn on and be ready to play".'

Bickley cannot recall what his final words were to his men. As with most players to experience such a day, he has stored glimpses of the game in his memory, complemented by an overall emotion. 'We were okay early, but then [St Kilda forward] Barry Hall got off the chain for a bit,' he said. 'That was indicative of our year. We just hung in there and put pressure on.'

Hall was just twenty. Though he was to become a consistent goalkicker for more than a decade, he had kicked just 14 goals in fifteen games that season. Teammate Jason Heatley was a more traditional forward threat—he'd booted 73 goals that year—and the Saints' pairing was looking increasingly dangerous as the second quarter wore on. Robert Harvey and Nathan Burke were damaging (incredibly, those two earned more than a quarter of the Saints' entire kicks total that day), and Alves took his men to the rooms at half-time with the very real taste of the club's second-ever premiership. Ellen had kicked two important goals to keep the Crows within reach, but the margin was 13 points and momentum seemed to be running St Kilda's way.

As he wandered into the quiet MCG rooms at half-time, another of his dreams from the night before danced around in Malcolm Blight's mind. 'This is the truth, I had a dream about Darren Jarman in a grand final,' Blight said. 'I loved him around the middle because he was clever. So we ran him out of the centre square for his touch and smarts, then got him to run forward. Simon Goodwin came off the back of the square and basically onto the ball. No one picked it up except Leigh Matthews in the [commentary] call. Honestly, it came from a dream I had the night before.'

SEPTEMBER 1997

Goodwin remembers Blight being 'pretty animated' at the long change. 'He wanted to get a response from the group—I guess he felt we were shell-shocked in the first half and we were on the back foot the whole time. He said something like, "If you keep playing like this you're going to be opened up". So he threw the team around. Jarman started centre bounce then pushed forward. Shane Ellen went to half-back for a while, McLeod into the middle. Getting clever guys around the footy. Mainly, we needed to get more proactive.'

On reflection, Blight believes one of the strongest lessons the game has taught him took place at half-time of the 1992 grand final. His Geelong team had led by 12 points at the long change. 'This sounds easy to say now, but as a coach I'd rather be a goal down at half-time of a grand final, because it makes you really think about things,' he said. 'When you're two or three up, you don't change it because you might stuff things up … and you're thinking, "What are they going to do?" In 1992, we led by two goals and I did nothing, except wait for them to come at us. And they did.'

Having sent Jarman in for the bounce and Goodwin off the back of the square, 'Nigel Smart went forward on a young Max Hudghton. I told Nigel to stand near Jamie Shanahan, and it freed up Darren to get space when he slipped forward. Simon got seven or eight touches and set us up, and suddenly we were controlling the ball'.

Putting Jarman and Andrew McLeod into the centre square perfectly suited Blight's philosophy that no matter what was happening around the ground in a game of football, when the ball was bounced in the centre square it was a 50–50 contest. So put your best talent there. Having rearranged his team, Blight then sold a basic message to his team: 'You're a couple of goals down, win this quarter by a couple of goals,' the coach demanded, 'then I'll see you at three-quarter time.' It is one of Bickley's strongest memories of the day: 'It was all about bite-sized pieces'.

'And in that first five minutes after half-time we felt we were away,' Goodwin added.

In the sixty minutes that followed the long break, McLeod inked his name in the game's history. He would close his afternoon with 31 possessions, finding space wherever he liked. He took 11 marks that afternoon; no other player on the ground, *for either side*, took more than six. Less than two months past his twenty-first birthday, it was a rollicking, breathtaking coming-of-age for one of the game's greatest talents. 'No one really knew who Andrew was until that afternoon,' Blight said. 'Well, no one out of Adelaide.'

The Crows kicked 6 goals to 2 for the third quarter. At the last change, they led by 10 points. 'At three-quarter time Blighty said, "Now, you've got thirty minutes",' Bickley said. '"Just win the quarter and the premiership is yours." It was the first time he had ever mentioned winning.'

* * *

Malcolm Blight believes coaching has its place in the game, but talent shines through. 'The simplistic view is that coaching is overrated,' he said. 'Good players win games.'

Darren Jarman is more than a good player. His first grand final medal was earned off the back of a 41-goal season for the Hawks, although he gained only 5 possessions in an ordinary grand final

SEPTEMBER 1997

showing. Six years later, at age thirty, he was primed to share the premiership feeling with his Crows teammates. Blight's dream was playing out before the eyes of 98,828 fans. 'There was space for Darren because he was just running forward without a hard tag,' the coach said. 'Give a good player space and time and he'll hurt you. And Darren was a very good player.'

The fall guy for the quarter was Shanahan, a classic 192-centimetre full-back who played a serviceable 162 games of League football, all bar two for St Kilda. When Jarman slipped Tony Brown after the bounce and headed forward, Shanahan found himself lined up against a more nimble and gifted opponent, often one-out. Early in the final term, he found himself trapped on the wrong side of a forward line entry and gave away a free kick.

Jarman goal, his second.

Caven then burst clear of the last line of defence and took several bounces before finding Kim Koster. As Jarman stalled his lead he weaved around Shanahan, almost mesmerising the Saints' key defender. Finally, he broke as Shanahan lost his man. Lead, mark, goal. Textbook. His third.

Jarman then added 2 goals sharked in general traffic. If Shanahan had no chance in a one-on-one, he looked completely lost in traffic as the ball was contested on the ground. Jarman booted his fourth.

There were still ten minutes to play, but the Crows had blown the game open. Ellen then burst into an open goal to kick his fifth for the day, as unlikely a scenario as even Blight could have imagined; Ellen was playing his thirty-eighth AFL game and had kicked a total of 3 goals to that stage. He played another twenty-seven and managed just 8 more before injury and form ended his career after season 2000.

The Crows now held sway by 27 points. On the next forward entry, four men flew for the ball. The contested ball landed in Jarman's hands. He casually—seriously, watch the replay—snapped his fifth goal for the term, and sixth for the afternoon.

'That'll do!' yelled commentator McAvaney. 'That. Will. Do!'

Bickley watched his teammate with equal parts awe and delight. 'It was just one of those days where he just had the ball on a string', he said of Jarman. 'I've watched the game back a few times since and I remember Bruce McAvaney in his commentary saying, "That will do". And it did. When you watch it back we probably had the game won before that, but you don't feel that when you're out there playing your first grand final.'

With three seconds remaining on the clock, Nigel Smart drifted forward and, in McAvaney's words, 'put the icing on the cake'. The small pockets of Crows fans in the MCG were by now ecstatic, heartily belting out a theme song AFL fans would come to know much better in the coming year or so.

The ball returned to the centre square. When the siren sounded, the ball was in Andrew McLeod's hands. And the world was in those of his coach. The final margin was 31 points; Adelaide had kicked 8 straight goals in the final quarter to make the result decisive, but Blight had not been able to relax until deep into time-on. 'The margin got away from me a bit,' he said. 'I was surprised we won by six goals, I felt on the edge of my seat for the whole game. I'm sure I would have relaxed a bit earlier if I realised we were four or five goals up, but I didn't know.'

SEPTEMBER 1997

On the siren, he remained in the coach's box and hugged his support staff.

'[Carlton coach] Robert Walls once said it was relief,' he said of coaching of a premiership. 'For me, it was absolute, pure bloody joy. It was amazing; so were the days that followed. The cavalcade through the streets, the tickertape parade, fire hoses over the plane as we got back. For the first two or three days, no one's feet touched the ground, nor should they have.'

For all of the joy, Blight still found one aspect of the post-match celebrations odd. 'I hadn't spent a lifetime there [coaching Adelaide] so it was a surreal feeling. I'd have loved to have done it at Woodville or Geelong. And I was sharing it with these blokes I'd basically known for twelve months. By the end of a footy season you know blokes pretty well and you become family quickly, but it was still a bit strange.'

Not strange enough that he did not find time to kiss Simon Goodwin in the raucous dressing rooms. The youngster's journey had been remarkable. 'Leading into 97 in the pre-season period I didn't think I'd get a game,' he said. 'I only got my first trial game against Essendon in Alice Springs, two weeks before the season started. I had no idea where I would play, what role, I just lobbed on a half-back flank. And Blighty just made me believe in myself.'

Football manager John Reid then instigated what has become a grand final tradition. With the ground empty and the main lights dimmed, the Crows filed back onto the ground and gathered around the centre circle. Blight joined them, enjoying a beer and a cigarette. 'We put our arms around each other,' Bickley said. 'Then Malcolm spoke. "This feels so good, why don't we make a pact to

279

come back and be here next year?" We were living in the moment, he was thinking about 1998.'

It perfectly summarised an extraordinary season in the life of the Adelaide Football Club, and the football life of Malcolm Blight. 'We were looking for someone to cling to, someone with a track record to sell us hope', Bickley continued. 'Blighty was really clear in what he wanted to do. His rules were set in stone. There was no grey; it was black or white. We jumped in behind him and never missed a beat.'

18

BACK-TO-BACK

KEVIN SHEEDY IS credited with saying he enjoyed coaching
for the sum total of eight hours during his twenty-seven
years as head coach of Essendon. That was, Sheedy explained, the
two hours after each of his four successful Bomber trips to the
grand final. Then the reality of defending a premiership kicked in.

Sheedy was exaggerating. But his thoughts do correlate with a
saying about coaching that rings true: defeat is never fatal, success
is never final. I'm sure Malcolm Blight could empathise. Even in
the days that followed the Crows' historic win, he was beginning
to focus on a meeting that would take place in the middle of the
week. The match committee would sit down and assess the list for
1998 and, inevitably, a handful of players would have their careers
terminated.

'One of the hardest things after a grand final, win or lose, was
then going to a meeting to find out who you had to get rid of.
I struggled with that, always,' he said.

'By later that week I wanted to finish. I suppose I was like the dog that barked at the car finally catching the car, and I felt in a strange place, particularly after that Wednesday meeting. For all the celebrations, the realisation was that we had to do it again. It was awkward ... you were making decisions on people's lives.' Not one of the players who had figured in the premiership twenty-two was delisted or retired—Blight's senior list would return largely intact. Yet his lack of motivation was such that he felt a disconnect with the need to prepare for the 1998 season, and it concerned him deeply. 'There was a bit, or a lot, of "Can I still do it?" I sensed I had the know-how but not the enthusiasm.'

Late in the week, Blight broached the subject with close allies within the coaching circle. Both Neil Craig and close friend John Reid suggested that Blight take his customary break before Christmas—he would surely come back refreshed. After much soul-searching he returned after his break, not entirely refreshed but accepting that walking away after a single year in command was unacceptable. And he put his team to the torch.

'I was much harder on them in the 98 pre-season; that came from the 1990 lesson from Geelong,' Blight said, referring to the Cats' rapid decline from second to tenth after a rare grand final appearance and overly casual preparation for the following year's campaign. 'My message was, "They're coming after us, it's going to be harder".' With purpose renewed, Blight made another internal commitment that would come back to haunt his final season at Football Park.

'I decided that I wouldn't refer to the year before,' he said. 'I never said, "You're a premiership player, you should be playing better," and I consciously went out of my way not to do it. I reckon we all knew we had some legs to go a bit further and give ourselves another opportunity. There was obviously talent in the group, but was there hunger and desire? Or any complacency? I'll fix that up.'

He did that by setting extraordinarily high benchmarks in pre-season testing. The Crows had to better their fitness times from the previous off-season or they would be denied skills work until they did. And if that dragged into the home and away season, the coach was determined to continue his ban until the player measured up. 'If anyone was going to miss the boat, they were really going to get left behind. I didn't mind, but everyone was still pretty genuine about having another crack,' he said.

Not one of his men let him down. 'Which is all about good character and leaders,' he continued. 'If you're an honest football club all the way through, eventually it shines through. Your playing leaders, if they're honest and of good character, it flows down from them. That's exactly why you win.'

Well, not at first. For the second consecutive season, the Crows stumbled out of the blocks. In an eerily similar scenario to that of 1997, they were 1–2 as they prepared for the Round 4 Showdown against Port Adelaide. Rain and wind dominated the day, and the Crows' inaccuracy didn't help—they booted 8.16 to lose by 9 points. The game threw up just one significant moment for Blight's team: rookie Nathan Bassett, playing in his fourth game, secured three Brownlow Medal votes for compiling 8 kicks, 2 marks and 3 handballs. In his 210-game career, he would earn best afield honours from the umpires just twice more.

The season did not improve. By the time Richmond visited Football Park in Round 8, the Crows were 3–4 and could gain no momentum in their title defence. The Tigers arrived with a 4–3 record and sat one place above Adelaide on the ladder. While early in the season, it had the makings of a statement game. And did Malcolm Blight make a statement.

Late in the final term, Richmond simply overran the home side by repeatedly winning first use of the ball in the middle. The Tigers kicked 7 goals to 2 in the fourth term to win by 13 points. When the final siren blew, the home team's coach was nowhere to be seen—Blight had seen enough as his men were outworked by a more industrious opposition. He claims to have glanced at the scoreboard and thought time was near enough to expired. So, with John Reid in tow, he stormed out. Blight and Reid walked down to the ground surface and started around the boundary line in front of a disbelieving home crowd.

'It was a really bad day,' he recalled. 'I looked up at the screen and saw the clock running down, I thought there was thirty seconds left. Maybe I got the "3" in the wrong spot. But I thought, "I've had enough of this". John marched down behind me. My thinking was that by the time I got to the ground it would be perfect, I could walk in and eyeball them straight after the siren. But I was walking around the ground and the game kept on going, and going … and going … and going. I thought, "What have I done here?"'

Television cameras caught Blight as he headed up the players' race. Still no siren.

'We couldn't exactly turn back, could we? So I went into the rooms. It seemed like forever until the siren went.'

BACK-TO-BACK

As the players prepared to head up the race, CEO Bill Sanders appeared at the door. 'What was all that about?' he demanded. 'Who was in charge of the team?'

Reid jumped in to save his coach the embarrassment. 'It's all under control, Bill, we set it all up with the guys.'

But 'under control' was not a status you would associate with the Crows' 1998 home and away season.

Andrew McLeod missed the middle month with injury. Kane Johnson managed twelve games all year. Goodwin was absent for a month, while Jameson, who had kicked 6 goals against the Tigers, compiled nine games for the entire campaign. By Round 11, the turning point for home, Adelaide faced a test that in all likelihood would determine perhaps not their season, but their contender legitimacy: the top of the table Western Bulldogs. Twelve months earlier, a Princes Park win over the fancied Dogs had kickstarted their season. This time, they lost by 11 goals at the same venue. Without McLeod and the injured Ricciuto, they were monstered.

But two things were working for Blight's team that season: first, it was an incredibly even competition. When Adelaide squeezed past Essendon by 2 points in Round 12, the ailing Crows managed to remain within a game of the top eight, in tenth place. A fortnight later, due to wins over Collingwood and Sydney, they had climbed all the way to third, leading a pack of eight teams with seven or eight wins after fourteen games. It placed extra emphasis on their healthy for-and-against percentage, which was due to the aspect of that Crows era that gets the least respect: the back line.

In both 1997 and 1998, Adelaide finished the home and away season with the best percentage. In the latter season, it was not

285

even close—its 123.2 per cent figure was almost 6 per cent ahead of the next best. Technically, it was also the best defensive team in both years, conceding the lowest 'points against' tally. Given that Blight had cut his AFL coaching teeth on highly attacking Geelong teams—the running joke was that he didn't mind if you kicked 20 goals, as long as he kicked 22—it might be the most remarkable statistic of his time at Football Park.

Captain Mark Bickley was amazed by those numbers. 'Mainly because I don't think it was ever something Malcolm really high-lighted,' he said. 'He always talked about how important it was to have a good defence, but equally we were encouraged to back ourselves. Blighty was huge on keeping the ball to the front in defence, and run to support your teammate. We were united with these simple rules—you didn't need to be a superstar to do them, you just had to contribute. I suppose we had Hart, Smart, Caven, Jameson; we had six guys who played a lot of footy together. Plus, Ricciuto and Goodwin, even McLeod, played a lot of half-back.

'Our midfield was a pretty accountable bunch, too. We were very competitive and prided ourselves on it through the middle of the ground, and obviously that's going to help any back line if that pressure is being put on.'

The same message that had salvaged Peter Caven's career was the foundation of Blight's defensive philosophy. He largely applied a man-on-man approach, imploring his defenders to stand in front of their opponent whenever there was a stoppage at any part of the ground. Read the ball and back yourself in open play, but be accountable. Simple but unbreakable rules.

'They came from just watching enough games of football,'

Blight explained. 'Having played both full-back and full-forward, as the ball went up to the top of the bounce, I always tried to just move slowly to the front. And two or three times a game you'd get a cheap kick as the quick kick fell short. So I hardly ever got caught behind. I was playing on much bigger blokes at centre half-back so I almost had to, but you could not afford to get caught behind. Really, the same applies wherever you are.'

The other understated aspect of that team was its tackling pressure. A statistic that leapt off the page in the 1997 preliminary final win against the Western Bulldogs was a 43–17 tackle advantage. Of the teams that played more than one final in 1997, the Crows averaged 44 tackles, St Kilda 35, no one else more than 31. In the finals series of 1998, they were out-tackled only once, in a match where they controlled the ball and won.

Blight did not emphasise tackling, preferring the theory that depth of talent, fitness and commitment contributed to his team's admirable tackling record. 'Really good teams become good tackling teams because they've generally got twenty-two more honest players, better players, maybe quicker and fitter players,' he said. 'So they get to contests more often. Rather than just not get the footy, they might get the man. Pressure. So it's a by-product of being a good team. If anyone says, "If we have sixty tackles we'll win," that's rubbish.

'Plus, tackling is a by-product of training. We'd have competitive training each week, not for long, but it's a game of contact. I don't understand coaches and teams that don't do it.'

Rounds 16 and 17 further conspired to make the Crows' run home as difficult as possible. Carlton overcame a 4-goal deficit at quarter-time to sink Adelaide by 4 points at Football Park, one of only four Blues wins ever against the Crows at that venue. Then the unthinkable: the 4–12 Dockers outlasted Adelaide by a point at Subiaco. Suddenly, the very prospect of playing finals football, let alone defending a premiership, was being threatened, as the Crows remained in the eight on percentage only.

Late in that Subiaco game, both Darren Jarman and Nigel Smart had opportunities that would have edged their side ahead. Jarman tried a torpedo and failed to connect cleanly, kicking a point, while Smart failed to score. As the bus pulled up at the team hotel after the match, the players sat in silence as Blight stood to address his men. 'Darren, Nigel, you're with me! Get your roommates to take your bags up.' Blight led them into the foyer of the hotel and turned left.

'In here!' he said. Smart and Jarman realised they had walked into the hotel bar.

'I'm having a Crown Lager, what'll you have?' Blight asked, laughing.

'I missed a couple after the siren, too. It's a game,' he reflected. 'Eventually, all the boys came down and had a beer and a laugh about it. In a game like that, which we should have won, I legitimately could have gone off at some efforts of that night. But 80 per cent of the time you take the positive approach, especially because it felt like the season was still alive.

'We had a lot of injuries, a terrible run, so you never felt comfortable all year. It was a struggle.'

In Round 18, the unpredictable Crows fired a warning shot across the competition's bow, walloping St Kilda by 70 points at Football Park. McLeod was healthy again, while Rehn had re-discovered his All-Australian touch of four seasons earlier. Tony Modra had returned against Carlton, but the effects of a long lay-off from knee surgery were obvious; he had just 2 touches and kicked a single goal that day against the Saints, but there were eleven goalkickers that Saturday night.

Then, a sweet Sunday afternoon. In Showdown number four, the Crows humbled Port by 74 points, all but ending their cross-town rival's finals hopes while improving their percentage to a League-best 121. With three rounds to go, the Crows found themselves in fifth place, but in the eight only on percentage; admittedly, with a 25 per cent advantage over ninth-placed Melbourne, their advantage was effectively worth four premiership points.

A trip to Kardinia Park beckoned. Adelaide had never won there (and in their two decades of existence have suffered a 3–11 overall record), but they came back up the highway having given the Cats a 74-point hiding. Modra kicked 6, though Blight was unconvinced: 'He kicked them on a kid.' Plus, this was hardly the fearsome Geelong unit Blight had once steered—during this period of transition, only four of that day's Geelong players had managed more than 100 games.

Round 21 produced a classic Football Park meeting with first-placed premiership favourite North Melbourne. Behind their superstar centre half-forward, Wayne Carey, the visitors held on by 13 points, leaving seven days for the Crows to ponder their immediate future. It had been a bittersweet performance, all at once proving Adelaide might be competitive in September ... if only they could get there.

On Friday night of Round 22, the Cats did Adelaide a favour. By defeating Essendon by 10 points, Geelong ensured Adelaide could not fall out of the eight, easing the pressure on the Crows' trip to Subiaco to face West Coast. The result, however, would still mean the difference between finishing fifth and seventh. 'It typified the whole season, it was a touch and go year,' recalled Goodwin, who believed that stress was embodied by the coach. 'I felt Malcolm was a lot more aggressive and intense in his demeanour.'

The captain agreed, aware that those back-to-back campaigns rarely offered the chance to take a breath. 'Both years we tended to be under pressure. And it was constant pressure,' Bickley admitted. 'Injuries, slow start, whatever it was, we rarely got our best team on the park so it never felt like we were going really well. In 98 it wasn't about getting ready for the finals, it was more about, "Let's make sure we actually make them".'

The Crows led West Coast at every change to win by 25 points. Ricciuto and McLeod were their best, while Modra kicked four. It secured fifth place. In the multiple configurations of the finals— most tellingly since 1972, when a final five was installed—no VFL or AFL team had won a premiership after finishing the home and away season so low on the ladder.

*   *   *

Adelaide's qualifying final opponent was Melbourne. The Demons were laced with talent and experience, rolling out forwards Garry Lyon, David Neitz, David Schwarz, Jeff Farmer and Russell Robertson, ruckmen Jim Stynes and Jeff White and a midfield anchored on Todd Viney, Stephen Tingay and Shane Woewodin.

In their defence, the Crows, of course, were the reigning premiers
… but it sure didn't look like it that day.

Melbourne led by 28 points at quarter-time. It was never that
close again. 'In that first final, we got flogged,' Blight said. '[We
lost by] eight goals, but we were that far down halfway through the
second quarter. We were terrible.'

With the notable exception of Darren Jarman, the Crows were
outplayed in essentially every position on the ground. Especially
full-forward. You sense that Blight had been stewing on Modra
since the previous year, when his star spearhead had stopped dropping in to the coach's office from the mid-season point. On this
bleak afternoon at the MCG, he ran out of fuse. The runner sent
Modra to the half-back line, and changed the course of a career.

'He wasn't playing well—the whole team wasn't playing well—
so I put him at half-back just to see if he could get into the game,'
Blight explained. 'He dug his toes in. His body language, he didn't
chase, he didn't want to be there. You don't see players do that
very often. Sadly, after the result I had to do something. Tony's
form wasn't great so I got him in and showed him the tape [on the
Monday]—he was wandering around like a nomad, and I told him
he'd be playing at West Adelaide the next week.'

Blight told Modra that he should not consider his season over.
'Your form will dictate whether you come back,' Blight said.

Modra felt spurned. 'You won't play me,' he replied.

'You go back and play, attack the footy and enjoy your footy.
Show me you want to play, and why wouldn't I bring you back?'
was his coach's response, though in truth it seemed Blight had
played his ace, sacrificing the star to energise the team.

'That was the only time you saw that Blighty had an issue with him,' Goodwin said. 'Mods had never played in the back line in his life. Was he embarrassing him, teaching him a lesson, humiliating him? He must have done something to get up Blighty's nose.

'The media was all over Blighty: "What are you doing, you need your star forward to be playing well". But that was Blighty. It was a big call, but he was prepared to throw the team around. Given his reputation when he arrived, then what happened in 97, whatever he did was going to be all right. That got reaffirmed in 98. By then he was the Messiah over there. When you start getting called that you can do anything.'

Blight denies he dropped Modra purely to send a message to the team; he was omitted because the effort was lacking. But the coach also recognised the potential consequence of his actions. 'Part of it was, "How do we resurrect this?" Dropping Tony Modra, when I announced that to the group, and that he wouldn't even be training with us, I think I heard a pin drop. You should never blame one player after a loss, but he actually didn't try. To drop him and not let him train with us until he got a better attitude probably woke the group up.' And many players perhaps realised the absolute truth in what was unfolding. Tony Modra had played his last game for the Adelaide Football Club.

The coach then did some more prodding. No more beers and a laugh in the bar. 'He'd tried to take the casual approach in the first game of the finals against Melbourne, and we got flogged,' Goodwin said. 'Then it changed. He flogged us on the track [for] the rest of the finals. It was two completely different approaches. As soon as he saw things happening differently in 98, he hammered us. Maybe once he got a sniff that blokes thought it would just happen, he decided to keep us on edge.'

The significance of that Round 22 win at Subiaco was now evident. That win out west had earned for Adelaide a double chance, though the prize was hardly one to cherish: a trip to Sydney to tackle the Swans, who had finished third on the ladder and were as formidable at the SCG as the Crows were at Football Park. Blight is blunt in his recollection of how he felt his team would fare. 'If we had not much chance in any of the finals in 97, we had nil in that game. Less than nil, playing the Swans up there.'

In the pre-match build-up, Blight produced a comparatively traditional game plan to sink the home side, which wielded veterans Tony Lockett, who had kicked 109 goals that season, and defender Paul Roos, who was playing out his final season after seventeen years of senior football. Despite his pessimism, Blight had not installed any gimmicks in his plans; thirty minutes before the teams were due to run out, he reviewed his notes and felt comfortable, reiterating key points to the team as they mentally switched on. Then the heavens opened.

'After the meeting the skies opened up, it was a big electrical storm. The ground was under water,' Blight said. 'So I rounded up the players and said, "Everything I've just told you for the last half-hour; guess what? We're not doing it".'

Blight summoned the men he believed were the best two kicks on the team, Mark Ricciuto and Darren Jarman. 'Right, you blokes are going to kick out. Go on the ball and change at full-back. After you kick out, run down the ground.'

He then caught the attention of Peter Vardy, whom he

considered the longest kick in the team. 'Shaun Rehn, or whoever is rucking, knock the ball towards Vardy's wing. Knock the ball, everyone, out that side. Peter, you're just going to run onto the ball and kick goals. Simple plan. No one in the forward line lead, just stand there. If you want to run, run around in circles.'

As they watched the rain continue to turn the surface to slush, Blight then banned one of the two most basic methods of disposal in the game. 'And no one is going to handball,' he said. 'Anyone not understand this? No one handballs once. If you handball, you come off.'

Jarman and Ricciuto had 33 kicks between them. Vardy kicked 6 goals. The Crows defied their coach, dishing out 71 handballs, albeit a figure well below their season average of 97 per game. 'Ben Hart handballed in the second quarter so I dragged him to make a point,' Blight laughed. 'He got on the phone, "Sorry Malcolm, I'm sorry!"' Hart did not handball again.

The unwinnable game was won by 27 points.

Just as destiny had appeared to accompany the Crows a year earlier, they now felt momentum was swinging their way. Their preliminary final opponent would be the Western Bulldogs, a repeat of 1997's penultimate match-up in which the Bulldogs were run down at the death. This time, it wasn't even close. 'We never felt we would lose to the Bulldogs in that game,' Goodwin said. 'I couldn't wait to get to the game. From the year before, the confidence we took into the match, we felt unbeatable.'

The game is best remembered for the performance of Crows forward Matthew Robran. Growing up in Adelaide as the son of Barrie Robran—an official Legend of the AFL Hall of Fame—

would not have been easy, especially when you showed promise in football. Drafted by Hawthorn in 1989, he played seven games for the Hawks in season 1991, ironically making his debut against Adelaide in its inaugural appearance. He sat out the final year of his contract, 1992, in a bid to return to his home state, and he first ran out for the Crows in Round 5 of 1993.

At the first bounce, Robran headed to centre half-forward. While he had never been considered an elite talent, Blight loved Robran's presence as a key attacking option. 'He was a very good player, Matthew. If you undersold him, he got you,' the coach said. 'He could mark it and he was a beautiful kick. In fact it was a very good kicking team. Jarman and him, McLeod, Ricciuto, all beautiful kicks. He was a bit maligned, Matthew, but I kept on picking him. He was important to our structure.'

Dogs coach Terry Wallace tried something different, sending running defender Rohan Smith to Robran from the first bounce. The plan was to incessantly run off Robran but it came unstuck when the Adelaide forward started strongly. 'The idea was to bring the ball to ground and run off him,' Smith said. 'But he marked everything. Absolutely everything. He was kicking goals from outside fifty, you name it. Before long the game felt like it was over.' By the time Wallace conceded, moving Smith, the Crows were away. They led by 19 points at quarter-time and 34 at the half. Robran kicked 6 goals, dragging down 10 marks in perhaps his signature outing for the club.

For all his dominance, Robran was arguably not even best afield. McLeod was tagged by Tony Liberatore, and Blight sent him forward—out of the pesky Bulldog's comfort zone. 'They put

Libba on McLeod, so we sent Andrew to the half-forward flank,' Blight said. 'When Libba went to him I knew it wasn't his go.'

McLeod kicked 7 goals. A remarkably even team performance supported the Robran–McLeod one–two punch, and Adelaide cruised home by 68 points. The defending premiers were back in the grand final.

'That game was over early. Great,' Blight recalled. 'It was one of those games you can sit back and enjoy because it's up to the opposition to do something. They didn't happen often.'

* * *

On the other side of the draw, North Melbourne had accounted for Melbourne in the preliminary final. The final margin was 5 goals, a true indication of the distance between the sides as the Kangaroos appeared to hold sway for much of the evening. The result set up a grand final to be played between the premiers from the previous two years.

If the Crows had overachieved in returning to a grand final from fifth place, it was nothing compared to what they would have to produce to topple North. They had lost five in a row to Denis Pagan's men, falling both times in that home and away season. Yet there was life, and even hope, because the margins in those two games were only 13 and 4 points. And as he watched the game tape from their Round 21 meeting at Football Park, Malcolm Blight stumbled across something.

'In that game, for 80 per cent of their goals it struck me that there was no one between the North Melbourne player kicking the goal and the goals themselves,' he explained. 'We'd actually been sucked up the ground. Because I had that penchant to play in front from 50–50s, North was leaking back into space all the time.'

There was a name for it: 'Pagan's Paddock'. The Kangaroos coach designed the strategy primarily to exploit opposition defences. In Wayne Carey he had arguably the most lethal mix of athleticism and strength the game had seen. Carey rarely lost a one-on-one contest, and Pagan created the space to provide precisely that scenario. 'We employed a three-quarter ground squeeze on the opposition where we'd push the half-forward line up into the midfield and the full-forward line up to half-forward and we'd kick over their heads into space inside fifty so our forwards could run onto it,' Pagan once explained. 'We were lucky enough to have Wayne Carey running onto the ball towards goal. If he marked it, terrific; if he didn't mark it, he brought it to the ground and we had plenty of space to run on to the loose ball. It evolved and there were a lot of variations of it, with and without Wayne.'

Blight considered his options, but deep down he knew he had only one. After two years of hammering it into his defenders to play in front, he changed his instructions. At the pre-match meeting, he played the tape as a North Melbourne player ran into an open goal from 30 metres out. Blight hit the stop button.

'And Pagan's Paddock worked again,' he said to his players. 'What are we going to do about that?'

The coach made all six defenders stand up, collect their chairs and come to the front of the room. He then lined them up as they would play their positions: the half-back and full-back line. 'When it's a 50–50, where do we normally stand, and have done for the last two years?' he asked.

Every backman dutifully walked around and stood in front of the chair.

'That's right,' said Blight. 'For the last two years, we stood in front from a 50–50. Well, we're not going to do that today. Ben [Hart], march around the back. From 50–50 situations, they're not going to kick any more easy goals. They'll start kicking points, because we'll be up their ginger and putting pressure on them. I know you're programmed, now I'm going to de-program you.'

Blight three times made them move to the front of their chairs, then to the back again, driving home his point. Then the Crows boarded the bus to the game.

'I was never going to die wondering,' Blight said. 'If I thought something was worth a try, I tried it. I didn't think we could win the game playing the way we were playing because North was a great football team.'

Sitting in the front row of the bus with Terry Moore, a match committee member, Blight was pondering his options when Moore nudged his arm. 'Look at that,' he said, motioning his head to the police escort in front of them. The number plate read MAL 010.

'Malcolm, this is your tenth grand final', Moore said, clutching at whatever omen was on hand. It was true. Prior to the 1997 Adelaide success, Blight had visited September's big day five times as a player—he had missed the Roos' 1974 loss through illness—and taken Geelong to three as a coach. Moore concluded his observation with a definitive statement: 'We'll win'.

Early in the contest, his prediction seemed ill-founded. North entered the game on an eleven-match winning streak, having not been defeated since a 2-point loss to Hawthorn in Round 13.

The Roos brought that form into the game—they won the toss, then proceeded to win every contest in the hour that followed. Adelaide stayed in proximity in the first quarter, going to the huddle 8 points behind, but was obliterated in the thirty minutes that followed. There was only one solace, but it was an important one: North was not hurting the Crows where it counted—on the scoreboard. In the second quarter, North kicked 2.11 to 1.1, still good enough for a 24-point lead at the long break but hardly a defining margin.

'Have a look at the replay. For only two shots did they have a bloke clear,' Blight said. 'They've always got someone on their ginger. It worked a treat. The problem was, because we were playing behind they were getting the footy. Every time they got it forward, they were getting it.'

Blight believed he had proven his point, chipping away at North Melbourne's invincibility in the process. At half-time he surveyed a dressing room that should have been despondent, for the Roos had clearly outplayed them. But this Crows unit had a powerful sense of its capacity to overcome.

'We were playing really poorly,' Goodwin said. 'The experience from the year before gave us a sense that we could still win this. We just had to get a good start in the second half. I remember Blighty said, "We can't play any worse and they've kept us in it". We also had enormous belief in our fitness. We'd come from behind and won games throughout those two years. No matter what stage the game was at, we were still in it. Charlie Walsh [highly respected national cycling coach and Australian Institute of Sport figurehead] has been telling me for years: "Belief comes from doing".'

Blight asked his men to get ready for the feathers and tar if they continued to play as poorly as they had in the opening half. He then rang the changes, the most important one being in the back line. It was time to win the game.

'Guess what we're going to do now?' he said to his defenders. 'Go back to getting in front.'

Blight believed the opposition had spent a lot of energy and would have been frustrated. He also figured his men to have an edge in fitness and leg speed. It was time to release the hounds. 'Ricciuto went back to half-back, he'd been struggling to get a kick, and we moved Bickley onto the ball. We changed the midfield and the back line mentality. It highlighted that we were never, ever the best side, but we had change-up positions.' Plus, Blight had Andrew McLeod up his sleeve.

McLeod and Ben Hart had led the Crows through the first half. Now they took their teammates with them, the script playing out in a remarkably similar way to that of twelve months earlier. Fans of history watched with fascination as the second half mirrored the 1997 epic. Crows fans watched captivated as their heroes did what they were seemingly born to do—win in September. And North Melbourne fans could not look at all.

Adelaide kicked 5.8 to 2.0 in the third quarter, wresting away that all-critical momentum and entering the final quarter with a narrow edge. Just as North had squandered its first-half opportunities, the Crows' pressure swamped them in the final thirty minutes; the Kangaroos kicked 7 behinds in their final stanza of the season, while Adelaide poured through another 6 goals, blowing out the final margin to 35 points. The two teams had exactly the same number of scoring shots but, in terms of pressure and execution, were a class apart.

With 60 seconds remaining, Blight trotted down the steps from the coach's box to the boundary line to share the joy of the siren with his team. As the handshakes and hugs commenced, commentator Bruce McAvaney gave the moment—Blight's moment—context: 'One of the greatest footballers of all time and now, surely, one of the great coaches'.

Immediately after the siren, he headed to the jubilant players' huddle in the middle of the ground; almost comically, Blight could not initially break into the group, circling the huddle until he sniffed an opening. Once in the mix, his charges clearly returned the joy of the achievement with their coach.

Bickley reflects on that 1998 season with a mixture of pride and awe. 'We had to win in Perth to guarantee a finals spot, and we'd never beaten West Coast at Subiaco. Next week we went to Melbourne and lost but we stayed alive and went to Sydney. There'd been six inches of rain and it was still pouring, but we won. Back to the MCG, the fourth week in a row on the road and we beat the Bulldogs by 10 goals. Then the fifth week in a row, on the road, was the big one against North. And we still ran out the grand final in the second half and won the game.'

Blight, too, reserves a special place in his football history for that team's efforts over two seasons. 'That team doesn't get enough credit,' he said. 'Every finals series, all the talk is that you can't play four finals and win. It's handed down through the generations, it's written in stone. But this team did. And in the following one, we travelled five weeks in a row to beat North Melbourne.

'If the criticism of Geelong was that our bottom six or seven players never quite measured up, it's probably the harsh reality—we were just a bit underdone at the bottom end, although I reckon we had more at the top. At Adelaide, we had a more even group. In the end you had Jarman and McLeod, but there was a lot more under it, a really even lot.'

In modern football, Adelaide is the only team to have won a premiership after finishing lower than fourth in the home and away season. The Crows' finals performance across those two years was nonpareil ... and I doubt any team will ever repeat those two incredible Septembers. In fact, I had an on-air conversation with Leigh Matthews in the aftermath of the game, suggesting that the Crows were a 'super team'. Leigh replied that he felt they were simply a 'super September team'. I can look back on my response all these years later and realise I would not change a word: 'It's the only kind that matters'.

* * *

Before they broke for summer—or, at least, a form of temporary respite—there remained unfinished business. The question of Tony Modra loomed large over the football club. After much agonising, the Crows put him on the market, and Fremantle willingly took the bait. He kicked 148 goals in three seasons at Subiaco before his retirement at age thirty-two.

'I was bitterly disappointed when Tony left the football club,' said CEO Bill Sanders. 'I could understand Malcolm's reasons in running out of patience with Tony, because Malcolm expected his players to fill other spots on the ground. But once Tony got outside that arc of full-forward, he seemed to be in trouble. Ultimately it became the coach's decision. I was sitting in the car park with Tony and Max Stephens, his manager, saying, "We won't trade you or clear you to Fremantle. You're part of this group". But, in the end, Tony became a victim.'

Modra departed Adelaide a year short of his life membership. Given the excitement and performance he brought to Football Park for seven seasons through that period, it seems inconceivable that he departed without a premiership medallion, though he certainly left a legacy. 'Everyone remembers the marks but some of the soccer goals he used to kick were outstanding,' mused fellow forward Matthew Robran. 'His ability to control the football, kicking it off the ground from acute angles, was incredible. I remember a game in 97, he took this incredible hanger, then there was vision of Troy Bond walking across the camera with a smile on his face. He had that effect of lifting all the boys. He was a sight to behold when he was in full flight.'

Their pin-up boy had soured on the coach, and after consecutive premierships the coach was going nowhere. Or was he?

'I got closer to finishing after 98 than the year before', Blight conceded. 'Definitely closer. There was just an emotional feeling of "Here we go, got to get rid of some players," then the thought of another pre-season. It never left my body when I was coaching, I couldn't last the distance and do a Sheedy. Could not do it.'

Blight recalled former Collingwood captain and coach Tony Shaw interviewing his former assistant at Geelong, Gary Ayres. Shaw suggested—only partly tongue in cheek—that Blight would just roll down to training and kick a few dropkicks and training would get going.

'Gary pointed out that training was planned to the minute. I think Tony was taken aback by it,' Blight said. 'There was this image that I was pretty laissez-faire, but the game would not leave me, would not get out of me. The whole game. It's tiresome. I could move on, but I had to tear it apart before I could do that.'

Indeed, for all of the success, the game was tearing *him* apart, and it would draw every ounce of his strength to re-energise for the coming season.

Once again Blight consulted his inner circle. He surely knew no one would want him to draw the curtain after two wonderful seasons, but had genuine doubt about his physical capacity to continue. As far back as his playing days—even after his very first contract with the Kangaroos—he had sought the solace of Queensland beaches to rejuvenate his soul, so Blight again headed north. It took some weeks of internal back and forth, a 'will I, won't I?', but an idea eventually began to dawn on him. 'Three in a row?' he asked himself. 'That snaps you out of it. Can we? Hmmm … maybe we can.'

19

EXPIRY DATE

WHEN THE END came, it came quickly. Malcolm Blight should have listened to his own soul, rather than listened to those around him, those who sensed the magician could conjure one more genie from the bottle. And he should have taken his own advice. Because, over the summer of 1998–99, Blight convinced himself that the only way he could succeed yet again, to win a third unlikely straight premiership, was to never mention the first two.

The season had started well, which was unusual in itself for a slow-starting team. The Crows even beat Port in the Showdown in Round 6, improving to 4–2. They then lost, in consecutive weeks, to North Melbourne (by 56 points), West Coast (54 points), Richmond in the rain at Football Park (11 points), Essendon (48 points) and second-last team Fremantle, at Subiaco, by 39 points.

On the morning of 14 May, the day of the Essendon loss, Blight played golf with Bruce McAvaney at Kooyonga Golf Club.

305

The pair then joined cricket legend Sir Donald Bradman for lunch, a rare honour few got to enjoy. But McAvaney could tell his friend was distracted. 'Malcolm that day, I felt like he'd lost the desire to coach,' he said. 'I also had the feeling Patsy was pretty unwell. He was so concerned for her, plus he probably felt like he had achieved the ultimate not once but twice; he seemed like he'd run his race.'

The Bombers trounced Blight's men that night, another nail if ever there was one. Then, after the Dockers defeat, Blight betrayed himself. 'I swore I would never do it, but I did,' he said. 'During that five-in-a-row spell, I took all the players and board members into the boardroom. I could feel the whole thing changing, the snowball starting to reverse itself. I went through it all and individualised—there were nine players on the Crows list now on TV, writing for the media or doing radio jobs, so from this group that once had nothing, I now questioned whether we as a group were the same as we were twelve months ago.

'It was the first time I ever brought up the fact that they were premiership players, *the first time*, and I swore I'd never do it. Because I put a seed in their head that wasn't great, but it was truthful. If I had my time again I wouldn't have done that.'

The seed related to hunger. The coach had refused to acknowledge the back-to-back premierships, as such an admission recognised that the ultimate goal had been achieved, not once but twice. For motivation, things could never be the same. And they weren't.

In his heart, Blight knew the pattern that had played out at Geelong—the grumpy coach, the unforgiving coach who no longer made Monday fun—was recurring. By now, he was a victim of his own intensity, and what strikes me as unusual is that it was not quelled by two premierships in Adelaide, but exacerbated. Perhaps the premiership standard is impossible to maintain.

And there were other things on his mind.

'One of the things I always admired about Malcolm was that he didn't let outside opinion influence him,' said John Reid, Blight's closest ally and friend in Adelaide. 'He'd do it his way. The media and the distractions, he didn't let them get to him. But the public adulation in Adelaide became incredible. To walk down the shops and buy the paper became a pain in the arse, because he'd get stopped fourteen times on the way there, then get stuck talking in the shop forever. He'd go to the pictures and make sure the lights were down before he walked in so he didn't have people tapping him on the shoulder to talk about the Crows.'

Blight had a name for it: 'The autograph book in the main course' syndrome. 'And once might be fine, but twenty times a night? Come on.'

Then there was Patsy. Early that season, his wife suffered a heart complaint that was fleeting but greatly troubled the coach. Just as he felt he had missed half of his son's progressive years, he felt torn between his commitments to his football family and his own, knowing inside there was no real choice but the right one. 'That was a perspective check, a big one,' he said.

Unless you have lived the life of an AFL coach, it is difficult to understand the pull between these two families. On the one hand, you are responsible for forty or more children, in a sense, a playing list with its own set of individual issues, problems and challenges. And then, at home, there is your own family, in my case a wife and four children. Splitting these obligations is near impossible. And, unfortunately, coaching tends to win.

The coach of the US NFL team the New England Patriots, Bill Belichick, once said, 'It's not enough to love coaching, you've got love it more than anything else in the world'. While he was irresistibly drawn to it, I'm not sure Malcolm felt that way. Even when you are with your family, you're thinking about the team: how to prepare for this week, who is fit, who is not. It comes with guilt, and it never leaves you.

And a suffering wife would be the toughest guilt of all.

'Patsy was sick, which was a huge thing in his life, a big concern,' Reid noted. 'At the time no one seemed to pinpoint the problem and it was a genuine concern. She's a fair part of his program, of his success; she was a confidante. She'd been with him through a lot of footy; they left Adelaide as youngsters, playing in Melbourne, coaching everywhere ... coaching at Woodville was a tough gig. Then back to Geelong, all of that. They would sit and talk a lot. The uncertainty of her illness definitely had an influence on him.'

The grumpy coach was taking his frustration out on the playing group. As in 1993, when Geelong was slumping, the players found him withdrawing more, and lacking the compassion to 'make up on the Monday'.

'His downfall was when he lost the ability to win the players back,' captain Mark Bickley said. 'The season snowballed out of control, the aggressive, abusive stuff continued but there wasn't the consoling there had been in the previous two years. It doesn't prove anything when you yell and scream at people, and Blighty burnt some bridges he was unable to mend.'

Bizarrely, he might have burnt them from up a ladder. Having played for Kevin Sheedy for my entire career, I saw Sheeds do some left-field things, but they were more about on-field strategy or dealing with the media. Nothing I ever saw, or heard, came close to the now infamous ladder story.

In the midst of the losing run, having seen his boardroom talk fall on deaf ears, Blight gathered the players in the rooms after another loss. He produced a ladder from the property room, and climbed it, sitting on the top step. Then he told the players to form a large circle around him.

'One by one he called us out and berated each individual,' Simon Goodwin recalled. 'Then we had to face the wall.'

Every player who had played that day, plus the injured squad members, joined the circle. As captain, Bickley was targeted first. 'He called you by name, you'd step forward and he gave you a spray. Every one of us, and it was pretty cutting. Some of his criticisms were quite funny; it was like a roast. "You're from outer space, you're a drama queen" sort of stuff. But some of it was really personal.'

Troy Bond was injured that day. 'Bondy, were you meant to go to a physio appointment this week and you missed it?' Blight asked. Bond started explaining that he had suffered a problem with his car when Blight cut him off. 'Yes, or no, were you late for an appointment?' the coach inquired. Bond confirmed he was late.

'Okay, go get your bag, get back to Port Adelaide. Don't want to see you again.'

Blight eventually forgave Bond, who returned that season. He might have been the only player he made up with all year.

309

'He knew his time was done,' Goodwin said. 'We knew it as well.'

In Round 14, Geelong visited Football Park. The result should hardly have surprised Blight, for the Crows handed out their customary beating of Blight's former team. Adelaide improved to 6–8, and was a game and narrow percentage adrift of the finals. But Blight and his men weren't fooling anyone. They fell by 8 goals to Carlton the following week. And that was that.

'That Carlton game at Princes Park was the nail,' Blight said. 'We had a place at Blairgowrie, I stayed over for a day and decided, that's it. If they want to get someone in now, I reckon I've got to tell them so they can plan for the future. I was getting grumpy again. I thought, I've got to finish this.'

Blight contacted John Reid and club CEO and close friend Bill Sanders. 'I said to Reidy, "Look, I know I've wobbled before but this time I'm really wobbling. I'm not going to go through the charade". [Crows Chairman] Bob Hammond thought if I went away for three months at the end of the season it would help, but at the time I'd made my decision. The game was gnawing away at me. I couldn't help this team anymore.

'If you're not happy you can't pretend. How can you ask a player to be honest when you're not?'

Reid saw that his friend 'was mentally gone. Just shot'. He added, 'Some people reckon it was piss-weak, including some people in the club, even at board level. They were very much, "Hang on, that's poor, we need to hang tight and start again next year". But it got to Malcolm, he felt he had lost his drive that he knew you needed to do it'.

Sanders, too, was not shocked by the conversation. 'Malcolm was genuinely worn out', he said. 'When he came to us and explained that, we looked at options—maybe have a rest—but in our heart of hearts we knew he'd had enough. You need someone in a pretty clear frame of mind to do that job, and it was evident he wasn't right.'

After the Carlton game, the Crows made the announcement: Malcolm Blight would stand down as coach at season's end. He coached the rest of the year; he said, 'From that moment on it was a better place, a better finish to the season. If you go around the Adelaide people, everyone got the maximum out of themselves. I don't reckon anyone left anything anywhere; the tank was empty. Players, coaching group, we extracted the maximum out of it'.

If you need any indicator of Blight's feeling of relief, it came in Round 20 when Sydney beat the Crows by 118 points. It was easily the team's biggest loss in his time there—the next biggest was a 67-point loss to the Bulldogs the previous year—but Blight has no memory of the game. Plus, they lost five of their last seven after his announcement.

A better place? Mentally, he had clearly moved on.

* * *

The end was not pretty, but maybe the level of intensity at which Malcolm Blight coached meant it could finish no other way. It's a part of his story that fascinates me the most. The Geelong disappointments and subsequent irrational behaviour made sense. Losing can do that to someone when you care so much. But after winning consecutive flags, he still couldn't grant himself a leave pass, not even for a single year.

Which, of course, I understand. Coaching is a twenty-four-hour existence. You dream about it, and spend every waking moment thinking about next week, plus the week that has just passed. The joy of winning passes quickly, far more rapidly than the joy of winning as a player. When you play, at season's end you want to get your medical exit report completed and head off on a holiday. But Blight could never seem to cleanse himself of the game from year to year; it built up in his system, and came out fair in the face of his players.

'The dictatorial approach didn't seem to work anymore, and it had been generationally changing. Malcolm's coaching style was probably a rung or two down from Barassi in that sense, who was probably a rung or two down from Norm Smith,' Bickley said. 'The withdrawal in his relationships, his behaviour became more erratic, his outbursts were becoming more frequent. Plus, the Patsy situation—it really shook him up. I suppose in the end he thought, "Is all this worth it?"'

A memorable relationship had ended. Like his time in Geelong, there were times both good and bad, but the Crows experience also delivered the one thing he could not claim at Kardinia Park: a premiership, then another one.

Goodwin reflected that '1998 was more satisfying from the players' perspective, because we also had to deal with a sense of expectation that wasn't there the year before. Plus, people had thought 97 was a fluke'. He continued: 'Then we fell off the cliff. The coaching staff, players, everyone struggled to handle it in 99.

Blighty definitely got more personal. There were certainly periods where he lost the group with his message.

'The playing group was lost but I think he was lost as well. He didn't seem to have the hunger there—he seemed like a different person, a different coach. Whether that was because the players couldn't do what he wanted us to do, or he was just in a different headspace, I'm not sure.

'But for all of that, I still remember the 97–98 Malcolm Blight, not the 99 one. We were probably not the most talented group in the world, but they were the best two years of my life. He taught me about the game and he showed confidence in me at a young age. Why was he doing this or that? But as you get older you start piecing it all together ... I've got the utmost respect for him.'

McAvaney was not stunned that Blight walked away. He remains intrigued by the lightning caught in a bottle for two consecutive years, and by what he calls the 'illusions' Blight crafted in the process. 'Things like Shane Ellen going forward and kicking five goals, Matthew Robran becoming this successful centre half-forward in the finals series,' he explained.

'Look at 1996, then 1999, then those two years in the middle—those back-to-back premierships are among the most unusual in recent history. Look at the years on either side and you ask yourself, "How in the hell did they do that?"'

20

SAINTS OR SINNERS?

MALCOLM BLIGHT HAD promised himself he would never again coach after his tenure finished at Geelong. He broke his promise, seduced by an opportunity in his home town, and took Adelaide to consecutive premierships. Finally, the dog had caught the car.

'So it was "never again" after Adelaide, much more so than after Geelong,' he said of his coaching desires. 'That was it.'

Blight had settled into what he believed was life after the game. He returned to the transport industry, and his astute business sense saw him quickly climb the ladder to a senior position. Meanwhile, his AFL needs were being met by a media role, this time with the late-evening show *Talking Footy*.

SAINTS OR SINNERS?

Then, like the temptress that is football, St Kilda came calling.

'I was doing *Talking Footy*, and Mike Sheahan said, "Why don't you help St Kilda look for a new coach?"' Blight said. 'I dismissed it the first time, but he asked me again and I admitted to him and myself that, yeah, I would like to help out. Then he started: "What would you do here, what would you do there?"'

Sheahan recalls the conversation. There was no intent to drive Blight back to coaching, and he admits his brief was to 'prod' Blight to get a response. 'I almost felt he had an obligation because he was independent and had been across the spectrum, that he was the perfectly equipped bloke to give some guidance,' Sheahan said.

The discussion was a response to the Saints' search for a coach for the 2001 season, a position I had recently vacated after two fruitless and frustrating seasons at Moorabbin. Director of football Grant Thomas had been placed in charge of an ad hoc committee to source a replacement, and Blight was soon engaged as a sounding board. 'I actually phoned and contacted every single current AFL coach,' Thomas said of the search. 'I knew half of them were well in contract but I just wanted to be able to say to all the members and the board and everyone else that we contacted every single person.

'Of course, no one wanted to do it. [Blight] continually put a line through everyone I proposed. I said to him, "Well mate, there's no one left," and he said, "You're looking at the best one". Which we laughed about at the time but I think there was a bit more in it than that. So, incredibly, the adviser to the committee became the coach.'

Thomas's recollection sounds straightforward, but there must have been some wooing to be done. It was one thing for Blight to express interest but another to renounce his 'never again' declaration for a second time. Enlisting the aid of Blight ally Ron Joseph, the Saints set about selling their program to a man whose VFL/AFL coaching record at that point was a standout: six seasons in Geelong for three grand finals; three years in Adelaide for two premierships.

Just as Blight was emerging as a candidate, Rod Butters was beginning to warm the president's chair. Butters had that year taken over from Andrew Plympton in a less-than-bloodless board upheaval; a close friend of Thomas, he sensed the appointment of a new coach had to make a statement. They came close to signing impressive Carlton assistant Wayne Brittain, who had essentially been coaching the club in the previous season; at the eleventh hour, Brittain succeeded David Parkin as the Blues' head coach, and the chance evaporated.

'Grant was of the view, as director of footy, that we needed someone with presence, somebody with a name and reputation,' Butters said. 'Thommo was still very keen to land a big fish and to his eternal credit he persisted and wooed Malcolm.'

The logistics of Blight living interstate—he had moved to the Gold Coast after walking away from the Crows—was overcome by a 'Mountain to Mohammed' methodology. Thomas, Butters, football manager Brian Waldron and Joseph flew to Queensland to dine with Blight; for maximum impact, they also took along the club's elite playing talent, asking Robert Harvey, Stewart Loewe, Nathan Burke and Peter Everitt to wait in a side room at a Chinese restaurant while the officials enjoyed a drink at the bar. The party then converged on the room and the players met their prospective new coach for the first time. 'I sat there until five in the morning drinking gin and tonics with him, talking footy and our vision for the club, what we wanted to do and where we'd come from and where we thought we could go,' Butters recalled. 'He became interested in the concept of taking a team from last to first.'

The club had one more ace up their sleeve: on Joseph's recommendation, they put a deal to Blight that would make him the first million-dollar coach in the game. 'This is where Ron Joseph helped enormously,' Thomas explained. 'Ron said, "Knowing Blighty as I know him, he wants a million bucks … he'd be keen to be the first coach associated with that salary".'

It is part of club legend that a deal was hammered out at the table that night. The agreement was heavily weighted to the first year of the two-year contract, to the point that Blight was understood to be receiving the bulk of his salary in year one. Butters, Thomas and Blight were signatories to an agreement written on a napkin. One small problem existed, however: St Kilda Football Club had never been particularly commercially successful, and certainly did not have $1 million sitting in the bank. In a cart before horse sequence, the Saints now had to fund their golden goose. 'It was a really interesting time, there was a lot of celebration as far as the securing of Malcolm,' Thomas said. 'But I distinctly remember turning to Rod and saying, "Well that's all great, but how the fuck are we going to pay for it?" One thing I will give Rod a lot of credit for is [that] he engenders a lot of spirit and initiative and he believes you can do a lot of things that other people would probably just say, "Nah, too hard". Heads down and bums up. Away we went and raised the money and got Malcolm paid.'

Butters was ecstatic. There has been a lot of retrospective consideration about the Blight hiring, but at the time few could say that the vibe was not positive. 'I was thinking, "What a phenomenal hit rate [Blight had]," and, naively, as a young president, thinking, "Can't wait to get him into the gig, because we're almost certainly going to play finals and probably grand finals",' Butters said. 'That's how naive I was.'

Neither side will confirm the exact details of the contract, although Butters nods to the most pertinent point: 'I can confirm there was a million dollars deposited into [Blight's] account,' he said. 'It might have been in November. I don't know where the serviette is today ... I'd hope it would get to the St Kilda museum one day, I think it's an important piece of our history.'

Not surprisingly, Blight admits the money was appealing, but the challenge was the overriding factor in his decision to return to the coach's box. 'Money's important but it's just one of the things,' he said. 'The thing that engaged me was, I wonder if I can regenerate all that I know in the game and pass it on to a group of young blokes and do it again. It was the challenge of the chase again. [After] twelve months off it sort of needled me a bit. History says I don't mind saying no [Blight has turned down three other coaching offers across his career], but this seemed like a bit of fun and a challenge and a buzz to try to make it work. Eventually it got under my skin. The money was good, obviously. Very good. But the second year of the contract—which was never signed for whatever reason— I never asked for or went for, even though it was a two-year deal.'

Forget his two laps of Arden Street exactly two decades earlier. The hastily scribbled words on those napkins signalled the start of the most turbulent, testing and disappointing months in the football career of Malcolm Blight.

*   *   *

From a timing perspective, Blight had always identified the best coaching opportunities existing in clubs that were down and out. It had driven his return to Woodville, which had won a single game the previous season, and he saw a similar opportunity at Moorabbin.

'When I was thinking about coaching after playing,' recalled Ken Hinkley, 'Blighty said to me, "Find the worst job you can and go there and see if you like it".'

There were few more difficult challenges than St Kilda, which had two wins, one draw and nineteen losses in 2000, but look closer and the upside for the newcomer appeared substantial on paper. The Saints had secured Nick Riewoldt and Justin Koschitzke with the first two picks of the previous season's draft. Having hurt his knee the previous season, Riewoldt was essentially a first-year rookie for Blight. The core of the team was Robert Harvey—by then a two-time Brownlow Medallist—Nathan Burke, Stewart Loewe and Peter Everitt. Lenny Hayes was entering his third season, and the club had recruited well in the off-season, securing Aaron Hamill, Fraser Gehrig and Brett Voss, along with a buzzing small forward called Stephen Milne. Prospects for a rapid turnaround seemed fair, especially with Blight's record for having an immediate impact at a new club: he had taken Geelong from ninth to second, and Adelaide from twelfth to a premiership.

'Somewhere down the track it was going to be promising,' Blight conceded.

Having spent time with the new coach, Thomas sat down and detailed Blight's methodology to an expectant board. 'I remember explaining it to the board, and everyone else,' he said. 'I said, "Listen, if you think you are going to get a passionate, intense twenty-hour-a-day manic coach here, you're not. You are gonna get a guy who gets results but he gets them in a very, very different way. He is extremely left field. He is so chilled in his approach and everything else, you want to check his pulse". So he would be very, very different but I suppose because he is Malcolm Blight everyone says, "That's okay".'

First, there was a Blight pre-season to plan. He by now had his set ways, having developed a focus on fitness throughout the pre-Christmas period that had proven so fruitful in his last two coaching stops. Blight was commuting from the Gold Coast for much of that period, wrapping up his life in Queensland while keeping an eye on the proceedings at Moorabbin. His assistants, Hinkley and Peter Jones (an assistant from his Adelaide stint), took control of the sessions. 'When I got there it was Monday, Wednesday and Friday and the weekends were for yourself, which was kind of strange that a team that had finished sort of last didn't have the footy in their hands every day,' Hamill recalled.

'But he was pretty relaxed in the pre-season, Malcolm, he didn't have too many hang-ups. He had a really good structure and he just believed in his methods. We were doing one-kilometre time trials; until you got your [target] time you couldn't touch the footy. He was big on the basics, getting players fit in footy mode and conditions, then later on practising how you want to play. Weights in the morning, skills in the afternoon, three days a week.

SAINTS OR SINNERS?

Amongst the players, the general feeling was, "He knows what he's doing, let's get on board".'

By the time the real stuff arrived, the Saints were fit and fresh. Blight was by now a full-time Melburnian, and he was thriving on his return to the coaching game. St Kilda faced the Western Bulldogs in Round 1; they had played finals the season before, while Blight's men had finished last. When the Saints claimed a 5-point win, the hysteria surrounding his arrival was extraordinary. Indeed, there was a supporters' night later that week that Blight attended—it was my first time back at the club in any form. When Blight took to the stage, the audience hung on every word.

He was, to this downtrodden supporter base, every inch the Messiah.

But others remained unconvinced. Jim Watts was the CEO of the club that season. Butters remembers walking past his office even before the season had started. Watts motioned for Butters to come in and close the door. 'Malcolm's heart's not in it,' Watts said.

'What do you mean?' said a flabbergasted Butters. 'We've just paid him a million bucks!'

'His heart's not in it,' Watts repeated. 'He doesn't understand the size of the job.'

Butters today admits to being 'blinded by Malcolm's persona and status' and was tempted to dismiss the observation. Yet he also valued Watts' opinions, and believes that was the first sign that things were unsettled.

Then, after that Round 1 triumph, St Kilda lost nine of the next ten games. They defeated Sydney in Round 6, and were competitive in most of the other matches, leading Collingwood and

321

Melbourne at three-quarter time before losing. But the news only deteriorated when Burke and Loewe's seasons finished with injury in Round 10, Harvey's a fortnight later. In many ways, the Round 10 defeat by the Demons summed up the season; the Saints led by 19 points at three-quarter time, then conceded 10 goals in the final thirty minutes to lose by 31. Blight could not get to his men fast enough—he gathered them on the ground and handed out a lecture before they had even reached the dressing rooms.

By now, the mood among a selection of players had turned. Neither Blight nor management will confirm that Burke, Harvey and Loewe headed the disgruntled core of the playing group. Hamill, however, recalls some disgruntlement about the perceived future after Blight delivered some home truths. 'Malcolm certainly would have had a different outlook on the St Kilda footy club the following year if he had been there,' Hamill said. 'I think he would have done the same thing he did in 1997 and 98, got rid of some dead wood in Adelaide and I think the same was coming St Kilda's way in terms of Harvey being there and Burke and Loewe. Those three had a pretty heated discussion during the year with Malcolm and I don't think that went down all that well.

'That is when the hierarchy got involved ... you know, we have to keep Burke, Loewe and Harvey otherwise they will tear the joint down.'

This is one of two central themes in the breakdown between club and coach. The commitment, or perceived lack of it, is well documented. Also simmering away was conflict between the club's senior core—some of whom felt their final playing years were now threatened—and their new coach. In Adelaide, Blight had sacked the four fading senior players McGuinness, McDermott, Andrew Jarman and Anderson; it was not stretching belief to think he was considering a similar shake-up at Moorabbin.

In fact, Blight would have made changes had he remained, although he is adamant that Harvey, whom he had handed the captaincy to replace Burke, was not on the market. 'Robert Harvey was a champion,' he said. 'The other boys, their contracts were up either that year or the next year, and you would have had to discuss it, yeah. But not Harvey. No, never.'

Thomas remembers that Blight felt that senior trio had too much control in the playing group, a similar situation to that confronting him with the 'big four' on his arrival in Adelaide. 'He felt they were reluctant to change their playing habits to how he wanted them to play,' Thomas recalled. 'That all came to a head, which I suppose if anything was going to come to a head it's going to come to a head when you're winning one or two games in the first fifteen. I thought that was going to get very, very ugly for a while there.'

For his part, Harvey does not touch on any angst about the direction of the club. He stated that he 'thought Blighty was the man who was going to take us there, would have thought that was from the whole team'.

By now, there were clear signs that the relationship between the front office and the coach was strained. Thomas was not the full-time director of football—he ran his own business from the city. But he was becoming increasingly aware that Watts and Waldron had their concerns. 'They thought [Blight] was a bit of a part-time coach', he said. 'There is no book on winning a premiership. It's not a prescriptive pursuit. If it was prescriptive, well, everyone would take their turn, but they aren't. So, there are lots of different ways to do it. I think once you appoint someone, sure you give them counsel. You give them advice. You help as much as you possibly can and you smother them with support.' That said, Thomas believes that once you make the decision to employ a coach, you are the one responsible for their success. 'They don't fail, you fail, in essence.'

Thomas believes he remained the buffer between the coach and the front office. The pair chatted regularly (although Blight says he had 'no inkling whatsoever' of what was to come). 'We had many discussions about whether he was comfortable with the level of time he was putting in. And the level of support.'

Thomas even once directly asked Blight if the coach thought he needed to be more engaged with more of the players. 'Understand that a lot of me is thinking that this is a very, very different coach, we have known it from day one and he's only been here for four, five, six months, let it go a bit,' Thomas said. 'Just let it roll and let's find out a bit more about him. If year one is a bit of a write-off, well, that was going to be a write-off anyway, so take the draft choices and move to year two.'

Even Thomas recognised a value from the coach that was not being recognised by others in the football department. 'The [players] knew he was different but they balanced it by saying he was captivating,' he said. 'He was engaging. When he said something it stuck. In any advice or tuition or education or development, they got value and worth from it and they implemented it; it reinforced the relationship because they would say, "Gee, he just changed my ball-hold a few degrees and I'm kicking much better." He was a real technician.'

But the front office remained unconvinced, despite the Thomas 'buffer'. St Kilda beat the winless Dockers at Subiaco in Round 12. Two weeks later, at 2–11, they visited the Gabba in what would sound the death knell for Malcolm Blight at Moorabbin.

Blight flew to the Gold Coast on the Thursday before the Saturday night game, looking to squeeze in a round of golf—as was his custom wherever they were playing. He did not see the players until they arrived at the ground, by which point Thomas said the result felt inevitable as much due to the coach's absence as the quality of the opposition. 'We were just going to get throttled,' he said. 'There was no spirit. It was like there was a death. The players were just really withdrawn and sullen.'

Brisbane walloped St Kilda by 57 points. After the game, Thomas informed Blight that the coach was expected upstairs in a supporters' function. Instead, Blight headed back to the coast. 'I went to Blighty after the game and I said, "Blighty, mate. You better come up and face the music upstairs with the supporters",' Thomas recalled. 'He said, "Yeah, yeah, righto mate, no worries". And he didn't front up. And Jonas didn't come up and Hinkley didn't come up.'

Blight said he headed back to his Gold Coast house to 'do the tape' as he normally would after a match. But others, such as football manager Waldron, were simply stunned. 'All of us thought, "Crikey, what's going on here? Why aren't we seeing a commitment like we expect from others?" The Brisbane thing, probably to me, was the thing that broke the back.'

325

Thomas rang Blight, who was travelling in his car with Hinkley and Jonas. They spoke for some time, most of it Thomas venting his disappointment that Blight had ignored the supporters' function. Notably, the board also was present, and the coach's disappearance rated high in conversation that evening. On Thomas's insistence, Hinkley returned to Melbourne to watch the reserves play the following day, a critical issue in the club's eyes as Riewoldt was making his return from a long-term knee injury. But Blight stayed on the coast, cut his tape and played golf before a late Sunday return.

Several days later, he was interviewed on Adelaide radio and was asked about the culture at Moorabbin. His response only dug his grave deeper: 'I'd say it's been, oh, 500 per cent worse than I've seen anywhere else.'

It was an honest observation, but coming on the back of the weekend on the Gold Coast it seemed to essentially sever the relationship between the director of football and the coach. 'After all my discussions with him he showed a complete lack of consideration and I suppose a dilution of our relationship,' Thomas said.

The issue festered. The following week, St Kilda met Adelaide in Melbourne; Rod Butters approached Crows CEO Bill Sanders, who had been so close to Blight during his Woodville and Adelaide days. 'Rod said, how did we handle this guy?' Sanders said. 'The question caught me off guard; I said something like, "With the greatest of respect, that's your issue, not mine—I think you should have done your homework better".'

Sanders sidled over to Patsy Blight and queried the relationship between club and coach. 'She seemed completely surprised by the question,' he said.

Adelaide won by 97 points on that Friday night. On the Monday, Blight was called into a meeting with Waldron and Butters.

'I suppose the whole package we were starting to struggle with,' Butters said. 'Who's going to watch Riewoldt? Who's going to ring Mr Riewoldt and say, "Your boy's played his first game today and I just want you to know that your boy's going to be all right," that sort of softer stuff. A bit of that was missing … I think in hindsight [what we did] was still the right call, although we probably should have waited until the end of the year.

'Coming into the Adelaide game we knew that we'd probably have to make a change. It wasn't so much the Adelaide result, it was more that we felt we weren't being heard … At that point we'd been living with it for sixteen weeks and we just thought, "Let's move on".'

Blight was presented with a series of management concerns, most of them relating to the time he was spending at the club and his perceived lack of connection with the younger players on the list. His response bordered on nonchalant: 'There was a whole list of things,' Blight said. 'After that I thought, "Whatever"; I went to training.'

Twenty-four hours later, Thomas was called to the famous Melbourne restaurant The Flower Drum for dinner with Butters. 'Brian Waldron was there with Jim Watts and Ron Joseph and I thought, "What's going on?" I didn't know what I was going there for,' Thomas said.

'I just want to let you know that it is all over, boys. Blighty's finished,' Butters said. 'Malcolm's been terminated. I'm terminating his contract.'

An argument erupted between the president and Thomas, as much concerning the lack of consultation as the decision itself. 'I'm the director of footy, for God's sake,' Thomas implored.

Butters would not be swayed.

'On the Thursday, I got a phone call,' explained Blight, who was summoned to Butters' house. 'They said they were going to terminate me. There was no inkling before that. Apparently for all these issues that I had, I can't remember anyone sitting me down and talking to me about my performance until that Monday.

'I was doing what I was doing. I was enjoying working with the young blokes. But commitment issues? Because I played golf on a Thursday, because I had a day off? Like I had at Adelaide and Geelong? Come on.'

There is an undeniable sense of 'he said, she said' when intangibles such as commitment are considered. Thomas believes the pressure built slowly, and confirms Blight's suspicion that had the Saints been winning, the formula would never have been questioned. But that Saturday night in Brisbane was to be a critical turning point in the careers of both men.

'That sort of last, most recent act of "defiance" by Blighty, as individualism and quaintness or whatever the word is, probably wasn't the best thing he could have done at that time,' Thomas said of Blight snubbing the function, before expanding on the coach's overall performance. 'Footy had moved very quickly, it had really changed and the responsibilities and onus on a coach had moved quite dramatically,' he added. 'And it was moving at a great rate of knots. I think at that time that may have surprised Malcolm a little bit and he sort of rested on the "my way" morals, but probably in reality, if he was to be brutally fair to himself, there is no way known he could possibly stand in front of myself, or anyone at the club at that time, and say that he was 100 per cent committed.'

Blight still steams at the allegation, defending behaviour that had been perfectly acceptable at two others clubs—and that the Saints surely knew what they were employing. 'After a period of time, when I couldn't help St Kilda play in a grand final like I did with Adelaide and Geelong in the first year there—there's a good reason for that, they'd won two games [the year before], the others had won eight and ten—when that miracle worker didn't work his miracle, I guess people must have started looking at me and trying to find fault in me,' he said. 'That is their prerogative. Absolute prerogative. But whether I stayed or went, the timing was just stupid. Stupid.'

Blight had sensed the Thursday meeting was to be definitive—he had even taken Patsy with him as both support and witness. Butters recalls him responding to the news by saying, 'Well, I was always a square peg in a round hole, wasn't I?'

A press conference was hastily organised, and Butters dropped the axe. 'At the time of Malcolm's appointment it was agreed that if either party felt at any time that the relationship was not working, then either party could walk away,' he said. 'Accordingly, Malcolm Blight was terminated this morning ... Over the past two or three months we have concluded that Malcolm's essentially autonomous style simply does not fit with the direction we believe this club must pursue.'

Butters also addressed the issue of the radio interview: 'Malcolm Blight's comments on radio in Adelaide last week were nothing but a mosquito hitting the windscreen of a vehicle moving at 100 miles an hour.'

The departing coach was given the chance to speak to the players. Not one saw it coming, Harvey describing it as 'shock and anger ... everyone's head was spinning, almost like it wasn't happening'.

Some, such as Hamill, were as furious as they were stunned. ('I remember Aaron being fucking filthy, I thought he was going to tear my head off,' Butters said.) Lenny Hayes remembers Hamill speaking for the players. 'He got up and said there would want to be a pretty good reason as to why it happened,' Hayes said.

'They had invested so much in him financially that I would think that they would give him a fair tenure at the footy club,' Hamill explained. 'We needed a good kick in the arse as a footy club and a playing list, and Malcolm certainly delivered that. But the powers that be didn't see it.

'Grant Thomas, Waldron and Butters were in the room upstairs. Malcolm stormed in and said, "Let's get this over and done with". The playing group was in the theatre. Butters broke the news, said he didn't believe Malcolm was the one to nurture our younger list, or embrace what we wanted him to do. Then Malcolm departed, never to be seen again. The core of the playing group was pretty gutted. There were a lot of impressionable kids, but I assumed Burke, Harvey and Loewe knew it was coming.'

* * *

By the time the news broke, Malcolm and Patsy could barely enter their suburban street—media had blocked both ends, for this was

SAINTS OR SINNERS?

the largest football story of the year. The Messiah had lasted fifteen weeks, and was walking away with what on face value would be an enormous payout. But the terms and conditions of the split were the least intriguing aspects of the tale; Blight's insistence to this day that he had done no wrong—and the emotion it still dredges up within him—was the overriding story.

He spent the next few days in a daze, comparing the feeling to 'like a third person doing it. Like winning a Magarey, or a Brownlow. That's exactly how I felt the next day, like the world was happening all around you but you weren't actually that person, but you were looking into it. For all the things I've done and been involved in, I handled it better than if I was younger, like the North Melbourne experience. But I still didn't get it'.

Just as Ken Hinkley argues that the Saints did not comprehend the package they were hiring. 'They didn't understand him, and they couldn't have, because they got it so badly wrong with how they reacted,' said Hinkley, who resigned a week later (Jonas resigned on the day Blight was sacked). 'If he was so desperately sought-after nine months earlier, and so desperately wrong in the same people's eyes, a lot of people got away with a very bad decision. Malcolm Blight was the same Malcolm Blight that I knew, he coached the same way he coached in Geelong—I can't speak for Adelaide—and he was exactly what I thought he would be. The people at St Kilda got that wrong, they didn't understand Malcolm Blight. They made the poor decision.'

In many ways, Butters agrees. 'We didn't give enough consideration to matching the role at the time in terms of where was our list, in terms of its capacity, in terms of its quality, in terms of its development, and where did we want it to unfold over the next number of years,' Butters said. 'The truth was that it was only months later that we actually realised that our list was horribly underweight. We weren't a premiership unit, and we worked that part of it out quite scientifically—by measuring the ability of our entire list based on certain criteria and a very strict methodology, and compared it to the Brisbane premiership list of the year, and fuck, there was space. We deserved to be second last on the ladder, because that's how good we were.

'And, given our later understanding of where we were at as a club, Malcolm was never the right choice.'

While Butters was clearly aware of the conflict between his handful of senior talent and Blight's blunt approach, the president also recognised the Blight legend in play: 'Malcolm was not a nurturer of youngsters—he nurtured senior players, he nurtured Harvey, Burke and Loewe, he was tough on 'em, hard on 'em, but he was also one of their teachers. He could teach a Harvey, and I'll never forget watching him talk to Robert—Robert was in awe of him—but he didn't have the patience for the Jason Blakes who had a runny nose, or a Stephen Milne, who was basically still having his mum drop him off to training. He didn't have that patience, and that was one of my early observations … was that there was a massive gap between Malcolm's ability to relate to the kids [and the senior players].'

I'm not sure I entirely agree with that assessment. It was not about their age; it was about their potential—could the player, at whatever age, play a role in success for that football club at that particular time or in the immediate future? Isn't that a coach's job?

In a move that stunned Blight as much as his own dismissal had, Thomas was appointed interim coach for the remainder of the season, then full-time coach from 2002.

'They had the right to hire and fire,' Blight said. 'I've done it to people over my life; people have done it to me. If they didn't want me there, there was no point in my being there. You've got no support, so you're out. I don't have a problem with that. The problem I have, and I reckon the honest football world has, is that you are replaced by a guy who, nearly ten years ago, coached unsuccessfully at an amateur league club. How that ever happened ...'

Of everything Malcolm Blight talked about for this book, nothing touched a nerve as much as his dismissal from St Kilda. As Hinkley said, he was—and still is—a proud man not used to failing. 'He took a big hit, Malcolm, because people questioned his commitment. I still have this belief today that with the right amount of time the club would have won a premiership.'

There were no winners from the fallout; St Kilda was pilloried by the media, with Butters recalling one senior journalist chiding him by saying, 'Do you even know what you've done, son?' The president reflects on his handling of the situation, both the sacking and aftermath, as 'shocking, appalling'.

'It was a bunch of inexperienced people out of their depth,' Butters concluded. 'In hindsight, would it have been better to wait to the end of the year [to sack Blight]? It would have been less of a story. Again, I gladly accept full responsibility; I was out of my depth ... We were in the spotlight, we were young, we'd managed to disenfranchise a lot of our supporters, and a lot of the media, and we just became the laughing stock of the AFL.

'At the time I couldn't understand the criticism, because I just made a business decision—and you make them all day long—but all of a sudden you'd stepped into a whole new environment of this media frenzy of footy, and the richness and the rawness of it, and when I look back in hindsight, they were all right—we monumentally stuffed up.'

That might give Malcolm Blight some consolation, though I doubt it. He insists he coached the same way he had in Geelong and Adelaide, and the game had not moved on that dramatically in the twelve months from his departure from the Crows to his signing at St Kilda. 'The difference is the results', he said. 'It's a results-orientated business, and the magic wand wasn't there because the list wasn't there. I didn't do it any differently. If I was that bad—supposedly—and not capable, I must have been very lucky for the previous fifteen years.'

EPILOGUE

IT SAYS PLENTY that Bruce McAvaney once dined with Sir Donald Bradman and Malcolm Blight, yet McAvaney's enduring memories of the lunch were related to Blight, rather than the most famous sportsman in our history. And that Grant Thomas can only compare the Blight persona to that of Greg Norman. 'When they enter a room it's like *bang*, it's very electric,' Thomas said of running into Norman. 'Malcolm's like that, he is very charismatic and engaging.'

Which, ultimately, might have been the key to his coaching success.

Malcolm Blight *sold the dream.*

There is something seductive about his presence. Sitting and listening to someone talk about themselves for hours is not usually my idea of a good time. Malcolm admittedly was not fond of the

EPILOGUE

idea of this book—he did not chase me down to spill his life story, and it took some convincing for him to chat for any period of time. But once he started, he was fantastic company.

He was astute. Amusing. Still surprisingly passionate about the game. Disarmingly honest. Intelligent. Self-aware. Not exactly humble, but it's hard to be too self-effacing about a list of football achievements that has few equals in the history of the game. During that time, in his home, a thought dawned on me that three different people had expressed during the compilation of the book: 'I would have loved to have played under him'.

Above all, the overriding trait was his intensity. Malcolm Blight had to be a hard driver; you can't get to his heights as a player or coach if you are a soft touch. But his intensity away from the game took me completely by surprise. Like his late-night tape sessions, or his post-season agonising about such things as the time he decided to train on the heavily sanded Kardinia Park in the 1994 finals, a decision he now thinks cost his team dearly in the grand final three days later. Sixteen years on, Blight was moved to emotion regaling us with that story. (Ken Hinkley said his motivation for joining Blight at St Kilda was not only to be back in his former coach's company. 'I wanted to *be there* to see him win a premiership. Losing 94 was like a dagger in his heart.')

Also revealing was his attention to detail—Billy Brownless talking about tying shoes the right way, for instance.

'In a lot of eccentric geniuses the preparation is underrated,' McAvaney said. 'Malcolm might not be considered as diligent as a Ross Lyon. When you sum up Blighty as a coach, one of the last things you talk about is his attention to detail, but he had this

336

extraordinary ability to teach people how to do things. You think of Blighty as expansive, prepared to take a risk, pioneering, but not those things.'

So many people told stories of Blight's influence. And we have heard not a tenth of it; as Blight says, 'One of the things that people don't understand is that the best things you say are usually one-on-one, that no one else hears.'

Not long after Blight secured the head coach job in Adelaide, former Geelong centreman Paul Couch was speaking to his old teammate and captain at Kardinia Park, Mark Bairstow. 'They'll win the premiership next year,' Couch said. 'He'll get them playing well and they'll win.'

That's the sort of faith those Geelong players had in Blight, despite his not delivering a premiership. Couch had been dropped regularly under Blight's predecessor, John Devine. 'Early in the week leading up to a game Blighty said, "You're playing next week. Just get yourself right",' Couch recalled. '"Because if you are worried about being selected you worry about that instead of worrying about the game."'

It is insight into the way Blight thinks, which sometimes appears inconsistent but seems to ultimately make sense. He was convinced players like certainty, hence the Couch example, or the time he promised Barry Stoneham eight consecutive games at centre half-forward. Equally, he loved to catch them off-guard: up a ladder in the Crows' dressing rooms, for instance, the voice of their conscience.

And he always came prepared, even when he was working two jobs and could not get to training until late in the day. 'He would obviously mull over things after the match and before the next lot of training, maybe when he was at work or sitting at an airport,' said his right-hand man at Geelong, Greg Wells. 'We would have a clearly defined plan for that week. And he would walk around talking about contingencies. What ifs and Plan Bs, he was very good at that. That's where his real instinct came in.'

Yet the most prominent takeaway from sitting with Malcolm Blight is how much he hated to lose. Even today, on the golf course, friends describe him as 'super-competitive'. His former assistant and successor at both Geelong and Adelaide, Gary Ayres, saw it firsthand. 'The pain of defeat lingers a lot longer and is a far deeper feeling than the joy of winning,' Ayres said. 'You're riding every kick, mark, handball. Every dropped mark, every turnover, every positional change. Every rotation. Every umpire's decision. Every umpire's non-decision. Every missed shot on goal. Every shot on goal. That's you as a coach. It encompasses all those things. Malcolm is a very deep thinker about football. You can be away from the club but you are still thinking about it quite deeply; he took it all with him. And for him to come and give those players a vision or to give them ways and means of getting up and winning the next week ... you've got to sell that to those players. That was a real strength of his.'

His critics suggest he focused too much on the top ten to twelve players on his list. Thomas believes it was a function of his character as much as his coaching. 'I think he has a personality where he just wants to mix with the best,' he said. 'I don't think he tolerates anything less than top shelf. He hasn't got much time for it. People can be critical of that but if you set that high standard ...

EPILOGUE

maybe he was, "If you want me to respect you more or like you more, shift up a cog".'

* * *

Malcolm Blight is an enigma. Apparently uncaring and detached, but obsessed about the detail in the game. Easygoing with the media and fans, but highly intense during and after matches. A consummately fair player who once sent one of his players, Mark Yeates, onto a ground to deal with a (admittedly fair but marginal) vendetta. He interacted most with the senior talent, but adored teaching the youth. Blight played in an unstructured, freewheeling style but in each new coaching environment presented his players with a series of intractable rules.

Whatever he was, we know that, after those laps of Arden Street at the beginning of his coaching career, he tried to be his own man.

Yet he could, and still can, laugh at himself. Blight was a borderline chain-smoker even in the coach's box, and would have openly puffed away if he thought he could get away with it. Greg Wells recalls that Blight developed a strategy for sneaking in a cigarette during a game. 'He learnt, from his time as a commentator, all about the six- or seven-second delay,' Wells explained. 'He wouldn't abuse anyone or have a drag [of a cigarette] in the first six or seven seconds after a player had made a mistake or the opposition had kicked a goal because the cameras were always going to go on him. He'd go, "The camera will be off me now," then take a drag.'

Above all, few people seemed to think about the game as much as he did. During my time at Essendon, we always respected those

Geelong teams that he coached, not simply for their talent but for some of the things they tried. One wet winter there was no grass on the MCG; it was a mud heap. When we played the Cats, they kicked wobbly torpedoes all day against us, and we fumbled our way to a terrible loss. Blight had planted that seed at training, instructing his players to practise mongrel kicks to take advantage of the conditions.

'Blighty had said, "Essendon is going to switch the ball so we are going to be ready for that; they'll make mistakes because it's muddy",' Couch said. '"Plus, they won't hold their marks against us." We were rubbing our hands together, practising flat punts for an hour. We even knew to be in front because they drop short. We were laughing, we were actually thinking before the game, "Well, how much are we going to win by?" Because that was the way it was.'

Yet coaching took its toll. He referred to himself as 'the barking dog that caught the car' when he won a premiership. He hated making decisions on people's lives, finding the annual culling of a playing list the most difficult aspect of the game, a chore that drove him close to retirement after nearly every season of senior coaching. And he hated losing.

Everyone associated with his coaching noted that when his teams were winning, Blight's biggest weapon was silence. 'Change for change's sake?' Blight mused. 'I never did it. There's not one headline about the coach when you're winning. Whenever we got on a roll, no one ever heard from me. Quite frankly, I was probably a worse coach when we were winning because I didn't say anything. Why mess it up? Most of these stories come from losing, because I seriously didn't like it.'

EPILOGUE

When defeat came knocking, as it must, he managed to curb his manner ... but it took a lifetime of learning. 'I backed off my aggression maybe 15 or 20, maybe even 25 per cent over the years, because we played some sparkling footy in there so there was a lot to like. I said to the blokes at Woodville a number of times that I know I was pretty hard, but if we can't win a game, what are we there for?'

Blight concluded with a line that stuck in the mind. Any coach at any level would do well to jot it in his diary. 'If you're not serious with yourself, and can't get dark on yourself, why do it? You've got to improve, *somehow*.'

In 2011, his 'somehow' relates to the Gold Coast Football Club. A boy from a commission house in the modest Adelaide suburb of Woodville, Blight has enjoyed a connection to the Queensland sun throughout his adult life: during his off-seasons as a player he would head north to recuperate, and he eventually moved there between jobs. These days, he and Patsy have laid anchor in far north Queensland.

It only seemed natural, then, that he would throw himself into a position as a board member of the Gold Coast Suns when they became an AFL entity in 2010. In July 2009, the Suns announced they had lured Blight to their board. Chairman John Witheriff was delighted to secure Blight's 'decades of insight and knowledge into what makes a Club successful'. Inaugural Suns coach Guy McKenna need not be looking over his shoulder, though ... this time, at sixty-one, Blight's 'never again' coaching pledge would seem an actual promise. 'I suppose I'll have a quiet word with Bluey every now and then if I think it would help' is the extent of Blight's intrusion.

341

EPILOGUE

Should the Suns ultimately succeed, it would complete a circle of football influence of which he is keenly aware and which he openly states is a motivation for his involvement with the Suns: Blight played in North Melbourne's first premiership, coached Adelaide's first premiership and would be a director of a Gold Coast triumph. In the meantime, he remains in the news. A Channel 10 commentator, Blight delivered special comments for the Suns' AFL debut match against Carlton in Round 2. The Blues won by 119 points, and scorn was poured on Blight for his biased commentary. It was not so much what he said, rather the anguish in his voice (and the running stream of displeased grunts) that ignited the world of football blogs.

His commentary has always been a lightning rod for critiques, because Blight's approach has swung between the flippant and disgusted. But it's never bland; Malcolm has something to say without being controversial for controversy's sake. Whether you agree with him or not, isn't that what makes a good commentator?

*   *   *

A number of people have asked if the events towards the end of this book, detailing his St Kilda experience, soured his achievements. When considering its place, Blight referred to Moorabbin as 'fifteen weeks in forty years ... so it should only take up fifteen weeks of forty years in a book'. But he cannot deny the impact it had then, and still has now when it is raised.

Witness his infamous 2008 response to co-commentator Steve Quartermain during half-time of Channel 10's coverage of a game. Then-Saints president Rod Butters had commented on

342

Blight in an article in the *Herald Sun*, and again questioned Blight's commitment at the time. Blight had said nothing since departing the doors of Moorabbin seven years earlier. Now, the dam broke.

'I couldn't give a rat's tossbag whether he thought I could coach or whether anyone thinks I can coach or can play. I'm happy with what I did,' Blight fumed. 'When they talk about commitment, that's when I get steamed up,' he said. 'It was a team that had won two games the year before, it was a very ordinary football club, had some problems off the ground, [but my] commitment, no. You don't like the way I did it—stiff. Commitment? Never, no.'

A decade after he was sacked, I saw the same anger in his body language when we talked about the Saints for this book. He folded his arms, pursed his lips and lost his easygoing demeanour. Clearly, he finds it difficult to let this chapter of his life go, and rattling his cage on the topic will elicit a response. But to answer the question: does his sacking detract from his career?

I say, not in the slightest. To finish where I started: perfection in football, and life, is impossible.

Bruce McAvaney agrees, and he put it better than I ever could. 'Think of Muhammad Ali. Do we remember Trevor Berbick and Larry Holmes? No, you think of Sonny Liston, Joe Frazier, George Foreman,' he said, referring to Ali's glory days before inglorious defeats later in his career. 'Lance Armstrong, do you think of his last Tour de France or his seven wins? Michael Schumacher came back and has been unsuccessful. Do you think about his championships or his comeback?

'St Kilda adds flavour to Malcolm's story. It's sort of the intrigue that surrounds Blight the man.'

343

EPILOGUE

I did not know about Malcolm Blight when he won a Magarey Medal for Woodville. I played a handful of games against Blight the North Melbourne footballer before he headed back to South Australia. I played against his Geelong teams, and coached against his Crows. And I got to spend some time with him—intriguing time, as Bruce points out—over the summer of 2010–11. But supporters of his teams, wherever he played and coached, grew to know Malcolm Blight far better than I ever did, or will. For them, I hope this book has done justice to a fine career in football.

ACKNOWLEDGEMENTS

B OOKS SUCH AS this need a variety of things to work in their favour for them to get written. Most of those things centre on cooperation.

In essence, the project could not have worked without the assistance of Malcolm Blight, who gave me time out of a busy schedule to sit and talk at length about his forty years in the game. I thank Malcolm and Patsy for welcoming me into their home.

Then there was the task of building the picture of Malcolm through the eyes of others. We spoke to too many people to thank them all: many of them are quoted in this book; others simply offered advice and anecdotes that proved invaluable. Needless to say, our interviewees' enthusiasm about Malcolm and his achievements shone through in every discussion, providing ongoing encouragement throughout the writing of this book.

Finally, I credit the people at Hardie Grant, who allowed me to convince them of what I believe is one of the game's most intriguing stories. They, too, came to see that Blighty's story is one worth telling, and I thank them for their support.